y Hemming

Henry Hemmir ⟨ ⟩s in London. *Together* is his third book.

Praise for Henry Hemming

'Hemming is a fresh new voice, idealistic, engaging and human' *Spectator*

'Compulsively readable' *Sunday Times*

'Entertaining, intelligent' *The Times*

'Sparkles with colour, originality and sharp insights' *Evening Standard*

'Henry Hemming is an inspirational writer' *Liverpool Daily Post*

'Likeable tones, with whimsical historical details and a range of philosophical and sociological references' *Guardian*

'An intelligent and encouraging piece of writing' *Times Literary Supplement*

'It would have been easy to set these people up for ridicule, but Hemming sensitively delves into their psyches to offer a witty narrative' *Observer*

'Hemm NEWHAM LIBRARIES f people

9080 0100064286

TOGETHER

HENRY
HEMMING

HOW
SMALL GROUPS
ACHIEVE
BIG THINGS

JOHN MURRAY

First published in Great Britain in 2011 by John Murray (Publishers)
An Hachette UK Company

First published in paperback in 2011

1

© Henry Hemming 2011

The right of Henry Hemming to be identified as the Author of the Work
has been asserted by him in accordance with the Copyright,
Designs and Patents Act 1988.

A CIP catalogue record for this title is available from the British Library

ISBN 978-1-84854-056-9
Ebook ISBN 978-1-84854-513-7

Typeset in Plantin Light by Palimpsest Book Production Limited,
Falkirk, Stirlingshire

Printed and bound by Clays Ltd, St Ives plc

John Murray policy is to use papers that are natural, renewable and recyclable
products and made from wood grown in sustainable forests. The logging and
manufacturing processes are expected to conform to the environmental
regulations of the country of origin.

John Murray (Publishers)
338 Euston Road
London NW1 3BH

www.johnmurray.co.uk

For Helena

Contents

Introduction

Man is a city-dwelling creature whose nature is to live
with others.

Aristotle, *Nicomachean Ethics*

Some years ago a group of men met in a pub called The
Clarence. It was what you'd call an 'old man's pub'. Even
the owner would agree that it had seen better days. But on
that particular night, a Friday night, none of these men
minded too much where they met. After an hour in the
corner, one or two peeled off: they had children to look after,
wives and girlfriends to meet in town. This left an inner core
of about twelve, later nicknamed the 'dirty dozen', who left
the pub and moved on to a nearby curry house. There they
drank several jugs of beer, ate, paid and, before midnight,
they left.

This is hardly a remarkable sequence of events. In fact, it
is the kind of thing you can imagine happening all over the
country as the week draws to a close and the weekend begins.
But this particular gathering on the evening of Friday 13 May
2005 was different.

The men who came together in The Clarence had one
thing in common. They supported the same well-known
football club. Only the day before it had been sold off to
a family of foreign investors and saddled with debt. They
were in despair. Thousands of other fans were in the same

predicament, and doubtless many of them spent that night drowning in maudlin speculation as to what the future held.

This get-together finished on an altogether different note. By the time their food was served, these men had begun to discuss the idea of setting up a breakaway football club. It would be everything the other one had long ago ceased to be – a member-led co-operative in which major decisions were decided by ballot; a club run by the fans, for the fans. Rather than sit during matches, they would stand and sing until they were hoarse. There would be talent contests before each game, stalls selling home-made pies and local ales, financial transparency, no sponsorship.

You can imagine each of them waking up the next morning, heads a little heavy as they pieced together last night's conversation.

Did we *really* say that?

There were those who scoffed when they heard the plan. It was pie in the sky, they said. It would never work. Apart from anything else, where was the money going to come from? Exactly.

And yet, two months after filing out of Dildar Curry House in Rusholme, Manchester, this band of ex-Manchester United supporters had helped to cobble together a football team and persuaded a former fruit and veg man to become their manager.

F. C. United of Manchester, as it became known, played its first match, a friendly, in front of 2,500 people. Despite failing to score, the players were carried off the pitch shoulder-high by a sea of new believers, each alive to the possibility of it all, the endeavour and the gut-wrenching thrill of leaving behind the club that they had supported for so long.

Over the months that followed a group of volunteers with the 'dirty dozen' at their core would steer F. C. United through its first season. The club was promoted. The next season they were promoted again, and in their third season, amazingly,

F. C. United completed a hat-trick of promotions by making it out of the Unibond First Division into the Unibond Premier.

It takes most football clubs years to get promoted this far, if they ever get there. F. C. United had done it in no time at all. They had expanded beyond even the silliest parts of that conversation back in Dildar Curry House and now shared a stadium with a team that played in the third highest division of the Football League. The singing, the contests, the ballots, the lack of sponsorship, the principle of one-member-one-vote – all of this was happening.

There were other elements of their success that they had not foreseen. The members of F. C. United felt a powerful sense of belonging and identity, and during those first few years a visceral sense of camaraderie formed between these men and women.

Yet perhaps the strangest part of this story concerns money. The nay-sayers were right. There was no sudden injection of cash.

So how could a small group like this one with no financial backing achieve so much, and in such a short space of time? Why was it that together they seemed to be a great deal more than the sum of their parts and what does this tell us?

The Power of Association

Together is about the remarkable things that can happen when we come together in small groups. It is an account of the strange alchemy within an association, club or society that enables a group like F. C. United to go much further, faster. In a quite different sense, why is it that joining one of these groups – be it a breakaway football club or any other association, from a knitting circle to a death metal band, book club, protest group or Judy Garland Appreciation Society – can make you healthier and happier?

In this book, I want to show you a different way of seeing the world, one that is based on an understanding of the extraordinary potential of small groups. I am not talking about nationwide movements, word-of-mouth epidemics or what goes on within vast, de-individuated crowds. There are other books on these. I am interested in what happens when a room-sized group of people come together of their own volition and agree to work towards a specific end, as they did in that crumbling pub in Manchester in 2005. I want to show you the power of association.

Yet it seems we have lost sight of this and that we know surprisingly little about the mass of associations in Britain today. One of the only (and best) studies of these groups, published in 1986, described them as 'an area of social life which was massive in its proportions, rich in detail and of fascinating complexity' but 'almost completely overlooked'. Other social scientists have referred to them as 'the "lost continent" on the social landscape of modern society' or, rather wonderfully, 'a loose and baggy monster'. Although there may be as many as 1.5 million of these associations in Britain, as one report in 1995 suggested, we hear very little about them.

So what do I mean by an 'association'? I mean nothing more than a group whose members identify themselves as belonging to that unit and come together regularly and voluntarily, and do so without seeking profit. An association could be a football club like F. C. United, or any one of the countless reading groups or book clubs in Britain today, as well as the choirs, bands, beekeeping societies, volunteer-led charities, support groups, prayer groups, Jewish burial organizations, every amateur sporting team or club you can think of, or indeed the more traditional associations, the ones we all know, such as Women's Institutes, Masonic Lodges, gentlemen's clubs, Rotary Clubs and Working Men's Clubs and Institutes. Then there are the walking groups, community support groups, Meet-ups, literary societies, local residents' associations,

Transition Towns, protest groups, miners' welfare gro
user groups, associations dedicated to a shared love o1
particular breed of dog, doll's houses, auriculas, koi, fungus,
bell-ringing or embroidery; they might be naturalist societies,
badger protection societies, pigeon fancy clubs, horticultural
societies, therapeutic communities, druid orders, swingers
groups, ante-natal classes, amateur dramatic societies, civic
societies, allotment societies, historical re-enactment groups,
social clubs, knitting circles, guerrilla gardeners, car enthusiast
clubs, Neighbourhood Watch schemes, archaeological clubs,
motorcycle clubs or fraternities, birdwatching groups, Christian
naturist fellowships, appreciation societies, family history
societies, Young Farmers' clubs; the list goes on . . .

Not only have we lost sight of the huge range of associations in Britain today but we tend to brush over their role
in our past as well. Although the growth of these groups has
been described as 'one of the most pervasive, diffuse and
amorphous social developments of the last 200 years', they
barely feature on any national curriculum. Scan the shelves
in the History section of your local bookshop and you will
find only a handful of books, if any, that deal with particular
associations. As early as 1720, it was said that in London
'almost every parish hath its separate Club, where the Citizens,
after the Fatigue of the Day is over in their Shops, and on
the *Exchange*, unbend their Thoughts before they go to Bed.'
Later that century a historian in Birmingham wrote that
'the whole British empire . . . is subdivided into an infinity
of smaller fraternities'. By the start of the twentieth century
there were said to be 6 million members of the nation's
Friendly Societies. Think of the Royal Society, the Levellers,
the Diggers, the Kit-Cat Club, the Lunar Society, the Anti-
Corn Law League, the Tolpuddle Martyrs, the Anti-Slavery
Society, the Suffragettes, charities such as the Royal Society
for the Protection of Birds, the National Trust or any one of
the countless societies, organizations, clubs, collectives and

associations that make up our associational past. Each began when a room-sized group of people came together and agreed to pursue certain shared goals, just as those football supporters did in 2005. Over the last three centuries real change has often been about much more than Great Men or Great Women setting out to achieve Great Things. Small groups have also been at the heart of this. Associations form a key ingredient in the make-up of our national culture – one that we no longer seem to recognize or value in relation to what it is, has been and looks set to remain in coming years.

A Revival?

Without turning back to the Contents page, if I was to ask you now how you thought the rest of this book was going to play out, I wonder what you would say? I know that, had I read the last few pages, I would be pretty sure that what follows will be a hymn in praise of associations and their unsung role in society. That seems to be where we are heading. But there is another subject I want to address, and it changes the direction and scope of this book entirely.

You see, F. C. United was not the only voluntary group that came about in 2005. I think there is a series of compelling arguments to suggest that this club was in fact part of a nationwide phenomenon involving millions of Britons. All over the country small groups like F. C. United, along with hundreds of thousands of societies, community groups, clubs, bands, choirs, covens, circles and other informal associations appear to have formed for the first time or registered a significant growth. Crucially, this seems to have happened on a scale that had not been seen in years.

During the first decade of the twenty-first century Britain may have experienced an unexpected surge of associational activity. It was not universal, in that there were some associations whose numbers dipped or which were forced to close, but many more were either born, their numbers remained steady or they expanded.

The strangest thing about this associational surge – and for me what makes it intriguing – is that nobody noticed. You'll find no mention of it in the national or local media. Social scientists were reticent on the subject. There was no flood of government strategies, initiatives and statutes aimed at nurturing this great wave of associational interest. Instead a very different narrative emerged.

Broken Britain

From 2005, ironically the year that F. C. United came into existence, the term 'Broken Britain' began to be bandied about by politicians and journalists alike. As well as heightened social inequality and increasingly violent, feral youth, one of the principal elements of this loose, sponge-like doctrine was the idea that we no longer knew our neighbours. Community spirit, we were told, was either dead, dying or in its death throes. We were living alone more than ever before. There were fewer local activities and street parties. The internet was pulling us apart inexorably, while mobile phones and social networking sites seemed to disconnect us further from the places in which we lived.

Take the example of shopping. Rather than visit our local high streets, increasingly we preferred to shop from home or in out-of-town supermarkets. By 2011 an estimated 32 million Britons were shopping online, spending £52 billion in the process, while between 1986 and 1997 the number of out-of-town shopping centres quadrupled.

Or religion: 'if Christianity goes,' T. S. Eliot once wrote, 'the whole of our culture goes.' Between 1980 and 2000 alone church attendance fell by 21 per cent, while between 1998 and 2005 about half a million people stopped going to church on Sunday.

Statistics such as these buttressed the same ubiquitous argument – that by the start of the twenty-first century the fabric of community in Britain had worn perilously thin, and that since the 1960s we had become less neighbourly, less trusting of each other and socially more isolated.

The authors of *The Spirit Level*, a book charting the effects of social inequality in Britain, summed it up like this: by 2009 we had become 'anxiety-ridden, prone to depression, worried about how others see us, unsure of our friendships, driven to consume and with little or no community life'. A well-publicized report from the University of Sheffield in 2008 argued that for some time now 'the social glue and cohesion had been weakening' and 'Britain has been steadily moving towards a slightly more atomised society with each decade that passes.' In 2010 Phillip Blond explained in his book *Red Tory* that during the tail end of the twentieth century 'British civil society, which is the source and well-spring of our culture, has been flattened by the unleashed authoritarianism of the state and the unrestricted freedom granted to the market.'

The diagnosis could hardly be more grim: society was atomized; Britain was broken; community was on its last legs. So how on earth is it possible to argue that during the same period there was in fact a nationwide surge of associational activity, that *more* people were coming together in small groups than during the 1980s or 1990s? It seems an extraordinary claim. It certainly undermines one of the foundations of 'Broken Britain'. So what is the evidence for this and why has it gone unreported until now?

Kidnappings

The standard approach to a question like this one would be to hunt down the relevant data describing how many of us belong to associations, adjust the weighting and standardization, plot some graphs and see which way they point. What could be easier? Since the introduction of Mass Observation in the 1930s, government agencies and independent bodies have produced an impressive drip-feed of surveys, reports and data-sets monitoring and making estimations about our behaviour, from the number of hours we spend watching television to what we think of our neighbours. There is an Office for National Statistics, a National Census and a slush of reports such as the General Household Survey, General Lifestyle Survey or the Time Use Survey. These are useful and informative, but they do not cover everything.

It turns out that there are no systematic and quantitative data to describe how many Britons are involved in associations. Instead, most of the clubs, societies and other informal groups that we are interested in fly beneath the radar with which we analyse society. There are scraps of evidence, and these are promising, but they are not enough to support a conclusion. This is perhaps why so few social scientists tackle this subject.

Yet what we must not do – the mistake that others have made – is to accept a Positivist take on the world, whereby if something can't be measured, it doesn't exist. There are two ways to answer any question, be it a dilemma over which socks to wear in the morning, or whether there has been a surge of associational activity in twenty-first-century Britain. Only one of these involves evidence based on observation.

Think of a film about a kidnapping. At an early stage the kidnappers will often present a 'proof of life' – at least they should if they know their stuff. This is to show both that they have the missing person and that he or she is alive. They might get them to speak on the phone, record a piece to camera or take a picture of their hostage holding a recent newspaper. These are three evidence-based proofs of the kidnappers' assertion that a given individual is alive and in their custody.

But what makes one of these films gripping is the tension that follows between the kidnappers and their adversary – let's say it's a detective – as each is forced to make a series of judgements about what the other is about to do or has done. They might use their knowledge of the psychology of kidnap situations, just as they could turn to the history of similar kidnappings.

In other words, they speculate, based on a deeper understanding of situations like this one. In philosophical terms, if the kidnappers' 'proof of life' was *a posteriori*, what follows is *a priori*; it is based not on demonstrable proofs but on calculation. Where evidence is lacking, we turn to logic, deduction and reason. This gives us the second approach to any question.

The only way to make a persuasive argument about what happened to the mass of small groups in Britain during the first decade of the twenty-first century is to combine the evidence we have with a series of deductive arguments. We can only make these by gaining a much deeper understanding of how these associations work. By getting to grips with what goes on within them, how they operate and what causes them to appear, we should be able to calculate whether there was indeed a resurgence of these groups.

It's a bit like being the detective in one of those films. You don't have enough evidence to work out what the kidnapper is up to. So what do you do? You find out everything you can about your subject, until you can predict with a degree of confidence how they are likely to behave in certain situations.

To get a thorough understanding of how these groups work, I want to look at them from every possible angle. We will consider their history on these islands from the first association that appeared late in the first century AD, a band of metalworkers in what is now Chichester, through to present-day groups such as F. C. United. Also, we must look at the psychology that sheds light on our desire to join one of these groups, and how we behave within them. Finally, I want to look at where these associations sit in the context of broader shifts in British society. It may be that other factors which appear to have nothing to do with these groups are fuelling this revival.

Together

Using all of these approaches, I believe it is possible to work out what happened to this mass of small groups during the early twenty-first century. In Part One I will show you how these groups work and what I mean by the 'power' of association. You'll see why F. C. United achieved so much in such a short space of time, what it meant to belong to this group and exactly what it is about an association that allows us to take our interests much further. We'll meet a group of druids in Portsmouth, book enthusiasts in Edinburgh, climate change protesters in the West Country, anti-art campaigners in Wales and a Women's Institute in Yorkshire, among many others. We will also look at earlier groups such as the eighteenth-century musical club run by a coal-seller, or the secretive Apostles society in Cambridge during the 1930s. Along the way, I will reveal a series of rules that explain how these associations work and why.

In Part Two, using this understanding of associations, we can move on to the main question: namely, was there really a nationwide surge of associational activity during the 2000s, and if so, why did this go unreported?

In Part Three I want to explore the implications of all this. Does it actually matter whether or not there was an associational revival? Does this change anything about how we see society and our role within it?

Yes is the easy answer. First, it knocks out one of the legs of the 'Broken Britain' argument. But it can also change our understanding of 'community'. During the early twenty-first century, the British government poured billions of pounds into promoting an archaic and at times misguided vision of community. I will show you where that ideal came from and the worrying effects it has had in certain areas.

I think there is a very different way of talking about community. It is inspired by a simple idea: that a growing number of Britons now experience a sense of community not just in their neighbourhoods, or the ethnic and religious groups into which they are born, but the associations they belong to. In these small groups we forge meaningful and lasting connections to one another: we communicate, make decisions as one, we work together towards shared ends.

Is it possible that in Britain today these groups are beginning to take the place of the traditional local community? Could they be the modern-day answer to the medieval village? Not only did the members of F. C. United build a successful football team out of nothing, they formed a thriving community as well. This was something that most of them simply did not experience elsewhere. The same is true of countless men and women throughout Britain. *Together* is about the idea that when we come together in small groups like this, as well as being able to achieve much more, we feed the part of us that longs to belong, and that this is why these groups are flourishing.

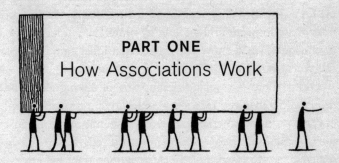

PART ONE

How Associations Work

1
Coming Together
Why We Form Associations

What life have you if you have not life together?

T. S. Eliot, *Choruses from The Rock*

In 1971 there was a military coup in Uganda. At the time East Africa was awash with coups and counter-coups, and it is unlikely that many people living in Leicester took much notice. Yet this power-grab was different. The man who took control was General Idi Amin. Tall and athletic, Amin was blessed with a physique 'like that of a Grecian sculpture'. He was cheery, plain-spoken and resolute – every inch the tribal chief. 'Amin *oyee!*' they cried. 'Praise to Amin!'

When Amin declared himself President, there were some 90,000 Gujaratis, Bangladeshis and Pakistanis living in Uganda. Most were descended from indentured labourers brought over by the British in the late nineteenth century. Since then they had come to form the backbone of society; they were the businessmen of Uganda, the shopkeepers, clerks, lawyers and teachers. Amin knew that Ugandans resented this easily identifiable but highly successful minority, and in 1972 he expelled them.

Kenya, Tanzania, India and Pakistan closed their borders immediately, leaving most of these exiles stateless. However, just under a third of them had British passports, and of those the majority moved to the United Kingdom. Many of them, including Raju Vora, went to Leicester.

'But I did not come straight away,' he corrected me. Now in his seventies, Vora has the manners of a statesman. He is a compact man, with a wave of salt-and-pepper hair that curves easily over his forehead. 'At the time I was a journalist in Kampala. Some friends and I ran *Transition*, a magazine hostile to General Amin. We had V. S. Naipaul write for us, Paul Theroux, Julius Nyerere and others. I did not want to leave Uganda. I felt it was an important time to be there. But under General Amin I was taken to prison, tortured and so forth. The same happened to my friends. When I was released I knew I had no option but to leave. So I moved here, to Leicester.'

Vora's attention returned to the plate in front of him. We were in a windowless, fawn-coloured room in one of Leicester's best-known hotels. Dinner had just been served. Around us were fifty men, most wearing dark single-breasted suits, ice-white shirts and ties. There was a hum of achievement in the room.

This was a meeting of the Thursday Club. I was surrounded by some of Leicester's most powerful and successful Asian businessmen and professionals, who for more than a quarter of a century had been gathering like this once a month for a meal followed by a talk. Most of the club's original members had, like Vora, grown up in East Africa before being forced to leave.

The Thursday Club is a classic example of the kind of association we are looking at. It is voluntary and part-time, its members recognize themselves as a group and they are not at all commercial. If we are to understand how these groups work, we must get to grips with the anatomy of a club like this one. What causes an association like this to appear? Exactly what was it that pulled together the members of the Thursday Club in the first place?

Immigrants

'The reason we formed the club?' repeated Gautam Bodiwala, a tall man with a magnificent, stentorian voice who kept a pipe in his left breast pocket. 'Well, I was the first Chairman-President, so I remember quite well the feeling back then. There was a need, I think, for Asian people in Leicester to get together. We wanted to learn from each other on matters such as how to succeed, how to get through an economic downturn, things like this. You see, for all of us this was a foreign land. We were new. There were those who had come from Uganda after General Amin came to power and had lost their savings. For them the challenge was to achieve the same quality of life they had enjoyed before. That, or better. So we invited bankers to our club to give talks, or estate agents, lawyers, medics, tax consultants, insurance brokers. We spoke about business problems. You could say the club allowed us to help each other.'

Clearly it worked. Of the original members of the Thursday Club many went on to be hugely successful. Bodiwala, for example, started out in 1970 as a junior NHS doctor. Four decades later he was Deputy Lieutenant of Leicestershire, a Commander of the British Empire, President and founder of the International Federation for Emergency Medicine, Fellow or Honorary Fellow of more medical institutions than you can recite in one breath and a doctor renowned for having pioneered the field of emergency medicine. He has even had the wing of a local hospital named after him.

'But I think the most important thing about the origins of the Thursday Club,' Vora chipped in, 'its strength really, it boils down to one thing. That we are immigrants.' He placed great stress on the last syllable, *grants*, as if to draw out the possibility of that sound and the idea that this shared status *granted* them a certain determination and resolve. 'This breeds a particular enthusiasm,' he went on. 'It is different for the next generation. But for people like myself, Gautam here, most of the original members of the club, what united us, if you like, was this experience.' Almost every member of the Thursday Club echoed this sentiment. Clearly what brought these men together was their shared experience.

You could say the same about the first association that appeared on these shores soon after the Roman invasion of AD 43. It was formed not by an enterprising band of native Britons but a group of metalworkers who migrated here from mainland Europe. They worked on ships and established a *collegium* in what is now Chichester, just a few miles from where part of the original invading force may have landed.

Yet for these two sets of immigrants, separated by almost two millennia, what was it about the experience of migration that inspired them to form an association? Why should this prove to be cohesive? We share plenty of experiences with others that elicit no pang of solidarity. If I was to get on a train with several hundred other passengers, it is unlikely that any of us would try to form an association at the end of the journey based on the experience we have shared. It feels a bit silly to talk about 'our' or 'us'. There would be no real sense of group-ness. Why? Because nothing happened to inspire a sense of solidarity.

Solidarity

In London, on 7 July 2005, three tube trains and a bus were attacked by suicidal militants in a series of co-ordinated bombings. Fifty-two people were killed, and more than 700 were injured. In the weeks that followed, journalists and commentators picked over the backgrounds of the bombers – why they had done this, where they came from, what could be read into it all. There were also accounts of the people who had been killed, and the lives they had led.

To a lesser extent there were articles about those who had survived. Some of these reports picked up on an unusual thing that had begun to happen in the weeks following these attacks. Clusters of survivors were coming together to form associations.

One of these was Kings Cross United. It was made up of about 100 of the 900 passengers who had been travelling on the 8.50 a.m. Piccadilly line train 311, attacked between King's Cross and Russell Square. As Rachel North, one founder member, explained, Kings Cross United involved 'dozens of passengers drawing together, caring for each other, comforting each other, remembering the dead and injured and bereaved'. They would meet in a pub to share stories and piece together what had happened that day. A private forum was set up for their conversations to continue online.

So why did Kings Cross United come about? On the face of it, that's easy. These people had survived the same traumatic ordeal and were united by a sense of solidarity. In the same sense, the members of the Thursday Club were bound by more than a shared experience of migration, it was the *nature* of this migration that mattered. Not only had they moved to a foreign land, but many of them had been forced out of their homes in East Africa. They too were survivors.

Kurt Lewin, now thought to be the father of social psychology, concluded in 1947 that what allows any set of humans to display a group mentality is their shared recognition of an '*interdependence of fate*'. This was later given the more clunky title 'Interdependence Perspective' and is shortened nowadays to I. P. The thrust of I. P. is straightforward: as humans, we feel closer to those who we think are in the same boat as us, and if that boat appears to be sinking, we feel closer still. This continues to be seen as one of the foundations of group identity.

But this is a book about associations rather than groups in general, and while every association is a group, not every group is an association. An association is a type of group, just as a thriller is a type of book. Lewin described Jews living in New York in the aftermath of the Second World War as a group. Of course they did not constitute an actual association. You could refer to the 90,000 Asians expelled from Uganda as a group, but only a tiny proportion went on to form the Thursday Club in Leicester. Again, while the 900 passengers on the tube train attacked near King's Cross constituted a group of sorts, only a fraction of these went on to form the association called Kings Cross United.

So this feeling of solidarity that comes with having survived an ordeal is merely a starting point. It is a foundation stone on which associations can be built. It does not follow that on feeling this we will automatically form these groups, but it becomes a possibility.

Yet the ordeal you share does not have to be anything like as traumatic as surviving a terrorist attack or being expelled from the country of your birth. Watching the football club you have supported all your life be sold off to a family of foreign investors is enough to inspire that sense of solidarity, as it was for the members of F. C. United. The same goes for a shared experience of military conflict, addiction, a devastating illness, the loss of a loved one, mass redundancy such as that which followed the pit closures of the 1980s, or being treated for mental health problems. These experiences have been the foundation stones on which countless associations have been built in recent decades.

Just as we associate in the wake of a disaster or an ordeal, so we club together in the face of one. In 2008 a proposal for a floating sculpture on the river running through Cardigan, in Wales, was given the go-ahead. Most 'Cardis', as they are sometimes known, were against it. They wanted to protect their town from this sculpture; they felt a wave of defensive solidarity towards each other. Some acted on this and formed a group to fight against the proposed installation. The sculpture was later abandoned.

The South Essex Natural History Society came about in the 1930s when a series of local residents came together in protest at plans to build over Hadleigh Great Wood in Essex. That wood still stands.

When plans are announced to build a factory, power plant, wind farm or airport almost anywhere in Britain today, within weeks a cluster of local residents are bound to have formed a protest group. Or if it is not environmental, then the threat might be political. In the 2010 general election Nick Griffin, the leader of the far-right British National Party, stood for the seat of Barking. Teams of volunteers campaigned against his candidacy, and Griffin duly came third, with only 16 per cent of the vote.

It was this same protective urge, this sense of solidarity, that inspired a mass of mutual aid societies during the nineteenth century, including Co-operative Societies, trades unions, benefit societies and Friendly Societies. Although there had been just seventy-one of these by the end of the seventeenth century, at the start of the twentieth century their membership may have included 'one-half of all adult males' in Britain.

If some of us come together in the face of a threat that is personal or local, others team up to fight a global danger such as climate change. Or there are those who unite to address a national issue, such as the members of the Campaign for an English Parliament, who see a constitutional injustice in the fact that Scotland, Wales and Northern Ireland have their own national assemblies while England does not.

It seems pretty clear that one of the reasons we form associations is as a response to a shared threat or the experience of an ordeal. So the urge to associate is protective. We form these groups in self-defence. But there is more to it than that.

In each of the groups I have described so far, those involved have been personally at risk. Either they were the ones to have suffered, or it was their lifestyle, their beliefs or their environment that was endangered. But as humans we have a remarkable and consistent ability to club together with the same vigour and imagination around a threat that does not affect us in the slightest. We are altruistic. We form groups to protect those who cannot help themselves even when there is no short-term or long-term threat to ourselves, or to our genes.

What is now Europe's largest conservation society, the Royal Society for the Protection of Birds, began in 1889 when a handful of women from Cheshire started to campaign against the fashionable use of great crested grebe feathers. They were not battling to save their livelihood; there was no ordeal that they had endured. Nor was this an act of self-defence. Yet they campaigned with the vim and passion of those whose homes were about to be demolished.

Charitable associations and societies have played a seminal part in our society since they began to appear in much larger numbers during the second half of the eighteenth century. By 1862, as one report explained,

> it seemed that almost every want or ill that can distress human nature has some palatial institution for the mitiga-tion of it. We have rich societies for every conceivable form of benevolence – for the visitation of the sick; for the cure of the maimed, and the crippled; for the alleviation of the pangs of child-birth; for giving shelter to the houseless, support to the aged and the infirm, homes to the orphan and the foundling; for the reformation of juvenile offenders and prostitutes, the reception of the children of convicts, the liberation of debtors, the suppression of vice; for educating the ragged, teaching the blind, the deaf and the dumb; for guarding and soothing the mad; protecting the idiotic, clothing the naked, and feeding the hungry.

Although the state began to take on many of these roles in the wake of the Second World War, an event that helped to bring about a noticeable dip in our associational activity, by 2010 there were just over 180,000 charitable organizations, with a combined annual income of over £50 billion. Although some were run predominantly by paid employees – so we shouldn't think of them all as voluntary associations – most of these charities began when a group of like-minded people clubbed together to right a wrong or help those who could not help themselves. Again, what drew these people together was a sense of solidarity. It is this, rather than straight self-defence, that is one of the foundations on which we build associations.

And yet there is another reason why we form associations, one that has nothing at all to do with solidarity or feeling under attack.

The Small-Coal Man of Clerkenwell

Had you lived in Clerkenwell, in London, during the early eighteenth century, you'd almost certainly have recognized the name Thomas Britton. If for some reason the name was unfamiliar, you would at least know the voice. Britton was famous for what Jonathan Swift called his 'cadence deep'. He was a small-coal man, and most mornings he could be seen and heard tramping through Clerkenwell with a sack of coal over his shoulder, face *sfumato* with coal dust as he hawked his wares.

But a strange thing would happen to Thomas Britton on his daily round. As Ned Ward explained in *The Secret History of Clubs* (a wonderful, scurrilous account of London clubs published in 1709), wherever Britton went, he was greeted 'as if he had been a Noble Man in disguise, every one that knew him, pointing as he passed crying, *There goes the famous*

Small-Coal-Man, who is a Lover of Learning, a Performer in Music, and a Companion for a Gentleman.'

As well as being a small-coal man, Britton was a music lover. When not lugging about his sack of coal he devoted his time and meagre earnings to a collection of musical manuscripts and his legendary music society. For some forty years this association met on Thursdays (similar to Leicester's Thursday Club) in Britton's house – a residence Ward described as fit for 'old snarling *Diogenes*', with 'the window of his State-Room but very little bigger than the Bunghole of a Cask'. In order to get there, guests would clamber up a rickety staircase past Britton's cache of coal. You'd think this would put them off. Not at all. Britton's club attracted 'Men of the best Wit, as well as some of the best Quality', including a young Handel, the Duchess of Queensberry and many musicians 'of the highest quality desirous of honouring his humble cottage with their presence and attention'.

Of course, these musicians did not come together in the name of defence. There was no ordeal that they had endured – unless you include climbing into Britton's home – and this was not a charity. They associated around a shared love of music. That was it. Here, then, is the second foundation on which we form associations. If we are not united by a sense of protective solidarity, then a shared intellectual interest can be enough to bring us together and inspire an association.

By the start of the twenty-first century the range of subjects around which we formed clubs, societies, organizations, associations and teams was dizzying. From 2009 to 2010 I ran an online nationwide survey of associations in Britain. As far as I know it was the first of its kind. The responses were fascinating in their detail, but it was the range of groups that really surprised me. Here is a tiny selection of those that took part: the National Fancy Rat Society, the Desert Divas, the British Gladiolus Society, the Berkshire Family History Society, Apperley Cricket Club, Painswick Players, Essex Badger

Protection Society, Welford Women's Winter Reading Club, The Model Steam Road Vehicle Society, Mini-Ness Doll's House Club, Malvern Hills District Brass Band and the 32nd (Cornwall) Regt Foot 1805–1815. The members of these associations were united by nothing more than a shared interest in rats, belly-dancing, gladioli, family history, cricket, theatre, badgers, books, model engineering, building doll's houses, playing in brass bands and re-enacting one decade in the history of a British Army infantry regiment.

The Rise of the Virtuoso

For most of human history the idea of coming together like this in a voluntary fashion around a shared secular interest was bizarre. One of the things that made Thomas Britton's society so remarkable was that only a century earlier the thought of a small-coal man forming an association based on his love of fine music was unheard of. During the seventeenth century this changed.

Although on the eve of war in 1642 there were probably no more than twenty voluntary associations in Britain, by 1722 London was home to what one visitor described as 'an Infinity of CLUBS, or SOCIETIES'. A French visitor in 1784 was astonished to find that 'clubs are established in England in every province of the realm, in every town and every country district', adding that 'it is perhaps one of the most sensible institutions, the best mark of confidence felt in society and in general'.

What made this so startling was that there was nothing like this in Europe at the time. England was 'the sole home of the modern club,' confirmed Julius Rodenberg in 1875, 'which we find nowhere else as a popular element in public life'.

Many of these eighteenth-century clubs and societies were made up of individuals united by nothing more than their shared curiosity. These included artistic societies, musical groups and assemblies of people dedicated simply to 'keeping up good Humour and Mirth' – i.e., having a regular meal together and getting drunk. As Joseph Addison pointed out in the *Spectator* in 1711, these were 'points wherein most men agree, and in which the learned and the illiterate, the dull and the airy, the philosopher and the buffoon, can all of them bear a part'.

So what had changed to make these groups based on a shared interest so much more popular in the early eighteenth century? Why do we find a small-coal man running a music society in 1700 but none doing this a century earlier? First, in the years following the accession of Charles II the prerogative courts that had once been used by the Privy Council to abolish specific associations came to an end. The legal ability of the state to shut down clubs and societies was greatly reduced. The exchange of information and news was also transformed. Following an earlier parliamentary blunder, censorship had become even more relaxed by the start of the eighteenth century, and although the government could still prosecute printers and authors for blasphemous libel or sedition, works were no longer vetted prior to publication. Literacy improved, spelling continued to be more standardized and, as the number of printing presses grew and the cost of paper fell, the range of printed material that someone like Thomas Britton could get his hands on expanded at a terrific rate.

Another shift concerned one's personal mobility. As travel became easier and faster, men and women living in cities were no longer quite so rooted to where they lived. Of course, this did not stop them from socializing mainly with those who occupied the same street, members of their family, people they saw in church or their work colleagues. But there was at least the growing possibility of spending time beyond these social groupings. Some early eighteenth-century clubs even had rules against people from the same profession joining up, such as the Two-Penny Club in London with the statute:

'None shall be admitted into the club that is of the same trade with any member of it.'

The changing shape of religion also played a part in this. By the start of the eighteenth century religious belief had ceased to be the intellectual contraceptive it had once been. Although he meant it light-heartedly, when Montesquieu visited in 1730, he wrote that 'there is no religion in England', and 'if one speaks of religion, everybody begins to laugh'. The contrast with 1630 could hardly be more pronounced. Just as religion played less of a part in urban culture, so superstition began to fade as well. 'The divine art of printing and gunpowder have frighted away Robin-good-fellow and the fairies', wrote John Aubrey. All of this contributed to what marks one of the great shifts in the story of British associations: the rise of the 'virtuoso'.

When the small-coal man Thomas Britton died in 1714, there followed a stream of obituaries and appreciations by luminaries such as Thomas Hearne, Horace Walpole and John Hawkins. Almost all described Britton as a virtuoso. This sounds like high praise. But what does it mean?

A virtuoso was someone who learned for the love of it, a devotee, an enthusiast, someone who threw themselves wholeheartedly and without pretension into their chosen subject. Ned Ward once described a gathering of virtuosos, a 'Vertuoso's Club', in which

> happy was the Man that could find out a New Star in the Firmament; discover a wry step in the Suns progress; assign new Reasons for the spots of the Moon . . . or, indeed, impart any crooked Secret to the learn'd Society, that might puzzle their Brains, and disturb their Rest for a Month afterwards.

While the idea of a virtuoso had been around for some time, during the early eighteenth century the way the word was used began to evolve. Previously a virtuoso was either university-educated, wealthy or both. By the time of Britton's death this was in flux. A virtuoso could be an aristocrat just as he might be a small-coal man. Both could cultivate their intellectual gardens, and sometimes, just sometimes, they might end up doing so together. Hence why Britton was famous for being '*a Companion for a Gentleman*'.

The virtuoso is one of the first incarnations of what we would now call a hobbyist, an amateur or an enthusiast. The fact that a much broader range of Britons could be seen in these terms opened up a new continent in the world of associations. It precipitated the creation of countless hobby groups and clubs made up of fellow enthusiasts. We began to be a nation of hobbyists.

Being a virtuoso or an amateur was not only celebrated; during the eighteenth century it came to be seen as peculiarly British. In an age when many people were trying to articulate what it was to be British, what set us apart, here was an attitude that you did not find in mainland Europe. In 1713 Richard Steele wrote an article on this that began with an epigraph from *Phaedrus*: 'Every man has his particular way of thinking and acting.' It was precisely this sentiment, this ennoblement of intellectual individuality and the idea that 'every man' could be a virtuoso, whether aristocrat or small-coal man, that began to change the shape of our associational landscape. This is the origin of the second foundation on which we build associations today, that of a shared intellectual interest.

Of Their Own Volition

It seems that there are two foundations on which we build associations: either we come together around a sense of solidarity, such as that which united the Thursday Club or Kings Cross United, or, like Thomas Britton and his fellow music lovers, we associate around a shared enthusiasm.

But these are not mutually exclusive. It's perfectly possible to find both qualities in the same group. As you can guess from their title, the Essex Badger Protection Society attracts those who are keen to protect the badgers of Essex. So this group would appear to be based on sense of solidarity. But many of its members will also have an amateur interest in these nocturnal, striped animals. We must not be too rigid with these definitions.

What else can we say about the origins of any association? You would have noticed earlier that only one in nine of the passengers travelling on the Piccadilly line train attacked in July 2005 joined Kings Cross United. Similarly it was a tiny minority of those who moved to Leicester from East Africa who became members of the Thursday Club. Most of the Manchester United fans in anguish at the thought of their club being sold off to foreign investors did not join F. C. United and went on to renew their season tickets.

The point here is that associations are voluntary. If you start one, you do so of your own volition, and if you join, it is a personal choice. When you want to leave, you can. This is quite different from, say, being compelled to join a teenage gang, or joining one and then being unable to leave. Nor is it the same as being told that you belong to a particular grouping simply because of where you live or the colour of your skin. Joining or forming an association is often a response to a condition or experience that is not of your making. The fact that none of the people who joined Kings Cross United were required to do so was one of the things that gave it such strength.

Another is that it governed itself. Kings Cross United was not an initiative launched by well-meaning public sector employees or a charity run by those with experience in dealing with the trauma of surviving terrorist attacks. Associations often seem to work better and last longer when they are voluntary, autonomous and independent.

Among other things, this removes the possibility of there

being what the psychologist Morris Nitsun has called an 'anti-group'. This is the name given to those within a group who don't want to be there, the ones who have lost faith in the group process – if they ever had it in the first place – but are forced to take part anyway. As you can imagine, an anti-group can destroy or at least dampen the spirit of collaboration in any group.

What else is there to say about why these associations come about? There is one final point to make about how associations come about, and that's to do with how much of this might be 'instinctive' or 'natural'. One of the few characteristics that really distinguishes us from our closest primate relatives is our extraordinary facility for social cognition. We are ultra-social. What has been called the 'social' part of our brains, our neocortex, is much larger than that of any other primate. This makes it easier for us to operate in large groups or pick up on social cues and follow instructions. Aristotle was right: we really are social animals.

But there is nothing in our genetic code that impels us to form associations per se. F. C. United was not simply an instinctive response to the situation that those Manchester United fans found themselves in, and the fact that we form groups called 'clubs' and 'societies' that have meetings, committees, secretaries and logos tells us more about our cultural rather than biological inheritance.

While it may be tempting to think of our desire to join or start an association as something that is hard-wired into us, a universal trait that all humans display when they experience certain conditions, there's more to it than that. In Venezuela or Vietnam, Russia or Rwanda, there will be people right now who feel similar pangs of solidarity or intellectual curiosity but who are unlikely to form clubs based on these.

The groups we are looking at rarely appear *ex nihilo* among people with no history of this. They tend to form instead among individuals who have acquired what the sociologist

George Homans once called a 'capacity for membership'. Perhaps they belonged to a club or society when they were at school, or their parents did; they may have been a volunteer, scout, girl guide, cub or brownie. They might have read about a club later on in life. Either way, associational behaviour is not universal, and the act of joining or starting an association is bound up with one's cultural and social inheritance. For the members of Kings Cross United the idea of meeting up informally in a pub for conversations and support, and doing so under the auspices of the moniker 'Kings Cross United', was not a leap beyond the quotidian. It was sensible-sounding and familiar.

In many parts of the world, however, such an idea might have come across as a bit odd. Uganda, for example, is not famous for its associational tradition. So where did the idea for the Thursday Club come from?

'Back in the 1960s, before General Amin came to power,' Raju Vora began, always referring to the man responsible for his torture by his military rank, 'I travelled to London as part of a political delegation on behalf of Uganda's ruling party. There we met with Sir Harold Macmillan. He was Prime Minister. He gave us lunch at his club, the Reform Club, I think it was. And this was the first time I had seen something like this.' He smiled. 'So it gave me an idea. I thought, "one day it would be good to start something like this".'

If we are to understand how F. C. United achieved what it did without any backing, or how there came to be an undetected surge of associational activity in the early twenty-first century, we must know what causes these groups to form. There are four things to say about this. First, associations tend to appear among people with a 'capacity for membership'. Second, they are voluntary. Third, they generally govern themselves and are rarely engineered from above. Finally, we do not associate just for the sake of it. We are far too utilitarian for that! There must be a reason, and usually this will be a shared cause or interest that we care about enough to take it that little bit further.

But what happens beyond the point when we agree to come together? And why is it that, when bound together as a group, we can often become much more than the sum of our parts?

2

The Power of Giving
What Makes Associations Last

> Forsooth, brothers, fellowship is heaven, and lack of
> fellowship is hell: fellowship is life, and lack of fellowship
> is death: and the deeds that ye do upon the earth, it is
> for fellowship's sake that ye do them.
>
> William Morris, *A Dream of John Ball*

A few years ago Mel Houghton arranged to meet two strangers
in the back room of a pub. Thanks to the photographs posted
online, the three of them recognized each other easily enough.
Houghton was a university student with a blast of bleached
blonde hair and tattoos snaking up both forearms. Steve Jeal
was the eldest of the three: a shy, likeable man in his forties
living on incapacity benefits. The third spoke to this wheel
was James Lyons, an affable, gangly man in his early twenties
who made websites.

They met in the Barley Mow in Southsea, Portsmouth, a
low-slung pub set back from the seafront. Over the floor is
a swirling red carpet. Down one wall is a bank of fruit
machines that wink and blink in silence. Elsewhere the sound
is pacific – it is the soft, shingly burr of middle-aged men
gossiping without urgency.

Houghton, Jeal and Lyons were drawn together by their
shared interest in druidry. By the end of that night they had
agreed to form a new druid order in Portsmouth.

'It happened pretty quick,' Jeal began, 'but by the end of

that night in the Barley Mow, we'd said we'd give it a go. See what happens. We worked out that I'd be Archdruid, Mel the Archdruidess, and then James would be the Sword-bearer.'

In the weeks that followed, the three of them got to work. They gave themselves druid names, so Jeal became 'Stormwatch' while Houghton would be 'Morwen', and they arranged to have their first meeting – or 'moot', as they are known in pagan circles – in the Barley Mow. They spread the word as best they could, posting comments on internet forums giving the time and date of the moot, they told their friends and distributed flyers in what seemed to be the right places – tattoo parlours, alternative cafés, bookshops, that kind of thing.

'And it worked,' said Jeal, looking surprised. 'A good number of people turned up. We had the back room of the pub pretty much full. And at the end people started asking me when the next one was. I was amazed! So I lined up some more moots after that. Got some speakers sorted. Then we got the name worked out. Genesis. I wanted something that suggested a new start, you know, a new beginning. Plus, I was listening to a bit of Genesis at the time, as you do. But recently we've had to change the name to, let me see, the Genesis Order of Druids and Eclectic Pagans. Turns out that some of the members weren't happy about it as it was,' he added with a quick grin.

One year on, and the Genesis Order of Druids (and Eclectic Pagans) was flourishing. It had an inner core of about a dozen members based in Portsmouth, along with ten more living further afield, and another twenty peripheral attendees. They had a website, special costumes they'd wear for ceremonies and a logo. But what Jeal had found most striking about that first year was not only how rapidly a sense of camaraderie had developed between them, but the fact that everyone kept turning up. Having spent hours promoting that first moot, the sessions that followed seemed to take care of themselves. The members were happy to take on responsibilities and give their time and effort. It was as though the Genesis Order had become self-sustaining. As long as everyone did their job, the group could motor along indefinitely.

'And then, after a few months, people started coming up to me and asking for more meetings. Seeing as there hadn't been any druid group in Portsmouth for a bit, and there weren't many of us, I was a bit surprised. But it just seemed as though the more we met, the more everyone wanted to get together.'

As well as the monthly moots, Jeal organized a series of meditation nights. Still, it wasn't enough. So he got permission to perform outdoor ceremonies in the grounds of a nearby park, and later a castle. There they celebrated the spring and autumn equinoxes, Beltane, Samhain and the summer solstice. During those first six months the number of times this association met soared.

But why did these druids and pagans want so many more meetings, and what was it that kept them coming back each time?

The Gift Cycle

Let's say I ask you round for dinner. I cook some food, make sure you have everything you want to drink and eat, we talk about this and that, and towards the end of the night you reach for your coat, say goodbye and head for the door. At this point I produce a bill.

At a guess, you'd be taken aback. I know I would be. Although we live in an age in which the idea of providing a service or buying a series of objects, adding value and capital-izing them is by no means alien, asking for a bill in this context is unusual to say the least. Custom dictates that the offer of a meal in someone's home is not a commercial exchange.

Now imagine a slightly different scenario. The same meal, only at the end of it I do not present a bill. The food, the time I spent preparing it, the gas used for cooking, the electricity that lit the room – all of these constitute a small gift of many parts.

We say goodbye, you wander out into the night, bored no doubt by the conversation but happy that you've eaten and almost certainly experiencing a mild sense of goodwill having received this small gift, the gift of the meal. There's a good chance that, having given it, I too will feel some kind of pleasure. It will register in the caudate nucleus in my brain and the nucleus accumbens. Three or four days later you send a note to say thank you. Again, when I receive this I am bound to experience a flash of goodwill, just as you might upon posting it.

Yet by sending that card have you paid for the meal? No is the easy answer. Card-for-meal is an asymmetric exchange. So this is not a commercial trade. Yet there is now a sense of parity between us. It is not as if you owe me anything. Plus, there seems to be a fractionally stronger bond between us now that we have exchanged these gifts.

In *The Gift*, a provocative and often brilliant analysis of creativity, Lewis Hyde described the notion of a gift cycle. As he explained, this appears when a series of people exchange gifts over an extended period. The gifts could be physical objects, or gifts of expertise, time, knowledge or a gift of many parts, such as a meal. When gifts pass between people, it is not a commercial exchange but a gift exchange. Once you and I have exchanged gifts, you could say that there was a gift cycle between us. It's not much of a gift cycle, but it'll do.

What makes a gift cycle so interesting from our point of view is how it can change the relationship between those involved. It is here that we begin to see why those druids wanted more meetings, what fuelled their sense of camaraderie and why it took so little persuasion to keep them coming back. The same principle applies to every association.

Fellowship

'During the first year we had all sorts of talks,' Jeal began, warming to his theme. 'Some of the members did demonstrations on how to make candles, things like that. James spoke about druid staffs. Someone else did one on meditation. And then at the actual events we'd share tips on ceremonies, rituals, that kind of thing,' he paused and looked around, before adding, as if in conspiracy, 'you see, there's quite a lot of back and forth when it comes to how you should do the different pagan rituals. Everyone's got their own opinion.'

They helped each other with their outfits. Nick, a man with ears full of silvery rings, would play with his band called Cool Banana after the ceremonies. Those who knew a thing or two about computers would help out others who did not – and there was always something that went wrong: an email address that didn't work or a website that had gone down. One druidess provided the use of her basement for meditation nights. Those who travelled to moots from afar were put up by fellow pagans.

'All in all, it's quite a little community.' Jeal nodded, brushing his hair forward. 'It helps you save money, that's one thing. Also, when people have personal problems we really try and help each other out. So if someone gets sick we'll send healing energy, call them up, that kind of thing.'

This is a classic gift cycle. Of course, it is more complex than the one we imagined earlier as it contains some twenty people rather than two. But the social implications are the same. Hyde argued that every time a gift is given, it 'bears fruit'.

There is an increase. Not a physical increase, obviously, but a social and spiritual one. The 'fruit' is the goodwill that appears between two people as the gift moves from one to the other. So when I gave you the gift of the meal, the 'fruit' was the goodwill that accrued like interest in the relationship between us. The same applies to the card you sent a little later. As it is given, there is a tiny increase that will reside in the relationship between us.

Gifts connote community. They strengthen the bonds between us, and within a small group such as the Genesis Order, every time one member helped out another, gave a talk or in any way contributed something to the group, they were giving a gift. It brought these people together. Each of these gifts was 'an agent of social cohesion'. Every pass within a football team is a gift exchanged between the members of this group, every cue met in an amateur dramatic society, every chord sung in harmony by a choir, or every tip passed from one beekeeper to another in a beekeeping association – these are all tiny gifts that feed into the gift cycles that keep these associations going.

With so many people giving these gifts, and many of them being directed at the group rather than a specific member, an interesting thing happens. The 'fruit' does not merely strengthen the bond between two people. Instead it exists more generally in the group. The result over a sustained period of time? A sense of fellowship. As gifts are passed around within any club, society or association, the spirit of cohesion and camaraderie grows. The fellowship you experience within a group is nothing more than an accumulation of the 'fruit' that appears every time a gift is given or received.

This is the Power of Giving. In any group whose members help each other out and do so consistently, the Power of Giving pulls them together. It generates fellowship, and it was this that bound the druids together as one.

There is nothing new about the Power of Giving. For

Aristotle, *koinôniai*, or 'communities', including associations and clubs, were those groups in which men and women were to be found 'sharing a good activity, feature of identity or any combination thereof'. Within each association that Edmund Burke called a 'little platoon' there was 'trust in the hands of all those who compose it'. In Alexis de Tocqueville's associations there was an 'understanding developed only by the reciprocal action of men one upon another'. In each case it is the 'sharing', 'trust' or 'reciprocal action' that brings us closer together. The Power of Giving sustained the members of the Thursday Club as they met more often, as well as Kings Cross United or Thomas Britton's musical society.

It also brought together the members of F. C. United during the months that followed their formation in 2005. As they beavered away at securing a ground, recruiting new members, dealing with the legal and administrative minutiae of establishing a football club as well as trying to lay the foundations for a successful team, those involved were pulled together by the Power of Giving. Each of these acts was a tiny gift, and the more of these gifts they gave, the stronger the sense of camaraderie between them. This is what kept the club going.

Boosting the Sense of Fellowship

There are some associations, however, that don't seem to be bound together like this. It can be down to nothing more than appearances. 'The foundation of cooperation is not really trust,' wrote game theorist Robert Axelrod, 'but the durability of the relationship'. If, on joining the Genesis Order, you got the impression that this group was unlikely to last more than a few months, you might not want to pour your time and energy into it. Selfish as it may sound, we are often less likely to give gifts to a group if that group is unable to give back to us. Have you ever exchanged presents with someone, only to find that one of you has put a lot more into it – be it time, money or thought? It's an awkward feeling, one that can put a dent in any relationship. The same principle applies within an association. There must be a degree of balance in the gift cycle. Had Jeal taken it upon himself to provide his home for others to sleep in, give each of the talks, build websites for others, make all the costumes, prepare and lead all the ceremonies and play music for the group afterwards as a one-man-band, the input of others might have cooled. The contribution of any individual to an association needs to be roughly in proportion to that of the others in the group. Otherwise the gift cycle becomes skewed. We end up feeling that we are not part of a fellowship and we give less.

At the other extreme, you might find that, while most people are helping out and giving gifts, there are one or two 'social loafers' lurking in the group. A social loafer is essentially a freeloader, someone who joins an association and is happy to benefit from the generosity of others without pulling their weight. As you can imagine, with too many social loafers in any group the balance of the gift cycle is lost. Again, the Power of Giving fails to kick in and the association may not last as long.

But for Lewis Hyde what really shatters the equanimity of any gift cycle is if one member exploits what the group has achieved together for his or her personal ends. When Edmund Burke eulogized the trust in an association, he warned that 'none but traitors would barter it away for their own personal advantage.' In the early seventeenth century Ben Jonson railed against the poet who used 'old ends [. . .] To stop gaps in his loose writing' or made 'his plays [from] jests, stolen from each table'. To steal from the table is to sell out. It is to join a lively conversation in which everyone is contributing before going home and writing down the best lines you have heard and claiming them as your own. It engenders a negative kind of reciprocity in the group, one that 'strengthens the spirits – constructive or destructive – of individualism and clannishness'. Again, when this happens, the gift cycle suffers, the Power of Giving cannot work its magic and the group becomes less sustainable.

What the Power of Giving Says about Voluntarism

I think the Power of Giving can tell us a great deal about how associations work and what keeps them going. For one thing, it shows us why the members of a group in which the leader is paid to be there – such as a keep-fit class or a creative writing course – are less likely to feel a strong sense of fellowship. In their landmark survey in 1986 Jeff Bishop and Paul Hoggett made a critical distinction between associations such as these, whose members felt the group was being run 'by them, for us', and those where the organization was 'by some of us, for all of us'. Having a paid leader is, really, allowing one person to take advantage of the gift cycle. That person profits from the group's collaboration, and therefore the Power of Giving is weakened.

If a band of rebellious fitness enthusiasts or budding writers were to break away from either group and form their own association, then the Power of Giving suggests you'd find a much stronger sense of camaraderie within each. This is why a group that makes its decisions collectively is bound to last longer and achieve more than one that does not. The bonds in these breakaway groups are horizontal rather than vertical. Naturally, the gift cycle is more balanced. They'd also save themselves the cost of hiring in a paid teacher, a reminder of the other benefit of a thriving gift cycle: you save money. This is what a gift cycle really is. At its simplest, it is a band of people doing favours for each other and in the process forming a lasting social connection.

A great example of this is what happens in one of the caving clubs based on the Mendips, in Somerset. Among the members of the Bristol Exploration Club there is what's known as the 'Bank of Mendip'. This is the name given to the club's gift cycle. Among these cavers there is at least one lawyer, teacher, doctor, vet, civil engineer, car mechanic, welder, accountant, carpenter, computer salesman, glazier, security systems operative and farmer. Whenever one of them needs a job done by someone with any of these skills, they turn to the Bank of Mendip. The 'bank' will give them a handsome discount, or they might get the work done for free. Not only does this save them money, but it strengthens the social ties within the group.

The Power of Giving has another implication for the way we see groups, one that I think is even more important. In Britain every year, millions of hours are devoted to the operation of hundreds of thousands of voluntary associations. Of course this time is given for free. What kept F. C. United going during its early years and allowed it to expand so quickly without financial backing were the thousands of hours given by its community of supporters. By the end of the club's third season there were as many as a hundred volunteers who would work five to six hours on each match day. It would have cost thousands of pounds to pay these men and women, but they did not want to be paid. At no cost to F. C. United they manned stalls, sold home-made food, attracted new members and ran the Megacabin – their tongue-in-cheek take on the Manchester United Megastore that was based in a Portakabin. They maintained an efficient website and email list, wrote accounts of each game and provided entertainment before and after the matches, as well as live online commentary for their rapidly expanding army of armchair fans.

What makes this all the more remarkable is that during the week, had any of these volunteers been asked to do five or six hours of unpaid labour by their employer, there would have been a bit of grumbling. Yet there was none of that at F. C. United. These supporters gave their time gladly and did not want to be paid for it.

The reason appears to be simple. They were amateurs. F. C. United was their passion, so they were doing this for the love of it. But there's more to it than that. If every favour you do for the group is a gift, then just as you give to the group, it gives back to you in kind. When you have received something from the group, you are bound to feel the urge to return this favour and to give to the group again. This can keep going indefinitely, with each member giving, receiving and giving again, until you have a self-perpetuating gift cycle.

If the gift cycle remains balanced, an association like F. C. United or the Genesis Order can run for many years without the people who pour their energy into the group asking to be paid. They are compensated in a different way. Their salary, if you like, comes in the form of the favours, expertise and knowledge that they receive. The fellowship between members is a regular bonus.

This gives us a crucial insight into what fuels so many associations. The Power of Giving means that these groups will often be driven by more than their members' commitment to a certain cause, it is their social connection to one another that matters just as much. What keeps them coming back is both a belief in a certain ideal or an interest in a given subject, as well as the gifts they receive from the group and the camaraderie this creates.

The New Economics Foundation once described voluntary associations as 'disproportionately effective'. They meant this in a financial sense. The Power of Giving means that these groups can do much, much more with less. F. C. United could expand at such speed purely because it had a community of volunteers bound together by the Power of Giving. This is why the club did not require major financial backing.

So far we have seen this work only in groups such as F. C. United or the Genesis Order. These are essentially self-help groups in the sense that their members come together to help each other out and further their own interests. But does the Power of Giving apply to groups with more altruistic aims? Does it keep them going in the same way?

Chevra Kadisha

In north London there are a number of *Chevra Kadishas*, or Jewish burial societies. Chayim Gershon is a long-standing member of one. 'We have about twenty people involved in our locality,' he told me. 'So when someone in the local community dies, about five or six of us will come together to prepare the body for burial. In the Jewish faith this has to happen within twenty-four hours of death. It means you need to be on call all the time.' He paused. 'People don't often let you know when they plan to die. So you come together, you prepare the body, then you'll go to the funeral. But of course you don't tell anyone in the family what you've done.'

Within Judaism, belonging to a *Chevra Kadisha* is one of the great acts of charity. It is known as *Chesed Shel Emet*, or 'the truest act of Kindness', because the person on whom this favour is bestowed cannot pay you back. Nor should you boast about it or look for praise, which is why you do not tell the family what you have done at the funeral. It also explains why Chayim Gershon would give only a pseudonym, lest it appeared that he was taking credit for his role in his local *Chevra Kadisha*.

It is hard to think of a more altruistic association. But even here the Power of Giving was at work. A clear sense of fellowship had developed between the members of this group over the years.

'Once a month we meet in each other's homes for religious discussion, hospitality,' Chayim went on, 'and I've been doing it for twenty-six years now, so yes, you form a powerful bond with the others.'

This is important. In charitable groups as much as those dedicated to their own ends, if there is a balanced gift cycle, it will strengthen the camaraderie among the members. This can keep them coming back for many years. It allows the group to keep going.

The government is almost always looking to encourage civic participation, especially in a time of economic recession. The Power of Giving can make this easier. The personal commitment of even the most upstanding, virtuous citizen to a civic cause is bound to wax and wane. Yet if you apply the Power of Giving to this it becomes possible to make civic participation last longer. How? You ensure that the urge to help is funnelled into a voluntary group. Associations act as insurances against caprice. If our passion for any cause or subject wavers over the years, the social connection we feel towards others in an association tends to grow steadily.

The Preston Stroke Club was set up in 1975. One of the volunteers in this group, Edna Greenwood, has been helping out for the last thirty-five years. She is now in her nineties. Until very recently Edna was the group driver. She has now decided to stay off the roads, although she remains the club's Treasurer. Violet Birchall has volunteered for the club for more than fifteen years and is well over eighty-five (she keeps her exact age to herself). When asked what they enjoy about belonging to this club, both say it is the friendship and the relationship within the group that keeps them coming back.

A thriving gift cycle is valuable because it inspires us to keep going. So it makes sense that corporations all over the world long to inspire among their staff the camaraderie of a voluntary organization. They may take their employees on 'away days' that focus on team-building and exercises that have them problem-solving together – building things, falling backwards into each other's arms or running around firing paintballs together at a rival team. Essentially they are playing at giving each other gifts. A gift cycle may ensue, and this in turn can inspire more effort. At least, that's the idea.

Here, then, is the practical value of association. At its best, the Power of Giving allows a small group to keep going for longer. It means we can plug away at a particular interest or cause for an indefinite period and at negligible cost. The key to this is the social connection we feel.

Bonding and Bridging

So far this has all been one-way traffic. It is hard to imagine a dark side to the Power of Giving. If we help each other out within an association – be it a charity, social club, community group, football team or musical society – there follows a sense of fellowship, and this motivates us to do more. It generates trust and cohesion. These all sound like Good Things. But there is a different way of seeing this.

Bowling Alone is Robert Putnam's best-selling account of the collapse of civic society in the United States during the late twentieth century. Throughout, he refers to 'social capital'. This is the term used to describe the value of anyone's social connections or the networks to which they belong. If you want to calculate your financial capital, you would get in touch with your bank manager and tot up the value of any assets you own. To estimate your social capital, you would evaluate the relationships you have with neighbours, family, friends, work colleagues, acquaintances, business contacts and any broader social networks you may belong to.

Although the concept of social capital was not originally Putnam's, in *Bowling Alone* he gives it his own spin. He introduces the idea of 'bridging' social capital and that which merely 'bonds'. According to Putnam, bridging social capital occurs in relationships between professional contacts and acquaintances. It implies loose, non-associative ties that allow you to 'get ahead' in life. Putnam calls it 'sociological WD40'. He is clearly a fan.

By contrast, bonding social capital is 'a kind of sociological superglue' that is geared less towards getting ahead in life than to 'getting by'. As Putnam has it, bonding social capital lingers like a bedsore in long-standing relationships between people who have grown up around each other, those who belong to the same clubs or associations and any other close-knit group with a pronounced boundary. So the social capital you'd find in the Genesis Order, the *Chevra Kadisha* we looked at, or any other group bound by the Power of Giving, is bonding, not bridging, and bonding is to be avoided. Why does Putnam have it in for this kind of social capital?

There are several reasons. The first is speculative: he is imposing his political values on his analysis by setting up 'getting ahead' as an ideal to which we should all aspire. You could easily argue that 'getting ahead' is anything but a universal ideal, and that it implies a materialist, short-term and often selfish approach to life, one that rarely induces lasting happiness. Nevertheless this may explain why Putnam prefers bridging social capital to that which bonds. The second reason why he is set against bonding social capital is more explicit. He feels that a powerful sense of loyalty within any club or association 'may also create strong out-group antagonism', and that it may have 'negative external effects'.

In other words, the greater the camaraderie you feel within a tightly knit association, the more likely you are to be hostile to those who don't belong to your group. In-group bias can lead to out-group antagonism. That is the idea. In the past, tribal violence, rioting and gang warfare have been attributed to this strong feeling of in-group bias. But surely it does not follow that feeling great loyalty towards the members of your group compels you to discriminate against those beyond? Think of the *Chevra Kadisha* in north London, a group that combines a strong sense of fellowship with extreme altruism. Their social capital is bonded, and yet they display out-group *co-operation*.

Putnam's perspective would not concern us, but for the fact that it has had a considerable impact on social policy-makers in Britain during the early twenty-first century. Between 2000, the year *Bowling Alone* was published, and 2008 the number of annual references to 'social capital' in academic publications more than doubled. Social capital became fashionable. It was also integral to the delivery of New Labour's community agenda which accelerated after 2002. The understanding of this term in Whitehall was essentially Putnam's. Within most government papers or policy documents produced between 2000 and 2010 that contain a detailed reference to social capital you will also find a few words describing the difference between bonding and bridging social capital with the same implication that bridging social capital is preferable to that which bonds. For example, in his introductory essay to the 2003 edition of the Office for National Statistics' *Social Trends*, Paul Haezewindt assures his readers that 'negative effects occur when social capital is used as a private rather than a public good' and that 'in some instances it could be argued that the stronger the social capital within a group, the greater the hostility to outsiders.' The message here is plain: from the government's point of view, small, tightly knit associations can become insular and hostile as a result of the loyalty their members feel towards each other. Perhaps by helping each other out, the men and women of F. C. United were becoming more hostile towards those outside the group? Perhaps one leads automatically to the other and that counter-example of the *Chevra Kadisha* is really an anomaly?

This raises a much bigger question, one that takes us to the heart of how we think about human nature and what our evolution as a species has involved. Put simply, if you belong to a group with a strong sense of fellowship, camaraderie, cohesion or what the great Arab historian Ibn Khaldun called *asabiyyah*, does this mean that you are more inclined to discriminate against those outside your group? Do you automatically begin to see them in a different light, a more negative one? Is it possible, even in a time of crisis, to feel a sense of camaraderie within your group *and* to co-operate with those outside it?

Tit for Tat

During the first few years of the First World War a curious thing happened along the Western Front. Informal and tacit truces frequently broke out between opposing units of British and German troops pitched on either side of no-man's-land. 'In one section the hour of 8 to 9 A.M. was regarded as consecrated to "private business",' wrote one officer, 'and certain places indicated by a flag were regarded as out of bounds by the snipers on both sides.' Rather than shoot at the first opportunity, the two sides 'usually forbore to inter-fere with one another'.

'Mr Boche ain't a bad feller,' one British NCO explained. 'You leave 'im alone: 'e'll leave you alone.'

A typical reaction to the sight of twenty Germans cutting the grass behind their trench was 'Let 'em, by all means!' The most famous examples of these tacit truces were those that swept along the Western Front like a benign virus on Christmas Day 1914, including several that involved games of football.

It was not to last. As one commanding officer fumed, 'these people evidently did not know there was a war on. Both sides apparently believed in the policy of "live and let live".' Over the years that followed senior figures on both sides did whatever they could to stamp it out. Although 'live and let live' was a superb survival strategy for the troops involved, it was not helping either nation to win the war.

The story of these tacit truces appeared in the 1980s in *The Evolution of Cooperation*, by game theorist and political scientist Robert Axelrod. This book went on to be cited in more than 500 other books and 4,000 articles. Richard Dawkins thought it was so important that it should 'replace the Gideon Bible'.

So what did it say? Axelrod had set out to explore the idea that, when faced with limited resources, humans become selfish and antagonistic in the name of survival, and that during our evolution this strategy was dominant. Those tacit truces during the First World War provided him with a perfect example of something else: in-group bias leading not to out-group antagonism but out-group co-operation. What's more, it was highly effective. For both sides in-group bias combined with out-group co-operation constituted the most successful strategy for long-term survival.

More than a decade after *The Evolution of Cooperation* came out, a freelance journalist named Wendy Barnaby wrote a book on biological warfare. Her publishers liked it so much they asked her to write another one, this time about 'water wars'. At the time, there were plenty of prophetic statements being made about how the conflicts of the future would involve water rights. In 1995 the former World Bank vice-president Ismail Serageldin had suggested that although 'the wars of this century were fought over oil, the wars of the next century will be fought over water'. Barnaby got to work. Soon she had a structure in place and a rough outline of what each chapter would contain. Suddenly she ground to a halt.

This was not due to a lack of inspiration, time or will. The problem was the evidence, or rather the lack of it. Having looked much harder at the subject, Barnaby was forced to conclude that neighbouring 'countries do not go to war over water, they solve their water shortages through trade and international agreements. Cooperation, in fact, is the dominant response to shared water resources.' As she explained:

> between 1948 and 1999, cooperation over water, including the signing of treaties, far outweighed conflict over water and violent conflict in particular. Of 1,831 instances of inter-actions over international freshwater resources tallied over that time period (including everything from unofficial verbal exchanges to economic agreements or military action), 67% were cooperative, only 28% were conflictive, and the remaining 5% were neutral or insignificant. In those five decades, there were no formal declarations of war over water.

This was not for lack of motive. Some of the states worst hit by water shortages had burgeoning populations and experienced increasingly variable or reduced levels of precipitation. Water was becoming scarce. But this did not lead automatically to violent out-group antagonism on a national scale. Instead it seemed to encourage the opposite: out-group co-operation. As Barnaby explained, this 'killed my book'. Sadly the publisher was not interested in an account of regular, small-scale co-operation. 'An absence of war over water would not sell.' In due course she found another publisher for the revised work.

The story of those opposing units during the early years of the First World War and Barnaby's account of 'water wars' are unusual. Yet they embody the same idea. Each seemed to suggest that in-group bias and out-group co-operation were not only a good fit, but they represented a very successful strategy.

Axelrod took this further. He wanted to see just how successful it was. He developed a computerized adaptation of something called the 'Prisoner's Dilemma'. This is an imaginary scenario beloved of game theorists, in part because for so long it resisted the hoary embrace of mathematics. The dilemma is this: two individuals team up to commit a crime; they get caught and are sentenced to a year in jail, whereupon they are separated and told that if either of them implicates the other, then their sentence will be halved while their fellow inmate will have his or her term increased to five years. Both prisoners understand that their colleague faces the same dilemma. The drama begins.

Axelrod took this problem beyond the paradigm of a conventional psychological experiment. Rather than see it as a one-off decision, he pictured the same choice occurring repeatedly between a single pair of prisoners. Each would have to live with the consequences of their actions. Axelrod created a computer programme that played out the Prisoner's Dilemma several hundred times. He christened it the 'Iterated Prisoner's Dilemma' and put out a call to game theorists and mathematicians worldwide to come up with the best strategy to survive this scenario.

The responses flooded in, many of them laborious and complex. Yet the one that proved to be unbeatable was also the simplest: co-operation followed by reciprocation. The best advice you could give to either prisoner was that they should start by co-operating with their fellow inmate and from that moment merely mimic what the other one did. Axelrod called this 'tit for tat'. It remains the most successful strategy for surviving the Iterated Prisoner's Dilemma.

But what does this have to do with the Western Front, water wars (or a lack of) and Putnam's idea that in-group bias leads to out-group antagonism? Axelrod demonstrated in a theoretical sense that in-group bias and out-group co-operation were in fact natural bedfellows. Together, they represented a highly successful strategy, one that may have been dominant during the course of our evolution.

What Axelrod also argued was that this kind of co-operative relationship was more likely when each side recognized some kind of parity with the other. The opposing military units in the First World War would often remind each other of their strength, with German snipers illustrating 'their prowess to the British by aiming at spots on the walls of cottages and firing until they had cut a hole'. When they did not shoot, it was a co-operative gesture rather than an act of laziness or ineptitude. Equally, in the Iterated Prisoner's Dilemma each side is just as powerful as the other.

Time also played a part in this. What distinguished Axelrod's version of the Prisoner's Dilemma from its earlier incarnation was that each prisoner knew that his or her actions had repercussions. Their relationship with their former colleague was going to last, no matter what. In the trenches, co-operation was far more common where 'the same small units faced each other in immobile sectors for extended periods of time'.

This suggests that in the right circumstances we are quite capable of feeling a great sense of loyalty within a group and of co-operating with those who do not belong to it. Not only are we capable of this, but it can be a highly successful strategy. For Axelrod this combination of in-group bias and out-group co-operation was so advantageous that it must have played a significant part in our evolution. Others have since echoed this, including Martin Nowak, of Harvard University, who has placed co-operation alongside natural selection and mutation as the third great pillar of evolution.

Is it possible, as Amartya Sen once suggested, that 'enmity has not been the general condition of the relationship between people across the world in history'? Rather than think of our distant, prehistoric past in terms of the 'survival of the fittest', and buying into the crude Hobbesian notion of life before civilization as one long-drawn-out bloodbath, perhaps we can recast it in terms of the survival of the fittest *strategy*. Often this would involve co-operating with those outside your group.

On reading *Mutual Aid*, Peter Kropotkin's classic account of collective, sociable behaviour among indigenous peoples, a book that stressed the role of co-operation in our pre-industrial past, the naturalist Henry Bates wrote to Kropotkin, calling his book the 'most beautiful proof of the truth of the theory of natural selection'. It was 'true Darwinism', he wrote, adding, 'it is a shame to think what they have made of Darwin's ideas.' 'They' refers to the ideologues who took Darwin's account of evolution to be proof of all things individualistic, anti-collective and belligerent.

It seems that Putnam's attitude to small groups came from a very similar place. Look beyond this and it becomes clear that a strong sense of fellowship within any association – be it a club, society, choir, community group, football team or burial organization – does not mean that its members will automatically start to discriminate against those outside their group. It does not rule out that possibility, but if it happens, it is not simply an account of the bonded nature of the group.

This is important. It suggests that bonding social capital is not something to be wary of. What keeps an association like F. C. United going is the Power of Giving. With that goes a fantastic sense of camaraderie and trust among the members. Without this, the group would fall apart. If we are to understand the power of association, we must not think of fellowship as a negative force, but recognize it as evidence of a thriving group.

3

The Hothouse Effect
Why We Take Things Further in Groups

A club is neither a series of individuals attending a series
of classes, a place for eternal billiards, dancing, and
bean-bag hurling, nor is a club a club leader. A club is a
community engaged in the task of educating itself.
Josephine Macalister Brew, *In the Service of Youth*

For most of her life Laura Wilkie has lived in or around
Edinburgh. She has a chunk of blonde hair, and her speech
is peppered with lovely jolts of laughter, so you see her teeth
a lot – and they are great teeth, rounded and white. Wilkie
is one of those people who sweeps others along with her;
she's enthusiastic and infectious without being earnest.

Several years ago Wilkie arrived at what she would later
call 'a bit of a strange place'. There she was, a woman in
her early thirties doing a job that she enjoyed. She was in
a loving relationship living in the city of her birth and was
surrounded by friends. But something was missing. 'There
were moments when I felt life was rushing by too fast,' she
said. 'So I asked myself what was important in life? What
do I love doing, and how can I do more of it?'

The answer, at least one of them, was that she loved to
read. Opening into a smile, she said, 'I've always wanted a
book group. Ever since I was little. I love the way you read
a book when you know you'll be talking about it afterwards.
You get so much more out of it! Also that sense of being

with others and having a shared purpose. There's something almost, well, utopian about that, about like-minded
individuals coming together with a commitment to something
they love.'

So she started a book group. Less than two years later
what had become known as Laura's Book Group won the
Penguin Readers' Group Prize. It was thought to be the
nation's most interesting and dedicated reading group. And
yet winning that prize was not what really surprised Wilkie
about starting a book group.

'What I don't think I'd realized beforehand was just how
easy it was to get the group going. It took about half an hour
of organization, if that.'

Wilkie, her sister and a friend simply agreed on a venue,
a date and a book. They then sent group emails to friends
who they thought would be interested.

'That was it. All done. The hardest bit was waiting for the
first meeting. I remember getting so worried that we'd have
nothing to say. "So what did you think of the book?" "Er,
great. How about you?" "Yeah, really good." "Right," pause,
"more wine anyone?"'

On the agreed evening a room-sized group of women and
one or two men met in a flat in Edinburgh. Just as the members
of Britton's music society came together around nothing more
than a love of music, so these people were united simply by
their passion for books. They were neither kin nor neighbours, and this was not a reunion of old friends so nobody
there knew everyone in the room.

'And it started slowly,' she said thoughtfully. 'But there was
one person, Marla, who I remember making a couple of
provocative comments quite early on. After that it just got
going.' They began to laugh, to make fun of each other, talk,
drink, think, talk some more, and, as those who were there
that night will tell you, the next four hours flew by.

By the end of the night it was clear that there was

something about this blend of people that worked. They clicked. The discussion was passionate, funny and interesting. At no point did it teeter into pretentiousness. Nor did the night become a succession of self-revelatory monologues. There was a seductive mixture of analysis, gossip and silliness that left each one wanting more – more books, more discussion and more about their fellow readers. As Margaret Atwood put it, 'I suppose you could say that the real, hidden subject of a book group discussion is the book group members themselves.' Like the best opening chapter, that initial meeting suggested much more than it revealed.

The Next Level

There was one other element of this book group that surprised Wilkie, and it tells us a great deal about how associations work. Early on, the members of Laura's Book Group agreed to take it in turns to host meetings. Without realizing it, they had established a gift cycle. After the second or third session an interesting thing began to happen. Members started to theme the meeting to the book they were discussing. So for a session on *Friday Night Lights*, H. G. Bissinger's account of an American high-school football team in the late 1980s, they came dressed as cheerleaders and high-school jocks. To eat, they picked at a smorgasbord of iced buns, burgers and hot dogs, all washed down with Dr Pepper.

'The food was foul,' Wilkie assured me, pulling a face at the memory of it, 'but authentic to the book.'

For the discussion of Geoff Ryman's *The King's Last Song*, set in Cambodia, Jon, the host, served deep-fried crickets ordered in from South-East Asia. When it was their turn, others put up posters or played music in keeping with the period of the book being discussed, or they arranged slide-shows to give a loose *mise-en-scène*. A discussion of *The Thirty-Nine Steps* took place in a pub below the Forth Road Bridge. When I joined them for a conversation on *Time's Arrow*, Martin Amis's novel about a German doctor which plays out in reverse, from end to beginning, the meal was served backwards.

Now, if you were reading *The King's Last Song* by yourself, and you did not belong to a book group, although you might wonder to yourself what a deep-fried cricket tastes like – what its texture was, the sound your teeth would make as they collapse on to it – you are unlikely to order in a bag of them from South-East Asia just to find out. That would be taking things too far, surely? If you belonged to a book group like Wilkie's, though, that calculation is turned on its head. For them, this kind of behaviour is not only legitimate but encouraged. The group had become what is sometimes called an 'interpretive community', in which each member is surrounded by others who share their particular passion. Order in a bag of crickets and you'd be congratulated. Your fellow enthusiasts would remind you of this feat at later meetings, they might pat you on the back, crack a joke about it. They'll want to outdo you when it's their turn to host a meeting.

So what really surprised Wilkie about her book group was just how dedicated everyone became and how far they were prepared to take their passion for reading. 'Fearless' was the word she used. But it rarely feels like that. For those involved it is a release rather than an act of bravery. At last a weight is lifted. As Marla hissed to Wilkie during that first meeting, 'this is so indulgent!'

Not only could these book enthusiasts go a little bit further in their response to a book, but they were required to read more often and to take on a wider range of material. One month they could be discussing a work of mass-market contemporary fiction such as Khaled Hosseini's *The Kite Runner*, the next it could be Toni Morrison's *Song of*

Solomon, John Buchan's *The Thirty-Nine Steps*, Italo Calvino's *If on a Winter's Night a Traveller* or Mikhail Bulgakov's *The Master and Margarita*. If before you stuck to one genre, joining this group was the beginning of a journey around the world of literature. You became a more seasoned reader.

When the *Times* columnist Alyson Rudd joined a reading group one of the first titles she read was Niall Williams's *Four Letters of Love*. When she found out what the book was, as she recalled, 'my heart sank, it sounded awful. It would surely be whimsical and soppy and indulgent and quite possibly dull and earnest to boot. One love letter is more than enough for me, I thought.' She read it all the same.

'That was when I became a true, even zealous, book club fan. *Four Letters* is remarkable; a moving and quietly beautiful novel and one I would never have read without my book club.'

A number of things will often happen when you join an association of fellow enthusiasts. First, your knowledge of that subject tends to broaden. Second, you are free to take your interest to a new level and to do things that before you might have stopped yourself from doing. Finally, your understanding of the subject will almost certainly deepen. Why? Because of the dizzying, protean possibilities of what goes on within a group discussion. For me, this is where associations really come into their own.

As the social psychologist Jay Hall has shown, in any group that is accustomed to debate you will usually find better and more accurate judgements emerging out of a group discussion than you would if you had asked the most talented member of the group. 'We call this happy event *synergy*,' he wrote: 'Conflict, effectively managed, is a necessary precondition for creativity.' Around the grit of conversational disagreement forms a pearl of collaborative wisdom.

The discussion in Laura's Book Group was fascinating for

several reasons. The participants were articulate. They could express their opinions and seemed to enjoy doing so. They were certainly well practised. As the dandy Sebastian Horsley once said, 'the tongue is the only weapon that sharpens with use.' They could adopt other ideas, adapt to them, change course, move up a gear as well as down, and in every sense throw themselves into the helter-skelter of a lively debate. During the discussion of *Time's Arrow* that I witnessed, my understanding of that book improved hugely.

Incidentally, the nature of one of these discussions is such that it is rarely a good idea to have your reading group discuss a book that you love. This was something that almost every member of Laura's Book Group explained to me. In most debates there will be such a range of opinions that by the end of it the book you once loved unconditionally begins to feel tainted.

Yet none of this can happen without the Power of Giving. It is the gift cycle within a group that keeps you coming back month after month, and gives the group some kind of durability. In Laura's Book Group, for example, when it was your turn to host the group, you would pour energy into it partly because the group had given you so much in the past. This was your chance to return these favours. The evening you prepare is a gift to the group, and if you are on the receiving end, then that meal only adds to your desire to give back at a later date.

As we know, a thriving gift cycle also draws its members together. Two years after starting the association, the members of this group were going to each other's weddings, and they saw each other more than many of their close friends. It was this social connection that ensured the group would keep going. When this happens, it becomes much easier to take your interest further.

But does this principle apply elsewhere? What happens in a group that is not dedicated to a shared interest? Does the

Power of Giving mean that an association of protesters, for example, will take their protest to a new level, just as readers in a book group acquire a deeper and broader understanding of books?

Turbulence in Cardigan

In 2005 Channel 4 launched 'The Big Art Project'. The idea was for 'communities' all over Britain to propose sites for the installation of public works of art. The community would then work with an established artist to realize a permanent installation.

In Wales a property developer who lived near Cardigan suggested a prominent stretch of the River Teifi at the heart of this small medieval town as a potential location for one of these installations. This happened to be right next to a stretch of quayside that he had recently developed. Unaware of this, or just unconcerned, the Channel 4 judges chose Cardigan as one of the seven winning venues. Most residents still had no idea that anything was afoot.

Next, the Mexican-Canadian artist Rafael Lozano-Hemmer was selected to work on the project. He came to Cardigan, had a look at the river and came up with the concept for *Turbulence*, an interactive sculpture involving 127 flashing buoys that would be rigged up to audio equipment and anchored to the riverbed in Cardigan. As Lozano-Hemmer explained:

> a number of microphones placed at various locations around the quayside will record people's voices and automatically convert them into blinking lights within the buoys. The stored voices stay quietly in the buoys until the river's periodic turbulence – caused by the constant ebb and flow of the river Teifi – activates the buoys to 'release' the stored sounds,

which can be heard from the shore. A website will likewise allow people from all over the world to add their voices to the project.

It was to be 'a reflection on Welsh oral traditions, poetry and song'. The organizers loved it. The services of a public art consultancy were secured. The Art Fund set aside most of the £600,000 it would cost. All was set.

There was just one problem. The residents of Cardigan were dead against it. Many of them hated the idea of these blinking balls cluttering up their river. The property developer who had proposed the site did not in any way represent the 'community' of Cardigan. He represented himself. There was a flurry of letters to local newspapers. In *The Times* this was described as 'a minor civil war'. And yet somehow the project remained on course.

At this point three men and one woman came together to fight the proposed art installation. Peter James, Tim White, Janet Paynter and Ralph Rea – a glazier, two retired builders and a housewife – had never met before. They were united by their fierce opposition to the idea of Lozano-Hemmer's buoys. They thought this sculpture was a hazard to the local environment, a waste of money, and, crucially, they were adamant that the residents of Cardigan did not want it.

Over the next eighteen months this quartet mounted a sustained and co-ordinated campaign. They wrote to every councillor and public official involved in the project (as well as many who were not), they bombarded the organizations and agencies that had agreed to take part, they contacted the relevant ombudsman, they staged protests, gathered names for a petition, painted banners, printed and distributed fliers, and they did this at very little cost.

In March 2010 they won. Channel 4 and The Art Fund acknowledged that the views of the local property developer did not reflect those of most people living in Cardigan, and *Turbulence* was abandoned. Calm was restored.

'But I'm not sure if we would have got there had we campaigned individually,' Rea mused, sitting at his kitchen table, flanked by Paynter and White. 'It's a lot easier with more of you involved. I guess you feel as though you can take things further, don't you?'

Hothousing

There is an African proverb that goes: 'if you want to go fast, go alone. If you want to go far, go together.' When you join an association whose members are bound by the Power of Giving, you develop a bond to the others that keeps you coming back. One of the effects of this longevity is that your relationship with the subject that brought you together will almost certainly change. In many associations it is as though it has been placed in a hothouse. The frequency of meetings, the shared wisdom of others and the insights achieved through group discussion allow your interest to flourish. It becomes more substantial. Not only has it been moved to a hothouse, but you could say that your enthusiasm has been re-potted, placed in a large container of premium compost and is now being watered daily.

I like to think of this as the Hothouse Effect. Joining an association in which the members help each other out over the years has the effect of placing your enthusiasm in a hothouse. It benefits from being within this group setting and with time it can become gigantic.

Of course, some plants don't take at all well to a sudden plethora of heat and moisture. Perhaps your interest in the subject is not strong enough to survive life within an association. The Hothouse Effect is such that it can push some people away. Or the hothouse may not be that hot. If you join a group that is not used to debate, or one that is not bound by the Power of Giving, then your understanding of that subject may not improve dramatically, but it is still bound to grow.

Other hothouses are like rainforests. For many years Matthew Syed was England's leading table tennis player. In *Bounce*, his account of what makes a sporting champion, Syed described the role of his local table tennis club in his development as a player. At one point most of the country's leading table tennis players belonged to this one club – six of them lived on Syed's street. Clearly this association was a very hot hothouse. By joining this club, each player's enthusiasm for the game entered an intense associational environment that allowed it to blossom.

There are many ways in which we can see the Hothouse Effect at work in associations. By providing an economy of scale, an association acts as a hothouse. Joining a group may give you access to equipment that you might not have been able to use otherwise. For example, many members of Syed's table tennis club did not have a table-tennis table at home, so joining the club meant they could play more often.

If you were interested in cave-diving, for example, by joining an association of cave-divers you could share the cost of specialist equipment. Again, the Hothouse Effect is such that within a small group you end up taking your interest much further.

Equally there are some tropical plants that cannot survive in these climes *unless* they are in a hothouse. Let's say you had a profound interest in what it was to be a British army rifleman during the Napoleonic Wars. There are only so many re-runs of *Sharpe* that you can watch with the volume turned up to full. For your interest in this area of re-enactment to flourish you would need to join one of the three historical re-enactment groups dedicated to this – the 1st, 2nd and 3rd Battalions, 95th Rifles Re-enactment Groups. Unless you place certain interests in an associational hothouse they will wither.

An Odd Mixture of Mankind

The Hothouse Effect can also change our social horizons. Yet this is something we rarely acknowledge. When describing the seventeenth-century Vertuoso's Club, Ned Ward explained that its members were 'such an odd mixture of Mankind'. By this, he did not mean that each member was particularly strange, but that this combination of men was unusual. Next to 'a nice Beau', Ward wrote, you would find 'a dirty Blacksmith; there a purblind Philosopher next to a talkative Spectacle-maker; yonder a half-witted Whim of Quality, next to a ragged Mathematician; on the other side, a consumptive Astronomer next to a water-gruel Physician'. The 'Bird-Fanciers' he had such fun describing were 'as odd a Mixture as a Broker's Wardrobe [. . .] where a Beauish Sute, sold by a Gentleman's Vallet, shall hang up in View between a Patch'd Double and a Leathern Pair of breaches'.

During the first decade of the twenty-first century, the broadcaster Clare Balding presented more than 200 episodes of *Ramblings*, a programme for BBC Radio 4 in which she accompanied individuals and groups on long country walks.

'One of the things that always struck me about these groups,' she told me, 'was the mixture of ages, but also of backgrounds. They would often come from different places socially, much more so than within a typical circle of friends. Their shared interest in walking seemed to make these things irrelevant. By having something in common like this, it seems you don't have to constantly justify why you're together.'

For one member of the North Leigh Short Mat Bowls Club the main advantage of belonging to the group was 'meeting different people from different walks of life'. Several members of Laura's Book Group said exactly the same thing.

For Aristotle, social heterogeneity was vital, it was what made clubs and associations work. He believed that 'those who resemble one another grate upon one another'. Heterogeneity was to be cherished. We should not simply stick to our own. Quoting Heraclitus, he went on: 'the finest harmony is born from differences, and that discord is the law of all becoming.'

Without getting into why this is, and what it says about the judgements we make in British society to do with social background and age – not because there is nothing to say, but it would take too long to explore this – it seems that the Hothouse Effect will keep the focus within a group on the subject that binds its members together. Other things, such as one's age or background, become less important. But not everyone sees it like that.

'When people have the chance to choose who they socialize with, they choose people like themselves,' said the chair of the Commission for Equalities and Human Rights, Trevor Phillips, back in 2008. 'This is the cancer eating away at our society.'

If so, then in associations we have a cure. When it is at all strong, the Hothouse Effect ensures that clubs, societies and other associations dedicated to a shared interest become spaces in which interests are more important than back-grounds and any other inherited identities. This is one of the defining characteristics of any small voluntary group.

There are just two more things to say about the Hothouse Effect. One of these is that it can allow our money to go further. But not in the way you might think. Pretend that one afternoon Den Rayfield of the 2nd Battalion, 95th Rifles Re-enactment Group, goes shopping. This, by the way, is a group that meets regularly to recreate as faithfully as possible episodes in that regiment's past. On this particular shopping expedition Rayfield spends £50 on a pair of jeans. On his way home, let's say he passes a shop specializing in antique Napoleonic gear. This shop happens to sell the right lapels for the coat Rayfield wears when re-enacting. Each costs £25. He buys two.

According to work done by Jonathan Gershuny at the University of Essex, we can be confident that Rayfield would get far more pleasure from the £50 he spent on those lapels than the jeans. This is not a reflection on the use of either purchase, or on the value for money. It is to do with what happens when you spend money on 'a knowledge-intensive activity' such as Napoleonic re-enactment, if that is your passion. As Gershuny writes, 'specific knowledge *about* consumption contributes to [an] individual's satisfaction *with* their consumption.' Belonging to a group dedicated to a particular subject improves and broadens your understanding of it, and this is bound to increase the satisfaction you get from any money you spend on it.

Amateurs

There is one other element to the Hothouse Effect. Many, many books have been written about happiness and how to find it. This is not one of them. But for a moment I want to look at the pleasure that can come from taking an amateur interest further, and doing so within a group.

Like every professional cricketer, Ed Smith started out as a highly successful amateur. In 1996, aged nineteen, he turned professional. But of his maiden match as a salaried cricketer he wrote, 'for the first time in my life, I didn't enjoy the game. I feared falling short and worried about the consequences. I made an undignified three. But far worse was the manner of my failure. I felt as if I was in a strait-jacket. I had lost my voice.'

Smith later adjusted to life as a professional and went on to play for England. He is now a successful author. But what's so interesting about his account of turning professional is the way he describes the amateur world he left behind. At one point he quotes the former Chelsea football manager Luiz Felipe Scolari, who said that his priority was 'to ensure that players feel more amateur than professional [. . .] Now there is so much professionalism, we have to revert to urging players to like the game, love it, do it with joy.'

On the face of it, this is an unusual line. The word 'amateur' is often used pejoratively. It has come to mean slapdash or light-hearted. This is usually based on two assumptions: first, that only the most skilful and talented individuals will have their exploits rewarded with cash; and second, that no one would turn down the chance to be paid for doing something they love.

Yet there is another way of seeing this. What happens if we think of pursuing an interest within an amateur group as an ideal, rather than something you do if you are not good enough to go professional? Scolari's point was that the professional footballers he was coaching had forgotten how to play as amateurs. As such there was a joylessness to their game. Smith experienced a similar thing when he began his professional career. Both men seem to suggest that there is a certain pleasure that comes from pursuing an interest in an amateur fashion, a lightness of touch that can be lost when you turn professional.

Yet Scolari and Smith are talking about something more specific than the transition from amateur to professional. In both cases they refer to the shift from an amateur *group* to a professional one. Scolari wanted his charges to remember what it was to play in an amateur football team, a group bound by the Power of Giving in which the Hothouse Effect was evident. The same goes for Smith, who had left behind the world of amateur cricket. The joy he refers to was the joy that can come about when you pursue your interest in an amateur group, one in which there is a thriving gift cycle.

The Austrian neurologist Victor Frankl once wrote that 'success, like happiness, cannot be pursued; it must ensue, and it only does so as the unintended side-effect of one's personal dedication to a cause greater than oneself or as the by-product of one's surrender to a person other than oneself.' One part of the Hothouse Effect is that we dedicate ourselves more fully to our chosen interest. When that happens, this interest can become a cause much greater than we are. If we take Frankl's idea and apply it to the world of amateur groups, then perhaps the Hothouse Effect can elicit a unique kind of joy among those who experience it

It seems that within any amateur group experiencing the Hothouse Effect – be it a village cricket team, a football team, a reading group or a band of druids – a particular pleasure ensues when everyone in the group takes their interest further. If you leave that group to become professional, this is something you are bound to miss. Already we know that the Power of Giving can keep a group going. When this happens, the Hothouse Effect will often kick in. We end up taking our enthusiasms further. Social background becomes less important, we get more out of the money we spend on the interest that has brought us together, and there follows a unique amateur pleasure.

Here we can see associations at their best. These are just some of the things that can make belonging to an association so rewarding. But there are times when we can take this too far.

4

Going to Extremes
Anthony Blunt and the Danger of Detachment

> We felt we were acting like them.
>> Anthony Blunt, on the Cambridge Four and those
>> persecuted during the sixteenth century for their
>> religious beliefs

It is late November 1979, and in a windowless, panelled room on the Gray's Inn Road in London a donnish septuagenarian sits down before several journalists. He is wearing a worsted jacket, V-neck jumper and a tie with the knot half an inch off-centre. His features are elongated, like those of a Byzantine icon, and they give him an air of supreme inscrutability.

This is Anthony Blunt, renowned art historian, knighted for his services to the country when in the employ of MI5, former Surveyor of the Queen's Pictures, world expert on Nicolas Poussin, retired Director of the Courtauld Institute and fellow of the British Academy and Trinity College, Cambridge. He has come to the offices of *The Times* to give an interview and confirm to the watching world that he was the 'fourth man'.

For more than fifteen years, including his time as an MI5 agent, Blunt had passed information to the NKVD (later the KGB). In fact, he had transmitted so much during this period of his life that on at least one occasion the Soviets suspected him of being a double-agent.

The news came as a shock to the British system. It was

the most serious breach of security in living memory. Long
before I knew what a 'fourth man' was, let alone who 'Blunt'
might be, I remember my mother describing the reaction of
her father, someone who knew Blunt and was of his generation, and how he had sat alone in his study saying only to
himself, like a mantra, soft, 'a traitor is a traitor is a traitor.'
Elsewhere the reaction was more furious and sudden.
Immediately Blunt was stripped of his knighthood. A former
pupil who spoke out in his defence received death threats.
There were speeches in Parliament denouncing this elderly
academic, while the nation's newspapers produced a glut of
thunderous editorials and leaders. One of these appeared in
The Times on 21 November 1979.

It begins as a *cri de coeur* against Blunt and his betrayal,
until about half-way through when the focus adjusts to include
a group called the Cambridge Apostles. Blunt, you gather,
was a member of this clandestine society. The article then lays
into the Apostles, blasting their 'supercilious lack of patriotism in the First World War, personified in Lytton Strachey',
and their 'cult of personal relations, supported by an arrogant
cult of the intellect'. At one point Blunt had explained that
he did not inform the authorities of the defection of two fellow
spies, Maclean and Burgess, 'because they were my friends'.
For the author, or more likely authors, of this piece here was
Blunt's great solecism. To choose personal 'ties of friendship'
over loyalty to one's country was not only endemic to 'homo-
sexual culture', it was a threat to democracy and civilization.
But what exactly did the Apostles have to do with all this?

The Cambridge Apostles

The Cambridge Conversazione Society, also known as the
Apostles, is a secretive debating society at Cambridge
University dedicated to 'the pursuit of truth with absolute

devotion and unreserve', as one adept put it many years ago. I say 'is' because the Apostles are probably still active today.

In a spirit of wide-eyed inquiry I wrote to various people connected to Trinity and other Cambridge colleges, asking after the Apostles. The only replies I received came either from those who had never heard of the society or knew nothing about its current state.

Sending off a batch of letters like this was probably not the brightest idea. As Sir Frederick Pollock wrote to fellow Apostle F.W. Maitland in 1906, 'Did I tell you that a phenomenal person very slightly known to me tried some time ago to get materials for a book about the Society? I choked it off not without showing my sense of the impertinence, and I don't think the book will be written.'

All was not in vain. One of the men I wrote to kindly agreed to have lunch. Sir Andrew Huxley, Nobel prizewinner and grandson of T. H. Huxley, explained with care that, although he was not aware of the current activities of the Apostles, 'I think it very unlikely that they do not still exist.'

By the time Blunt joined, in 1928, the Apostles had been meeting on Saturday evenings during term-time since the 1820s. They enjoyed discussions fuelled by coffee, tea and 'whales' made from anchovies or sardines on toast. Like any group encumbered with secrecy, incidental habits had long ago become traditions. The order of each meeting followed a set pattern in which a 'moderator' delivered a paper on a subject proposed during the last meeting, Apostles and 'angels' (emeritus Apostles) then took to the floor, or the 'hearthrug', in a sequence decided by lot where they would respond to the original paper. The discussion ended with a vote, the results were stored in an ageing cedar trunk called 'the ark' and lots were drawn to determine who would play the part of moderator next week.

If the activities and structure of this society are unremarkable – and they are – the list of former members is spectacular. It includes John Maynard Keynes, Lytton Strachey, Leonard

Woolf, E. M. Forster, G. M. Trevelyan, Bertrand Russell, G. E. Moore, Erasmus Darwin, Rupert Brooke, Roger Fry and Alfred, Lord Tennyson.

But none of this explains why the society was savaged in *The Times*. Part of the reason was that four of the eight Cambridge graduates employed by the Soviet Union were Apostles. At one estimate, almost half of those 'born' into the society between 1927 and 1939 had Marxist or Communist sympathies. The article implied a link between Blunt's actions and his membership of the Apostles. Was it right to do so, and, if so, what can this tell us about associations?

For Blunt there was no connection whatsoever between his membership of this society and his decision to work for the Comintern. Instead he blamed the political atmosphere in Cambridge. On returning there in 1934 from what we would call a sabbatical, he found the place 'seething with Communist enthusiasm'. All of 'my friends – that is an enormous amount of my friends and almost all the intelligent and bright young undergraduates who had come up to Cambridge – had suddenly become Marxists under the impact of Hitler coming to power'. Many were persuasive and magnetic. They were figures such as James Klugman, John Cornford and Guy Burgess – another Apostle, and for Blunt the most charismatic of the lot.

This may explain why he developed Marxist sympathies. But it does not begin to unravel why Blunt became an agent of the Soviet Union, nor why he remained so after the shock of the Molotov–Ribbentrop Pact in 1939 and Chamberlain's subsequent declaration of war. You see, there is a problem with Blunt's argument that his decision to work for the Russian state, what he would later call 'the biggest mistake of my life', was the result of nothing more than the atmosphere in Cambridge at the time. By his own admission, Blunt was 'so naive politically that I was not justified in committing myself to any political action of this kind'. When touring Germany in 1934, although 'aware of the presence of the Nazis [I] did not really understand the political implications of what was taking place'.

These are hardly the words of a man whose Marxist sympathies were so advanced that he was about to betray his country in order to take them further. I believe that Blunt's sudden conversion to extreme Marxism makes sense only in terms of his membership of the Apostles and a phenomenon that psychologists call 'group polarization'.

Group Polarization

In 1961 the psychologist James Stoner argued in an unpublished thesis that small groups were prone to what he called a 'risky shift'. Stoner found that in certain situations groups would take collective decisions that were much riskier and more extreme than any course of action advocated by an individual member of the group. This flew in the face of received wisdom. Until then it had been thought that group discussion generally mollified one's views. They became more balanced. Apparently not, at least not as a rule.

Stoner's risky shift phenomenon later came to be known as group polarization once other psychologists found that the shift could go in many different directions. To understand how it works, imagine a group of women who belong to an association. For the sake of argument, let's pretend it is a Women's Institute. One of its members is recently bereaved and wants to raise money for a charity funding research into her late husband's illness. She proposes this to the group. Another member introduces the idea of a calendar. A third member suggests that they pose nude – she probably means it as a joke. They laugh. It's funny because it is so unlikely. And yet during that meeting and various others a calendar's worth of women agree to be photographed naked for a publicly available calendar.

This is a précis of *Calendar Girls*, a film and, more recently, a play based on the true story of a WI whose members posed nude for a calendar, raising over £1 million for charity. What's so interesting about this from an associational point of view is that had you asked any of these women beforehand to pose nude for a calendar, few would have agreed. The decision to do this was inspired partly by their membership of the group. It was this that allowed their attitudes to the idea of posing nude to polarize and become more extreme.

There are several reasons why this may have happened. In the case of the calendar girls, some of them might have acted simply out of loyalty to the WI itself. Others may have been driven by their sympathy for the woman whose husband had died, or solidarity with those who had already said 'yes'. Others might have been persuaded by arguments presented during the group discussions. Or it could have been any combination of the above.

These are the bare bones of group polarization. As you can see, it can be perfectly benign. In Laura's Book Group the decision to dress up as high-school cheerleaders for their discussion of *Friday Night Lights* could be described as an example of group polarization. But when you combine this phenomenon with the feeling that your group is cut off, excluded or in other ways detached from the world beyond, it can have a strange and more insidious effect.

As a typical Apostle during the mid-1930s there were at least four exclusions that could set you apart from mainstream British society. The first concerned the oath that accompanied one's entry into the Apostles. This probably involved 'the usual paraphernalia of the secret curse and other time-hallowed rituals'. At a guess, to be 'born' into the society involved swearing loyalty to the group in front of the other members. There would have been several readings. Perhaps a blindfold was produced. It is not important. What matters is that these men were bound to one another and the society itself by a self-imposed act of secrecy. Every secret is a burden, one that is relieved only by revelation or being surrounded by those who share it. By keeping this secret, not only did each Apostle reiterate his commitment to the society whenever he exercised discretion, but this deepened the divide between those within the society and those without.

Another exclusion was that of intellect. Most Apostles hailed from Trinity or King's. As an Apostle you were not only bright enough to be accepted into one of these colleges, but out of this élite pool you had been singled out for your exceptional intelligence and conversational acuity.

A third exclusion, though patchy, was that of birth. Most Apostles belonged to an intellectual aristocracy with its roots in nineteenth-century philanthropy, Quakerism and evangelicalism. It included the Huxleys, Darwins, Stracheys, Trevelyans and other names with an equally Bloomsbury ring to them. Theirs was a tradition that aspired to learning over the accumulation of wealth; it was largely suspicious of industrialization, modernity and the other English élite that sent its eldest sons to Oxford. Elysium on the Cam continued to have 'the more pleasant associations for nonconformist families', as it had done since the Civil War, all of which only buttressed the Apostolic sense of detachment during that period in the group's history.

Finally, a number of Apostles were set apart from traditional society by their shared criminality. Although no more than five of the forty-four Apostles elected between the wars were what Noel Annan called 'lifelong homosexuals' – as Robert Skidelsky delicately put it, 'a question-begging phrase' – 'the higher sodomy' was 'a favourite Apostolic topic' at a time when homosexuality remained a criminal offence.

Together these factors must have created at the very least a mild sense of detachment. The Apostles had a Kantian in-joke that summed this up. They would call everything connected to the society 'real', while the world beyond and all its accessories were merely 'phenomenal'. 'Is it mono-mania', Apostle no. 243, John Maynard Keynes, once wrote, 'this colossal moral superiority that we feel?'

By the 1930s there seems to have been within the group an almost Gnostic sense of their heightened perception, and a conviction that their interpretation of reality was so shrewd, so adroit, that phenomenal morality and phenomenal laws did not really apply to them. It is likely that what began as a sense of intellectual superiority had morphed by then into a feeling of moral detachment.

When Blunt returned to Cambridge in 1934, he had no intention of becoming a Soviet spy. Among the Apostles it seems that opinion became polarized, and he became far more inclined to make a decision that he would not have contemplated otherwise.

If the Power of Giving and the resulting Hothouse Effect illustrate human association at its best, the combination of group polarization and a profound sense of detachment reveal a very different side. The terrorist cell responsible for the 7 July terrorist attacks on London in 2005 was a group that meets almost all our criteria for an association. It was part-time, voluntary (as far as we know), independent and it was not geared towards financial profit. Its members went on to kill fifty-two people.

Stop Huntingdon Animal Cruelty (SHAC) is another asso-ciation whose members came together around a shared cause and were bound by the Power of Giving. The Hothouse Effect was such that they took their common interest much further than they would individually. In 2009 seven members of the association were convicted of conducting a vicious six-year campaign against employees of companies associated with the Huntingdon Life Sciences research facility. Their actions were described in court as 'urban terrorism'.

In neither case was there any evidence to suggest that these people decided to commit their crimes *before* joining their associations. The groups they belonged to were more than vehicles. Instead the actions of these individuals must be attributed, in part, to the dynamics of a small group. The combination of group polarization and a string of overlapping exclusions allowed the members of each association to drift away from the morality of the society in which they lived.

This is what I think happened to Anthony Blunt. Of course, his membership of the Apostles was not the only factor governing his decision, nor does it follow that everyone else in that group had the same experience. But it is highly likely that his membership of this secret society allowed his opinions to become more extreme in a very short space of time.

This book is not a wide-eyed paean to associations. The power of association is not exclusively positive. Just as individualism at its most extreme can lead to self-obsession, megalomania and murderous pride, so belonging to an association that is detached from the world can have dangerous consequences. If we are to understand how these groups work and the implications of there being more of them, we must bear this in mind.

A strong sense of loyalty within an association is not a problem in itself. But when it is combined with the feeling that your group is cut off from the world beyond, that you are adrift and this is the only set of people that matters in your life, then belonging to an association can cause its members to lose sight of a broader shared morality.

We have seen roughly what causes an association to come about and what keeps one of these going. We have also had a taste of how these groups can encourage us to take our enthusiasms much further than we would do otherwise, that they can become hothouses in which we mix with a broader range of people. We have also seen that on some occasions this can go too far. But why is it that these groups inspire in us a sense of belonging?

5

The New Zealand Tendency
Belonging and the Need for Identity

> I don't want to belong to any club that will accept me as
> a member.
>
> Groucho Marx

The New Zealand Golf Club is hard to find. You pass through
an expressionless patch of suburbia, past dogs and dog-
walkers, women in fleeces and villages that melt into one
another, until you see a blue sign. You follow a lane that leads
to an electronic gate, where you give your name to a metallic
box. With a whirr the sets of railings drift apart at the speed
of a plane across the sky.

You arrive at a clubhouse. It is white and elegant, with a roof
that slopes like a shield over its western flank. Beyond is a golf
course that looks different from the ones that tend to appear
on television. There are no sculpted trees here, the greens are
not the colour of tennis balls and, unlike some courses, it has
none of the kitsch lustre of an architectural model. Instead
there are clumps of heather, brown as though charred, unruly
slugs of rhododendron and passages of clumpy grass. In the
distance you can make out great banks of bluish pine.

Ask anyone who plays golf in or around London, and there's
a good chance that they have heard of the New Zealand. It is
of a type. 'The club is very, very much old school tie,' explains
the club secretary, Roger Marrett, a well-mannered man with
a papery smile. 'Unashamedly really. But why not?' Most of

the members can be traced back to the same handful of schools. They are at home hunting, shooting, fishing, and many work in finance, or they are married to those that do. Yet there is very little trace of their accumulated wealth at the New Zealand Golf Club. The annual rates are low and there is nothing brash or flashy about either the course or the clubhouse.

'Nor is it social,' Marrett goes on, 'in the sense that you wouldn't get anyone coming down on the off-chance of meeting someone and playing a round of golf. The games here are pre-arranged and we don't have many competitions, nor have there ever been evening functions. The club has always been for gentlemen from London to come down, have lunch, play golf and return to their clubs in time for dinner. There is no captain, no committees, just a board of Directors and a Chairman. No website either.' I ask why. 'No need really.' He pauses. 'Also I don't suppose it would be in keeping with the character of the club.'

It is not the first time that Marrett has mentioned the *character* of the New Zealand. But what exactly does he mean? The members of the club do not meet as one, so he is not describing what happens when these golfers gather together. And yet, ask any member of the club and they too will tell you about its *character*. They might describe a 'New Zealand' way of doing things. Even those who do not belong to the club seem to know about the character of the New Zealand. What makes this remarkable is the consistency of these answers.

So what was going on here? How can anyone talk about the character of a group that does not meet as one? What are they really describing?

The Role of Comparison

Until the late nineteenth century, had you asked a typical Briton to describe the character of a group – any group –

they would have told you that it was the sum of its parts. How could it be anything else?

The character of Thomas Britton's musical society, for example, would be the combined character of its members. If you had an odd assortment of apples and wanted to describe their shared character, you could put them in a press and taste whatever came out. This makes sense.

But what if there were too many apples to fit into your press? How would you describe the character of a group that does not come together as one, such as the New Zealand Golf Club? In the seventeenth century Thomas Hobbes argued that for any group bound by a social contract you could estimate its character based on the members that you had met. You were taking a guess as to what would happen if they came together. The same principle applied: the character of a group was the sum of its parts.

In the late nineteenth century Émile Durkheim proposed something radically different. He argued that the character of any group, be it a nation-state or a golf club, was not the sum of its parts. Instead, each of these groups developed its own character, and this was passed on from one generation to the next. It might evolve along the way, but this character was still a *thing* that snowballed through history with the inevitability of a lumbering leviathan.

So the character of 'the English' in the late nineteenth century was much more than the sum of its many parts. Durkheim argued that instead there was a character that had emerged over the preceding centuries, and that as you grew up within this group – the English – you would encounter this character in a variety of different forms. Eventually you were bound to acquire parts of it. This identity or character was all around you. It was there in the stories you heard, the songs that were sung, the mythology of how the English came about, the history you learned, the rituals, customs, mores, idiosyncrasies, symbols, laws and, of course, the language you spoke.

It is in all these things that you will find the identity of a group such as the English, the Scottish, the Welsh or the Northern Irish. Durkheim was the first to understand this. He saw the character of a group as 'an entity *sui generis*', one that was as real as any of us but not something you could see or hold. By the close of the twentieth century most psychologists agreed with Durkheim that the character of a group was 'different from' and 'more than' the sum of its parts, that it was a *thing* in its own right.

But they were more divided when it came to just how important this thing might be. Would you agree with Jonathan Swift when he said, 'I hate and detest that animal called man, although I heartily love John, Peter, Thomas, and so forth'? Is it possible to be English and have plenty of English friends but dislike 'the English' and everything this identity brings to mind? As a member of the New Zealand Golf Club, could you feel a great affection for your fellow members but none at all for the club itself? In which case, why bother describing a shared identity? What purpose does it serve?

In the 1970s there was a breakthrough in our understanding of the psychology of groups. Henri Tajfel was a talented psychologist driven to understand group dynamics by what remains the defining event of the modern age: the Nazi Holocaust. Towards the end of the 1970s Tajfel and his student John Turner developed what they called 'Social Identity Theory' or 'S. I. T.'. The nub of S. I. T. was this: we go to extraordinary lengths to give identities to our groups. Our sense of belonging within a group depends on its having a clear identity or character. Tajfel and Turner also found that these identities were based primarily on social comparison. We compare the groups we belong to with other groups or to the world beyond in order to come up with that all-important identity.

This comparison does not have to be positive. Let's say

you belong to a five-a-side football team, and that you lose almost every match you play. The only points you register in your league come about when the other team fails to turn up – an experience I know all too well from the team I used to play for. In this case the identity of your team is bound to be about failure – heroic failure, but failure nonetheless. Glorious, shambolic, silly and occasionally frustrating failure.

The identities of the groups we belong to rely on comparison, and as such they can change. If your five-a-side football team moved to a different league – maybe one in which you played against eight-year-olds every week – then, who knows, you might start to win one or two matches. In that case the identity of your team would adjust to reflect your newfound success.

Tajfel and Turner argued that making this comparison is so important to us that we often take short cuts to get there. If a new team entered your league that was pretty much identical to yours, one that lost just as many games and talked about itself in similar terms, then according to S. I. T. you would go out of your way to give it a slightly different identity. The identity of your group depends on there being some kind of contrast between your team and the world beyond.

Being able to give our groups identities can be so important that in a situation like this we are bound to make tiny exaggerations and omissions when describing the other group. We might make out that its members are a bit older than ours (even if they are not), or younger, too keen, too lazy, not very efficient, hyper-organized. The only thing that matters is that the comparison can take place.

Snowballing through History

So how does this relate to the New Zealand Golf Club? At first blush, these two ideas seem to head off in different directions. Durkheim saw the character of a group as an entity that could outlive successive generations, one that snowballed through history over many years. That implies a character that is more or less inherited. Yet Tajfel and Turner's S. I. T. appears to suggest something else: that the identity of any group is based on comparison. You might therefore think that it is being constantly refreshed.

The reality is that both arguments are partly true. The character of the New Zealand was indeed rooted in comparison, but a comparison that began many years ago when the club was founded. Over the years, the fruits of this comparison were added to fractionally but for the most part they have been preserved and passed on from one set of members to the next like some holy pot of jam.

The New Zealand Golf Club came about in the late nineteenth century. At the time there was a spate of new golf clubs popping up around London. Fortescue Locke King was a young lawyer who enjoyed the game but felt that most of these new clubs were too competitive and overpriced. He had a clear sense of how he thought golf should be played. For him, the pleasure of the sport involved being outside and enjoying a beautiful course and interesting companions. It was not about the golfing calibre of your opponents or the thrill of winning.

Since none of the existing clubs seemed to offer this, Locke King had a golf course built on one of his two estates. In 1895 the first of many small white balls was thwacked and prodded around a patch of land a little west of London now known as the New Zealand Golf Club. From the outset, then, the character of this club was rooted in comparison. The New Zealand was less competitive than other clubs. It was more relaxed, cheaper, there was a greater emphasis on the naturalistic landscaping of the course, and the members were drawn mostly from Locke King's social circle.

Amazingly, this character has survived more or less intact.

It is amazing because Locke King's formal involvement in the club was short-lived. Only thirteen years after the club opened, he was forced to sell the New Zealand to its members. He did not set down in a book his feelings on how the club should be run. Nor will you find any trace of them in the rules of the New Zealand Golf Club. And yet, they stuck. From the moment this club began, a series of processes were set in motion, most of them subtle and at times imperceptible, and these combined to keep the character of the club alive.

None of this was unique to the New Zealand. You will find the same processes at work in almost every association or small group as it creates and then preserves its identity.

'Both'

Consider these two short anecdotes, both well-known within the New Zealand. The first involves Samuel 'Mure' Fergusson, the heavy-drinking Scot who designed the course and was club Chairman for the first thirty-three years of its existence. He was, by one account, 'tyrant Chairman, end-all and be-all of the Club. There was no Committee – he was the Committee – and because it was very difficult to get in, all the snobs in town and elsewhere clamoured to join.' Burly, ruddy-cheeked and a man of few words, Mure once received a letter from a young man asking why he had not been accepted as a member. Was he being excluded because of his golfing ability, he had inquired, or was it his lack of social graces? Mure sent him a postcard with a single word on the back: 'Both'.

Roger Marrett told me a similar story about another man desperate to join the New Zealand. One day he asked the Chairman – not Mure, a later Chairman – why he was not being asked to become a member, to which came the reply:

'if I liked you, you'd get in tomorrow.' And if he didn't? 'Well, you'd probably have to wait until I'm dead.'

Ah.

We can see here just one of the ways in which the character of any club is kept alive. Each of these tiny anecdotes contains the DNA of the club's identity. They tell you that if the New Zealand was a person, he would be forthright and unafraid of causing offence to those beyond his circle, someone who loathes pretension and cant, says what he means and gets to the point. Socially, he is assured. Meanwhile, the wretched ingénue trying to become a member is upwardly mobile, he is arriviste. Worse, he is unable to see that these are the very qualities that will keep him out of the New Zealand for good.

Join any association that has been going for more than a few years – be it a metal band, a gentlemen's club, a reading group or a football team – and at some point you are bound to hear stories about the group's past. Within each of these will be the DNA of the club's identity. Sometimes there are songs that serve the same purpose. These ditties or anecdotes may illustrate how much the group likes to drink compared with others, how efficient they are, how skilful, hopeless, hapless, silly, serious, jolly, working-class, aristocratic, middle-class, Northern, Southern, rugged, soft – whatever qualities the group wants to be known by, you will find them contained in these stories. What's more, that identity will be drawn out by comparison. Invariably these stories place the members of the group next to outsiders, so the character emerges in terms of what it is as much as that which it is not.

The identity of the Bristol Exploration Club (B. E. C.), a caving club on the Mendips, owes a lot to their light-hearted rivalry with the neighbouring Wessex Cave Club. Ask any member of the B. E. C. about the character of their club, and before long they'll be talking about 'the Wessex'. Over at the Wessex, you're told, they love to drink tea. In fact, they barely have time to do anything else they drink so much of the stuff. There is a catalogue of anecdotes to back this up. Most involve members of the B. E. C. sneaking into the Wessex clubhouse to steal kettles, hide treasured mugs down nearby caves or pinch teabags. Members of the B. E. C., by contrast, pride themselves on the Teutonic quantities of beer they like to drink.

'Hang up all the poor Hop-Drinkers', read the sign above the entrance to the Apollo Room, part of a seventeenth-century tavern off Fleet Street in London. This was the meeting place of the Sons of Ben, a band of gentleman-poets with Ben Jonson at the helm. Just as the B. E. C. identified itself, in part, by its members' love of beer, and their ability to drink lots of it, so the Sons of Ben found an element of their identity in a mutual loathing of beer and beer-drinkers. Although we do not know what stories they told, in Jonson's poetry and the rules he created for the group this is hard to miss. At one point Jonson rails against 'Luther's beer'. He forbids 'Sober Bigots' from joining his group. Rather than drink beer or spend the evening sober, these poets were to drink moderate amounts of wine. As Jonson wrote, wine, 'the Milk of *Venus*, / Cheers the Brains, makes Wit the quicker'. But they shouldn't get carried away, lest their gatherings resemble the scene in an alehouse. 'Let the Contests be rather of Books than of Wine', he warned, praising the 'moderate Bottle' and urging his Sons not to end up 'guilty' after 'drinking good Wine'.

Another way to keep the character of any group intact is to observe certain 'norms', or unwritten rules. If you go to the bar in the New Zealand Golf Club, you will see a partition bisecting the room. It has a door in the middle, and next to it a bell. On one side the furnishings are dark, clubbish and heavy-set. Elsewhere the colours are more gamine and light. On entering the bar, you're told that women do not go beyond the partition into the more masculine-looking area. That's not to say they *can't*, but they don't. As a woman, if you want a drink you are to ring the bell and the barman will come to take your order.

There is no rule enforcing this; it is just one of those things that has gone on for as long as anyone can remember. Nobody really knows why it began, or precisely how old the tradition is. That's not the point. A norm like this may appear to have no practical use, but it helps to keep the character of a club alive. It reinforces the connection between the club's present and its past, and it distinguishes that group further from the world beyond. The more idiosyncratic traditions a group has, the more distinct its identity becomes.

The third way to keep the character of your group alive involves objects and symbols. For many years the New Zealand Golf Club had a distant relationship with its past. 'No archive, no library,' Marrett nodded. 'Nothing was ever kept, which is rather symptomatic of the way the club was operating.' By 2000 that had begun to change. Marrett started to scour the internet for prints, artefacts and other golfing memorabilia relating to the club. He would hang them on the walls or position each in display cabinets as if ancient talismans. Not long ago he found a calendar dating back to 1900 that showed the great Mure in action. He emailed this to an artist in China, who turned it into a large oil painting that now hangs by the bar.

'Of course it's a total fake,' Marrett explained, 'but worth it for the history.'

This is the point. The history of a group – the group's authorized biography, its memoir, the history it has constructed for itself and would like to be remembered by – has enormous value. It embodies the group's character. In order to make that history feel more real we tell stories, we preserve traditions, and we collect objects and artefacts that can bring it to life. These could be flags, statues, busts, portraits, mascots, banners or any other physical memento of the group's past.

The way an association like the New Zealand Golf Club constructs its history is in fact a miniature version of how the members of a nation, religion, company, or even a marriage go about this. The same techniques are at work, we develop an identical attachment to the physical accoutrements of our shared identity. In time, these objects or locations begin to embody the group's history and its character. Take them away, and that history no longer feels so real. The identity flickers and thins.

Yet for a club like the New Zealand it is not just the objects that count but their setting. Although very few associations have the luxury of a clubhouse, for those that do, these structures become fabulous museums of their past, and as anyone who works in an actual museum will tell you, buildings like these are often critical to the way certain groups think about themselves, their past and their identity. In exactly the same sense each clubhouse is a walk-in archive in which you can store the objects that bring to life your group's history.

I can think of no better example of a clubhouse acting as a museum than the home of the B. E. C., the Belfry. It is a long farmhouse tucked away down a slender lane. Over the doorway is a maquette of a giant bat that grins down at you as you cross the threshold. Inside all is worn yet workable. The smell is that of stone, mud, wood-smoke, instant coffee, toast. Down one corridor is a dormitory stuffed with home-made bunks and sweaty sleeping bags. Grubby window-panes keep out the day. In another room there is a bookshelf containing old copies of the *Belfry Bulletin*, the club journal. Elsewhere the walls are covered with signs featuring bats and belfries, or they say 'No Dumping', 'Glamour Pit', 'Children's Playground', and there is an oddment of donated and salvaged furniture laid out over uncarpeted floors.

And yet, like a film set in which nothing appears in shot by accident, almost every object in the Belfry tells a story.

The giant bat above the door once adorned the Land Rover of Tony Jarratt, or 'J-Rat', a charismatic and much-loved Belfryite who died in 2008. Each of those signs on the walls was a souvenir of a certain incident or a night out. The club journals provided an extensive archive of the club's past. Even the aesthetic was in keeping with the character of the club – worn but workable. Outside there was a tree that had become a memorial to a former Belfryite. Not only was the Belfry an archive of the club's past, but, like a medieval parish church, it had begun to provide a certain continuity between the former members of this community, the present incumbents and those yet to come.

Having once been little more than a place to store caving equipment, change or sleep, the Belfry had become the physical embodiment of the club's character. Winston Churchill was right: 'we shape our buildings, and afterwards our buildings shape us.' When you join the B. E. C., one of the ways you get to learn about the character of this group is through the time you spend in that building. It is like visiting a museum to the club's past. The B. E. C.'s identity is tied up in everything the Belfry is as well as all the things it is not. The same goes for any clubhouse, be it a caving 'hut' on the Mendips or a gentlemen's club in St James's.

In the summer of 1838 work began on a building site on the south side of Pall Mall, in London. Slabs of Portland stone and cloth-bound crusts of marble began to arrive. A well was sunk. Floors of oak were laid. A steam engine was installed to heat and ventilate this new construction. Pillars and pilasters rose up with Palladian exactitude around a covered courtyard, their capitals laced together with strings of plasterwork, stucco and scagliola. As builders made way for decorators, bas-reliefs modelled on drawings from the Acropolis began to stretch out over bookcases soon to carry a mosaic of cloth- and leather-bound spines, each a veteran's breast of regimental blues, greens and browns set off by reds and worsted yellows. Elsewhere the palette was dark and more refined. Candelabras were winched into place, mirrored shutters installed and enormous carpets unrolled, the fabric falling into place with a tired harrumph.

At last, the Reform Club was complete. Even here, in a new building, the character of the club was articulated with precision. Every detail in Charles Barry's design played a part. They suggested connections to the Classical past and Renaissance architecture. One member thought the new clubhouse 'worthy of Michelangelo'. Otherwise the Reform gave off an air of political authority and learning. You entered this clubhouse up a flight of steps, and in every sense this space was elevated above street level. When it opened in 1841, one member described it as 'the political centre of the Empire', and for any visitor it was hard not to be impressed by the symmetry, weight and sheer nobility of this structure, lovingly described by Thackeray as the 'massive Reformatorium'.

The New Zealand Tendency

These are just some of the ways in which we keep the character of our groups alive. We tell stories that set them apart, we hang on to certain traditions or norms, we collect objects or artefacts that make the group's history feel more real, and if possible we create museum-like clubhouses in which we store these things and flesh out further the character of the association. Moreover, we go out of our way to do these things. The identities of our groups really matter to us. We have a consistent tendency to give our groups identities, and once these are established, to hang on to them.

I think this is one of the defining characteristics of small groups. In honour of the New Zealand Golf Club, I want to call it the New Zealand Tendency. The New Zealand Tendency is that when we form groups, we give them some kind of character, even if the group doesn't meet as one, and that we will go to great lengths to keep this character alive.*

Beneath the New Zealand Tendency lies something else: our axiomatic need to belong. While it may not be the reason why we join an association, we seem to relish the identity that they can provide. These groups give us a sense of belonging. In an age so often characterized as one in which we are all searching for identity, and are surrounded by the hollowed-out remains of traditional Victorian certainties, this element of life within an association has an added resonance.

Making an Entrance

In 1833 Alexis de Tocqueville spent five weeks travelling around England. He returned for a short period several years later, and there followed an account of his travels around England and Ireland. As ever, his observations were acute and delivered with brio.

But every now and again he came unstuck. At one point de Tocqueville wrote, 'I see many things in this country which I cannot yet completely understand'. One of these was 'how "the spirit of association" and "the spirit of exclusion" came to be so highly developed in the same people, and often to be so intimately combined. Example a club: what better example of association than the union of individuals who

* The members of some groups may take this further and think of the character of the group as a personality, like a guardian spirit. Indeed this may be one of the reasons why early humans began to worship moralizing gods. If you combine our tendency to see 'agents' in the world around us, in other words, to give personalities to inanimate objects, then it is quite possible that some of the earliest prehistoric groups began to think of their group identity as a deity. See the Source Notes for more.

form the club? What more exclusive than the corporate personality represented by the club?'

You can see what he meant. But what de Tocqueville failed to get was that every association is predicated on some kind of exclusion. The word 'association' implies both similarity and difference: similarity within and difference without. A group cannot be said to exist unless there are some people who do not belong to it.

Often that 'spirit of exclusion' is inspired by utterly mundane and practical concerns. The Dulwich Quilters, for example, have an upper limit to their membership of twenty-five, because they meet in each other's homes and with any more quilters than that it becomes impossible to fit everyone in. Laura's Book Group introduced a cap on numbers after one discussion with too many people didn't quite work. But there have always been some associations that *could* accommodate new members and yet choose not to. This is probably what de Tocqueville had in mind. The mistake it is so easy to make is to assume that this is driven by snobbery or selfishness, when in fact it is all about the New Zealand Tendency.

Think of the New Zealand Golf Club. To become a member, you must be proposed by an existing member and seconded by various others. 'There is then a vetting process,' Marrett explained. 'This involves the Chairman and one of the Directors taking the potential member out for a round of golf. There will also be a meal. The whole thing can take up to a year, as most members live far afield and are off shooting and fishing. But to be perfectly honest,' he said, his voice dropping a register, 'if the individual did not go to the same prep school, public school, or university, or they didn't work in the same field, or at least play some of the same sports as the Chairman – and I don't just mean golf! – then he hasn't a hope in hell of getting in.'

On the face of it this is bloody-minded élitism. But look

a little harder and you can see that really this is about our need to belong.

Pretend you run the five-a-side football team I mentioned earlier, the one that wasn't very good. Generally you lose. Sometimes you draw. Such is life. One of your players has a friend who comes along to play a game. It turns out that he or she is very good, much better than anyone else in the team. Yet what's interesting about this is that the rest of the team may not want the newcomer to come back the following week.

Why? Because the overall success of a team is often less important than its identity and the fun you have playing together. While you might be a big fan of Sir Salman Rushdie and read everything he writes, you may not want him to become a permanent member of your book group. Within most local natural history societies it would be a huge honour to have Sir David Attenborough come and give a talk to your group. But you might not want him there the following month, when it's your turn to give a presentation on the declining newt population in your village pond.

With an exceptionally good player in your midst, the failings of others become more apparent and vice versa. In both scenarios the character of the group is at risk. Of course, your five-a-side football team could accommodate this more skilful player, and with time it might slough off its weaker members. Eventually it would become a more successful team. But the character of the club would have to change. That is what is at stake. The New Zealand Tendency means that we will often prefer to preserve the character of our groups rather than adjust the quality of our performances.

This works both ways. By choosing only those undergraduates with a real talent for conversation and debate, the Cambridge Apostles were not being intellectual snobs. They wanted to preserve the character of their secret society. When

Jonson insisted that there would be no 'Dunces, Fools, sad, sordid men' in the Sons of Ben, and that instead the members should be 'Learned and Witty', 'Jovial and Gay', 'Generous and Honest', he was doing the same thing. Jonson wanted to preserve the character of his group.

This can also tell us a thing or two about the status that goes with belonging to certain clubs. Earlier we saw that at one point 'all the snobs in town and elsewhere clamoured to join' the New Zealand. This was because it was so hard to be accepted as a member. But there's more to it than that. It may be very hard to join an élite band of ascetic monks, a terrorist group or a band of bog-snorkellers. That does not mean that 'all the snobs in town' would be queuing up to join. They wanted to join the New Zealand not only because it was hard to get in, but also on account of the club's character. They aspired to that identity, and they knew that by becoming a member of this group they would acquire a tiny slice of it. We define ourselves, in part, by the groups we belong to.

If there was a sudden influx of new members who did not match the established New Zealand identity, then that character would start to change. As a member you might not like what it becomes. Perhaps you feel compelled to leave. The point here is that by protecting the character of a club that you belong to, you are protecting part of your own identity. This is why the characters of these groups can be so hallowed. We see ourselves in them. An attack on the club's character can feel like an assault on one's own identity.

The New Zealand Tendency means that not only do we keep out of our associations those who we think may pose a threat to its character, but also that, when an existing member undermines that character, they too could be kicked out.

In the 1860s Sir George Bowyer MP said that if women were to get the vote, it would be 'manifestly indecorous' to allow them into polling booths. Bowyer was promptly expelled from the Reform Club. There was no rule against saying this, but his 'illiberal' opinions were at odds with the character of the Reform. The New Zealand Tendency tells us that the character of this group was far more important than Bowyer's continued membership.

The Long Wait

Most associations are fairly easy to join, so long as you have a genuine interest in what they are doing and are roughly compatible with their character. While only a handful are 'closed shops', as Marrett put it, there are others that will simply involve a long wait. This can have a curious effect.

In 1959 the social psychologists Elliot Aronson and Judson Mills went to a female college in the United States and advertised a discussion on sex. Very soon they had a mass of volunteers. These were then divided into three groups. The first set underwent a 'severe' screening process, in which each participant had to recite in front of the others a series of swear words such as 'fuck, cock, and screw' and 'read aloud vivid descriptions of sexual activity from contemporary novels'. The idea was to make them feel uncomfortable. The second group experienced a 'mild' initiation, in which they read out words such as 'prostitute, virgin, and petting'. The third group went straight to the discussion without any initiation.

The talk turned out to be incredibly dull. 'Participants spoke dryly and haltingly [they] contradicted themselves and one another, mumbled several *non sequiturs*, started sentences that they never finished, hemmed, hawed, and in general conducted one of the most worthless and uninteresting discussions imaginable.'

But not everyone found it quite so boring. While the girls who experienced the mild or non-existent initiation agreed that it was 'worthless', most of those who went through the severe initiation, by contrast, were gripped. So why was this? It seems that enduring some kind of hardship or long-drawn-out process in order to take part in an activity – such as joining a club – makes our experience when we get there far more compelling.

The American social psychologist Leon Festinger called this 'cognitive dissonance'. It is the idea that we find it hard to hold two contradictory notions simultaneously and instead will try to reduce the dissonance between them. The girls who had undergone the severe initiation had two options. Either they could accept that the discussion was exception-ally boring, but tell themselves that it didn't matter so much, because reading out those swear words wasn't embarrassing, or they could do what most girls did and move in the opposite direction. They would convince themselves that the discussion was in fact well worth the ordeal.

When Aronson and Mills completed their experiment, the waiting list to join White's Club in London was said to be between fifteen and twenty years. Just think what the men on that list must have felt on finally becoming members of the club! The most drawn-out conversation with a club bore would be like talking to Socrates himself, the stodgiest mashed potatoes would be an epicurean delight, the wine ambrosian – and the armchairs! Where to begin? The upholstery, the burnished sheen of each leather arm, the heft, colour, hue, even the way they were positioned . . . Waiting lists can be very useful.

To sum up, we now know roughly why we form associ-ations, what keeps an association going and why it is that being in one of these can inspire a sense of fellowship. They may encourage us to mix with a wider range of people and take our interest in a cause or amateur subject to a new level. In this chapter we have seen just how important it is to us that our associations have some kind of character.

This is the New Zealand Tendency. Now I want to look at something else, an element of what happens in most associations that can leave some people bemused.

6

Rules and Roles
Order and the Importance of Play

IV. If any member swears or curses, his neighbour may
give him a kick upon the shins.

'Rules of the "Two-penny Club"'
Spectator, no. 9 (10 March 1711)

Pretend you live somewhere other than where you do and
that you don't speak English. I know, I know, you're reading
this, which suggests that English is a language you're pretty
good at. But for reasons that will become clear, pretend
otherwise and that early in 2010 you visit Britain for the
first time.

It is spring, and after a few days in London you head out
to get a taste of the legendary English countryside. Yorkshire
is the place to go – at least your guidebook seems to think
so – and you take a train to Leeds. The next morning you
are in the dales. Your afternoon is spent tacking back and
forth through glorious, open country, across fields that heave
and roll like waves in a swell, past sheep that have just
lambed, trees soon to leaf, and at the end of the day you
reach Leathley. It is a small village clustered around a road
that ribbons north. The buildings here are gated or have
been squirrelled away behind hedgerows of beech or horn-
beam. But for the cars and a lean-looking cat that follows
you with its eyes, both watchful and unimpressed, nothing
moves in Leathley.

You admire the church, with its squat tower and slit-windows. Then your attention turns to a series of benches on the other side of the road. You see a telephone box that was once a proud, fire-engine red. It is now an embarrassed pink. Behind this enfilade of benches is a hall. It is one storey tall and empty. You don't pay much attention to this and instead settle down before a sweeping, southerly view as the sun begins a melodramatic descent into the horizon and the sky becomes a Turner of colour and cloud.

Then a strange thing happens. Just as the sky begins to fizz and the temperature drops, a succession of cars pull up in front of you. Each contains several women. Some are elderly and take their time to get out of their vehicles. Others are more nimble. They are all shapes, ages and sizes, and they head without hesitation into the hall behind you. Soon you have counted at least two dozen of these women filing into that building.

It is not clear what they are up to. From their appearance you can see that they are not related, so this is not a family event. Nor is anyone to be married or buried, as far as you can tell. The fact that most have driven here would suggest that few live in Leathley, ruling out the possibility of a village meeting.

You climb on to one of the benches to peer in through the window. To your astonishment, the room has been transformed. Chairs once stacked up in the corner are now laid out in expectant rows. Tables mark the perimeter of the space. Some bear jars and pots; there are flowers, cards and in the middle distance you can make out an array of clipboards with official-looking documents attached. Perhaps it is a professional convention of some sort? On another surface printed reports have been arranged over each other like fallen dominoes, and up on the platform at the far end you can make out a table adorned with a cloth dominated by an embroidered logo; before it, a table covered in wreaths.

But still you can't work out what these women are up to, or what has drawn them together. Clearly it is not a public demonstration, as there are no posters advertising the event and the door is shut. Moreover, these women seem to know each other. Everywhere you look there are miniature reunions, greetings, pats on arms and short, affirmative bursts of laughter as they buzz merrily about, contented bees going about their business – but what is that business? What is their relationship to one another?

You tiptoe into the back of the hall and hide behind a stack of chairs. Just as you settle down, a woman ascends the platform. With a hush the group becomes silent. She begins to speak. This must be the leader. Her voice is thin but warm, and she pauses now and then to let her audience respond, something they do in a relaxed manner. Several go one further and stand up to make short declarations or speeches. You curse the fact that you have forgotten to bring your English phrasebook.

After a quarter of an hour the leader of the group descends the raised dais, whereupon a different woman moves into position behind a lower table. For the next hour the new leader of the group talks and creates dextrous constructions out of ivy and willow-strips. The audience is rapt. She decorates branches, blows an egg, and later the women start to move about as before. There is chatting, laughter, biscuits the colour of sand are passed around, and every woman is handed a mug of what you assume to be tea (it is the same colour as the biscuits, and to your horror you have found that they add milk to their tea in this country). This goes on for a while, there is more chatting, milling, smiling, the stalls are inspected, one or two of those pots are bought, and after several hours the women start to leave. Tables are packed up, chairs stacked and the heater is returned to its

home in the cupboard. All other traces of the evening are
boxed and bagged and placed in the boots of waiting cars.
You hear the friendly thump of car doors closing, and at last
this nomadic caravan departs into the night.

The hall is as it was before they arrived. There is no trace
of what has happened, and the space is silent but for the
decelerating tick of the heater that has just been switched off.
It sounds like an athlete catching her breath.

Their Fantastical Authority

On your way back to Leeds you reflect on what was a frustrating evening. You have travelled all over the world, and
usually when confronted with an indigenous custom or rite
you find it quite easy to work out what is going on and why.
The gathering in Leathley was different. What you could not
put your finger on was the nature of the relationship between
these women. There were no costumes or badges indicating
rank, and yet some of them appeared to have roles within
the group and responsibilities. But they were not related, nor
were they neighbours.

After months of diligent research back at home, you find
out that what bound the women you watched that evening
was their acceptance of a single document – the ten-page
constitution of their association, which contained fifty main
clauses and a tapestry of sub-clauses. These explained the
rules of this group, how its members should act, what titles
they could give each other, the number of meetings they
can have each year, their order, who can become a member
of this group, how expulsions should happen, the stated
spirit of the group, the cost of subscription, how many
individuals should be on a committee, how long they serve
in these positions, the minimum number of times the
committee must meet each year, which positions can be

combined, what makes a quorum, how to create bye-laws, who these should be sent to – all of this, and much more, was explained in the constitution of the Farnley Estate Women's Institute, one of 6,500 WIs active in Britain at the time of your visit.

Hundreds of thousands of associations all over the country are bound together like this by some kind of agreement. It might be a set of rules, a constitution, a manifesto, declaration or memorandum of objectives. Either way, this covenant will describe some sort of structure as well as certain offices and positions of responsibility. Eighty-one per cent of the associations in my survey were run by a committee of some sort and had a formal structure. But what is so interesting about this is that, apart from groups that have become limited companies or registered charities, none of these associations was actually required to do this by law.

There were those in the early eighteenth century, such as Ned Ward, who found the idea of a club or society with its '*President, Secretary, etc.*' inherently silly. As Ward wrote, even 'the most morose *Cynick* would be scarce able to hear their Titles without bursting into Laughter'. Equally pointless, he felt, were their rules, 'exemplify'd at large by some Scrivener's Apprentice, and Ostentatiously hung up in Lacquer'd Frames'. Nor could he understand the need for 'officious Stewards' with their 'ridiculous Chaplets' and 'honorary White-Wands, which [. . .] they wear as Badges of their fantastical Authority'.

So why do we create these rules and give ourselves grand-sounding titles when there is rarely any legal requirement to do this?

Why

'Why do we have rules? Because that's the way it's always been,' began Pat Schwarzenbach, a tall, elegant woman, the Secretary of the Farnley Estate WI. 'When the WIs began, a constitution was drawn up that every group had to take on. Obviously different Presidents of individual WIs can put their own slant on it, but we didn't come up with these rules, if that's what you mean. They were handed down.'

For any association with an inherited set of rules, keeping them alive is yet another way to connect to the group's past. Already we are back with the New Zealand Tendency. These rules become a part of the group's identity, and so we are often inclined to hang on to them.

But how about the original members of the WI – why would anyone draw up rules and roles where before there were none? 'Upon reaching a certain size', wrote the great German sociologist Georg Simmel, every group 'must develop forms and organs which serve its maintenance and promotion'. By these he meant 'offices and representations, laws and symbols of group life'. Simmel was one of the first to argue that we create these formal structures in response to the group's expansion. Rules are an attempt to ensure that the members of the group are treated fairly. They are symptomatic of our desire for justice. In the same sense, positions and roles tend to appear as the workload within an association increases.

But what Ned Ward was really getting at was the nature of these titles. As they do today, the positions he lampooned had an innate authority and grandeur. You don't find many clubs or societies with positions such as 'Meeting Organizer', 'Head-Person' or 'She Who Invites Speakers'. Instead we go for 'President' or 'Vice President', followed by 'Chairman' and 'Treasurer'.

There is nothing new about this. In the first and second centuries AD *collegia* appeared throughout Britannia in places such as Noviomagus Reginorum, Wendens Ambo, Birrens, Corbridge and Verulamium. The members of these groups also gave each other titles full of ersatz authority. *Collegia* were led by *decuriones*; their finances were looked after by *quaestores*; there were *curators* involved in the administration of these groups, as well as *procurators* and *curators honarati*, *praesides*, *praefecti* and *syndics*, along with *quinquennali*, *magistri* and *duumviri*. Each term was borrowed. They came from a vernacular of civic or military officialdom. Outside a *collegium*, *decuriones* referred to officers in command of ten cavalrymen, not humble artisans running a burial association. A *quaestor* was a low-ranking senatorial position. *Praesides* were provincial governors.

Yet the members of these *collegia* in Britannia did not choose their nomenclature. They merely followed suit. The same goes for associations today. In my nationwide survey most groups had an identical set of officers. Of course, there were deviations from this – the Dell Angling Society had a Fishery Officer Head Bailiff, the University of Edinburgh Humanist Society had a Chaplaincy Liaison Officer, the International Necronautical Society, one of my favourite groups, had a Chief Obituary Reviewer, Head Philosopher and Chief Cartographer – but otherwise most groups followed an identical pattern. They had a President and/or Chair(man), followed by a Treasurer, Secretary and a series of ordinary committee members.

This shape has barely changed over the last thousand years. A medieval guild or fraternity was run by an Alderman (sometimes called a Magister or Guardian), who was assisted by a Dean, a Clerk and a series of Stock-holders (known in some parts as Stewards, Custodes, Skymini or Scabini). These positions are almost identical in scope and authority to the modern-day quartet of Chairman, Treasurer, Secretary and ordinary committee members. Again you can see the role of our cultural inheritance in the reality of associations today.

Yet there are many small groups that do not bother with

titles, rules or any sort of constitution. They do not see the need. 'We didn't have any rules for the first three years,' said Anoushka Myers, founder of Knitting Hill, a knitting circle in Notting Hill. 'We would meet in the same pub at the same time each week, but,' she caught herself, 'when something became a problem we introduced one rule and I suppose you could say we gave someone a job to go with it. For a while there was a bit of media interest in what we were doing. Journalists would come and sit in on the group. That was fine. But the atmosphere changed. People couldn't really relax with a camera there. So we designated one person to deal with the media, and made the rule: no media at meetings.'

Just as some groups have rules and others don't, so our rules are not always geared towards maintenance. When Ben Jonson created a set of rules for his poetic tribe, he did more than warn them not to get too drunk; he had one statute suggesting that the atmosphere should be 'neither noisie nor mute' but free from the discussion of 'things serious, much less of Divine'. That's not to say that members shouldn't argue, but if they did, then let their disputes 'bear no unmusical sound'.

It is a wonderful instruction, reminiscent of the Qur'anic *aya* urging Muslims to explain their faith 'with wisdom and beautiful preaching; argue with them in ways that are best and most gracious'. It's also a reminder that rules can be about establishing ideals as well as restricting behaviour. But what is the effect on any association of having rules and a formal structure?

Homo Ludens

In the space of three years I visited many different clubs, societies and associations. Along the way I was able to speak to hundreds of people about why they belonged to their association and what they enjoyed about it. The sentiment that recurred throughout – whether talking to a band of transsexuals and transvestites as they adjusted their wigs in a low-lit club in east London before entering one of their play-rooms, or when gathered around a sturdy, polished table in the Beefsteak Club off Leicester Square, surrounded by eminent diplomats, authors, journalists and politicians – was that belonging to an association provided you with an escape.

I have lost count of the number of times I have heard associations described as havens or refuges. Just as Ben Jonson called his group a 'free state', so Bishop and Hoggett found that 'escaping the home' was one of the main reasons for joining a club. In 1905 a member of the Oriental Club wrote that this club was 'the only place in London where my wife cannot get at me' – something that may begin to explain why it is so rare to find a married couple in the same association. These groups work better when they represent a break from one's home, work and family. But how do rules and roles fit into this?

Homo Ludens was the last book by the Dutch historian Johan Huizinga. It remains the classic study of play. In it Huizinga argued that human culture owes much of its advance to play and the possibility of escaping one's ordinary life to enter spaces in which slightly different rules applied. 'It seems to me,' he wrote, 'that next to *Homo Faber*, and perhaps on the same level as *Homo Sapiens*, *Homo Ludens*, Man the Player, deserves a place in our nomenclature.'

By 'play' Huizinga was referring as much to playing a board game with written rules as to what happened when you began to read this chapter. By asking you to imagine yourself creeping into the back of that hall in Leathley, or proposing in English that you don't speak English, I was asking you to play. If for a moment you suspended your disbelief and pictured yourself in Leathley, unable to understand what was being said, then you were playing in the sense that Huizinga implied.

The same goes for watching a film, making meals, having sex, painting pictures, going to concerts, listening to stories or impersonations. In all of these we allow temporary and translucent walls to form around the court of our concentration. We block out parts of what we know to be true and allow slightly different rules to apply, and it is when this happens that we can escape.

The key to entering one of these playful worlds is being able to accept certain rules or norms that are quite separate to one's everyday existence. If you go to the theatre, you have to play along with the idea that the actor on stage is not an actor but the part he or she is trying to play. You abide by the unwritten rule that this person is who they say they are.

If you agree to follow an association's rules when you know that they have no authority outside the group, and if you are prepared to call someone 'Chairman' or 'Treasurer' when in fact you know their real name, then to a tiny extent you are playing along.

This is why rules and roles in an association can enhance the sense of escape you may feel within that group. They make your escape fractionally more complete.

This matters for all sorts of reasons. Play revitalizes us. It is why you might leave the meeting of an association feeling refreshed or recovered – from labour, from work or from the monotony of being in the same place, doing the same thing, day after day.

Just as we go on holiday to escape our ordinary lives knowing that we will return, and we come back reinvigorated, so we might choose to spend time in an association. An afternoon with F. C. United, a meeting of the Thursday

Club, an evening with Thomas Britton and his fellow musicians, a moot with the Genesis Order, a discussion with Laura's Book Group – for the members of these groups each session was a mini-mini-mini-break. Rules and roles enhance the sense of escape, even if this is rarely the reason why we set out constitutions in the first place.

Philia and the Power of Rules

What else can a formal structure change within a group? Well, strange as it may sound, according to Aristotle and Huizinga, a structure can also draw people closer together. In the *Nicomachean Ethics*, Aristotle described different types of *philia*, meaning friendship, affection or fondness. There was the *philia* you might find between young lovers, lifelong friends, business contacts, members of the same tribe or the *philia* between individuals who belonged to the same association. Aristotle saw this last bond as quite different from friendship, love or a business-based connection. To demonstrate your *philia* for a business contact, you might do them a favour or make a useful introduction. In a conventional friendship *philia* is often about emotional support and loyalty. Yet associational *philia* was different. For Aristotle it was based on the shared recognition of the same set of rules and offices. So by addressing the Vice-President of the Farnley Estate WI as 'the Vice-President of the Farnley Estate WI' rather than just 'Gail Webb' (for that was her name), or by following the designated order of the meeting and abiding by the WI constitution, not only were you making your escape more complete, but you expressed a certain affection for your fellow members.

Huizinga describes the same thing but in different terms. For him, those people who have played together or agreed to follow the same rules constitute a 'play-community'. In one of these, the feeling 'of sharing something important, of mutually withdrawing from the rest of the world and rejecting the usual norms, retains its magic beyond the duration of the individual game'. So not only is the escape more complete, but you are drawn closer to the other 'players' in the group.

Yet we can take our fascination with rules too far. In some cases the constitution of a group becomes an authority in its own right. The psychologist Stanley Milgram had a name for this. He called it 'counteranthropomorphism'. As well as being the longest word I have ever typed, a skyline of a word, this is what happens when we take a very human creation – such as a set of rules – and begin to see it as non-human. We invest it with a power of its own, one that was not there when it was created. Counteranthropomorphism can only occur when we forget that every authority has an author, or a series of them, and that those authors are human. Instead, as Milgram showed, we have a capacity to let ourselves be dictated to by a set of rules that may be of our own making. We lose sight of their origins.

If ever you hear the words 'because the rules say so' in the meeting of an association, then beware. The rules cannot 'say' anything. They are merely expressions of what other members have said or written down. The authority of these rules should not exceed that of their authors. After all, that is what author-ity is.

Rules should not become authorities in their own right, and yet this often happens. Throughout these islands, towards the end of the Middle Ages, guilds and fraternities began to be seen by many as 'Places where [. . .] Conspiracies were', or 'Structures of Superstition'. Their members succumbed to what Coleridge called 'the lethargy of custom'. Men and woman followed certain traditions and rules not because they enabled their groups to run more efficiently or they ensured justice but because *they were the rules*.

All of this might have been different had there been a Macher or two to shake things up.

7

Machers and Maintainers
Tamsin Omond and the Fine Art of Leadership

We have different gifts, according to the grace given us.
If a man's gift is prophesying, let him use it in proportion
to his faith. If it is serving, let him serve; if it is teaching,
let him teach; if it is encouraging, let him encourage; if
it is contributing to the needs of others, let him give
generously; if it is leadership, let him govern diligently.

Romans 12:6–8

At university Tamsin Omond had her heart set on becoming a priest. All that changed, however, after she read a book about climate change. There was nothing for it. She would become a green activist. Perhaps you saw her in the late 2000s on top of Parliament amid banners opposing the expansion of Heathrow Airport? Or when she chained herself to the railings outside? During those first few years as a climate change activist Omond was arrested, she spent a night in jail, appeared in court, organized a string of 'actions' and 'rushes' targeting airports, banks and politicians, and in the 2010 general election she stood for Parliament, unsuccessfully, in Hampstead.

To meet, she is bright and confident, someone who greets the world with a milky grin and has a laugh to match. A flump of golden corkscrews dangle over her forehead like those of a sheep soon to be shorn. Omond is tall and proportioned, with eyes that fizz, a straight back and a clear voice. The combination of her drive, her looks, her lineage – her grandfather was a baronet – and the fact that she was in her twenties ensured that Omond was written about endlessly during those early years. *Vogue* and *Tatler* wanted to use her as a model. A major fashion label asked her to be their 'face'.

Although she turned them down, Omond felt this attention could be put to good use. So she did not shun the limelight entirely. Instead she gave interviews in which she did her best to talk about her various causes. For a photo accompanying a profile in *The Times*, Omond wore a T-shirt that read: 'THIS IS NOT ABOUT ME'. But for the people writing these stories, as well as those who read them, clearly it was. Omond had become 'a bit of a starlet'.

Surely I'm guilty of doing the same thing here? Not once have I mentioned the gravity of man-made climate change or the details of what Omond campaigned for or against. This has been a thoroughly conventional introduction to Tamsin Omond, campaigner, and, like any other profile, it has been about her personality, her youth and those run-ins with the police. Even more peculiar is that in a book about associations there has been not one mention so far in this chapter of, well, associations.

There is a reason for this. The story of Tamsin Omond can do two things. It takes us to the heart of how an association begins as well as illustrating a much broader point about why we fail to recognize the power of association in our rush to focus on the stars, the figureheads and the lead singers.

When we read about a great campaigner, there is a certain narrative that most of us have come to expect. Think of Emmeline Pankhurst or William Wilberforce. The trajectory of a campaigner is generally wearisome and lonely. We like to think of their campaign as a Sisyphean crawl to a distant summit. There is an almost Protestant quality to this. We seem to be fascinated as much by what it is they are campaigning about as by the heroic singularity of their endeavour.

The same thing happens in the world of exploration and

adventure. We have an enduring appetite for tales of lone adventurers (who might call themselves explorers) walking to the North Pole, climbing mountains or sailing around the world by themselves. But we are much less interested when a team of scientists does something very similar, even if their work is more demanding and infinitely more worthwhile.

There is nothing unusual about our affinity for plucky loners. Nor is there anything wrong with it. But it certainly gets in the way of understanding the mechanics of change and what can happen when we come together in small groups. Very few campaigners act alone. Think of any historically significant British campaigner from the last three centuries and without exception – *almost* without exception – you'll find that they belonged to voluntary associations.

Chartism was powered by the National Charter Association, the London Working Men's Association and Feargus O'Connor's Marylebone Radical Association, just as the Abolitionist movement would have fallen apart but for the Committee for the Abolition of the Slave Trade, the Clapham Sect and, later, the Anti-Slavery Society. The repeal of the Corn Laws in 1846 was a triumph for the Anti-Corn Law League, and we must not see female suffrage as the work of the Pankhurst family alone. It was the result of years of assidu-ous campaigning by associations united within the National Union of Women's Suffrage Societies or the earlier National Society for Women's Suffrage, the Women's Franchise League, the Kensington Society, the Women's Co-operative Guild, the National Union of Women's Freedom League, the Women's Social and Political Union, the Women's Liberal Federation and the Independent Labour Party.

Being a great campaigner takes much more than rhetor-ical skill and a monomaniacal devotion to your cause. It requires the ability to work within an association. Great campaigners are great collaborators. They are associational creatures who are just as comfortable planning with others, discussing an issue as a group, delegating and adopting a consensus as they are giving a rousing speech.

Throughout her career as a climate change activist Tamsin Omond belonged to different associations. To begin with they were other people's groups, yet after several years she decided to start her own. This is where she began to play the role of Macher, a part she performed with aplomb. Every association needs a Macher if it is to get going.

Macher, singular

'Macher' (pronounced *macker* or *marker*) is a Yiddish word meaning a person who makes things happen. A Macher is a doer, a social operator, somebody who inspires action. Although there is a smudge of irony to it, in the sense that by calling someone a Macher you might be teasing them slightly, or making out that they are a busybody, these are the people who are prepared to put their heads above the social parapet in order to get things done.

I want to use the word in a slightly different sense, to describe not so much a person but a style of leadership. For any association to begin, there must be at least one person prepared to play the part of Macher.

Earlier we looked at how associations come about. But I feel as though I told you only half of the story. None of these associations simply *occurred* once there were enough people with the same interest or sense of solidarity. These are the raw materials, yes, but you need a spark if they are to ignite. For an association to come about there must be a Macher to inspire associational combustion and to steer the group through the vicissitudes of those first few years.

The Kit-Cat Club was one of the great associations of the eighteenth century. It inspired the *Spectator*, whose influence on British society at the time was thought to 'exceed that of any other work except the Bible'. In her wonderful biography of the Kit-Cat Club, Ophelia Field describes the style of the *Spectator* as 'a flower grown from the bed of Kit-Cat conversation'.

But how do we explain the genesis of the Kit-Cat Club? It was about more than a series of individuals coming together around a shared interest. While the social, political and economic conditions of the period were important, they do not adequately explain this, and nor does the thriving associational culture and the rise of the virtuoso. The Kit-Cat Club came about because of all these things as well as the presence of a gregarious, portly bookseller called Jacob Tonson. He played the part of Macher. In fact, he did it so well that without him the club could barely function. When Tonson went to Paris in 1703, a fellow Kit-Cat wrote to him, mournfully, 'Our club is dissolved till you revive it again, which we are impatient of', and when he left London for good several decades later, the Kit-Cat Club finished.

So what makes a Macher? On the face of it, this is about charisma. As far as we know, this is something Tonson had in spades. So did Omond. She is someone whose presence irons out the crinkles of an unfamiliar conversation. She inspires commitment. But this kind of charisma is often incidental to being a good Macher.

In my last book, about English eccentrics, I interviewed the musician Peter Doherty – not Pete, don't call him Pete whatever you do. He was by turns enigmatic, funny, violent when he wanted to be, and more than anyone else I have met, Doherty exerted a magnetic hold on those around him. He oozed charisma. Yet Doherty was no Macher. Omond was, and so was Tonson, or Fortescue Locke King, who started the New Zealand Golf Club, as well as Laura Wilkie, with her Edinburgh-based book group. Steve Jeal, the softly spoken leader of the Genesis Order, was another skilled Macher. What did these people have that Peter Doherty did not?

Climate Rush

'The idea for Climate Rush came about at one of the climate change camps, a few years ago,' Omond explained one bright afternoon, in a field near Heathrow. It had recently been bought by a consortium of protesters and celebrities in a bid to block the airport's expansion. 'At the time I was a bit fed up with the mentality there. It was very much,' she put on a cranky voice, '"keep the journalists off site" or "be quite aggressive with the police." And so on. There was an emphasis on not talking to people who didn't agree with you. It was about enclosing yourself with others and being quite self-righteous.' She looked quizzical. 'Which I didn't really get.'

Instead she felt the issue of climate change could become more fun, more womanly, and that the emphasis on self-denial and frugality – eat less meat, fly less, have fewer children, use less electricity – was unlikely to inspire many people to change their lifestyles. 'And at the end of that climate camp I realized the centenary of the Suffragettes' 1908 "Rush" was coming up. It was six weeks away. So I thought to myself, "how about staging another Rush on Parliament? A Rush about climate change. A Climate Rush!"'

Many of us prefer to read about activism in history books rather than newspapers. Having once been the scourge of Middle England – there was even a popular anti-suffragism movement dominated by women – by the start of the twenty-first century the Suffragettes were remembered as paragons of virtuous protest. Omond wanted to tap into that legitimacy.

Her first step was to form an association. To do that she needed a vision of what her group could be. This was something she already had. Her association would embody a different approach to climate change, one that made the issues more feminine and popular. It would also stress the analogy between what they were doing and the Suffragette movement.

Here we have the first quality of any Macher. They must

be able to articulate what an association *could* be. This is what Locke King was required to do when recruiting the first batch of members for the New Zealand Golf Club. He would have told them about the lack of competition and the beautiful course. Tonson inspired his Kit-Cats with the idea of a convivial, poetic brotherhood and delicious pies. Jeal presented a vision of a druid order without all the bickering of the last one in Portsmouth. Wilkie, meanwhile, had been telling her friends for many years about how wonderful a reading group could be before she sent that initial email. Like the others, she had an inspiring vision of what the group could be.

As well as having that vision, a Macher needs the courage to propose it and then defend it. There is an element of persuasion involved. This is something Omond relishes. She has always loved 'the kudos that comes with biting the bullet, swallowing my fear and uttering an idea into the silence'. This is what Machers do. They utter ideas into the silence.

Omond's first recruit was a girl called Lotti. 'She became Project Manager, and I was Event Co-ordinator,' she explained. 'I liked my title a lot.' They threw themselves into the logistics of staging their demonstration outside Parliament. 'Both of us worked for free, and both of us worked harder than we'd ever worked before.' Thanks to the Power of Giving and the Hothouse Effect, we know why.

But there was a limit to what the two of them could achieve in such a short space of time. Omond recruited nine more campaigners, again outlining to each newcomer a vision of what the group could be. In this new and enlarged collective there were those who concentrated on contacting different women's groups to tell them about the event, including mother and toddler groups, branches of the Women's Institute and other female associations. Others secured speakers, or dealt with the website and equipment hire.

It was during these weeks that Omond got to grips with

the second element of being a Macher. As well as outlining what your association could be, the Macher must co-ordinate their group and remind everyone of their responsibilities. This is not the same as making all the decisions – the group will usually do that together – but the Macher is there to ensure that whatever has been agreed is implemented.

Climate Rush took place on 13 October 2008 and attracted over a thousand protesters, most of them women – and the kind of women you would not usually see at a protest. Towards the end of the day they rushed Parliament. The objective was not to get inside, but to make those within aware of their presence and to generate positive media coverage. This they did. There were supportive pieces in the *Daily Telegraph*, *Guardian*, *Independent* and *Evening Standard*, and a gallery of televised news broadcasts.

Part of the reason for the coverage being so sympathetic was that Omond's group of organizers had delivered such a consistent message. They had urged everyone to wear Suffragette-style outfits. 'For most newspapers the photo makes the story', Omond wrote, and one of the aims of Climate Rush was to avoid any of the visual clichés of green activism. There were to be no photographs of angry young men waving misspelt placards. Instead, Parliament Square was a sea of washed-out approximations of Edwardian dress. Wherever you looked, there were rolls of creamy broderie anglaise, reclaimed bedsheets, calico, buttery satin, and over the flummery of lattice and lace went diagonal red sashes, the appropriated symbol of the beauty pageant, with slogans such as 'DEEDS NOT WORDS', 'TRAINS NOT PLANES' and 'CLIMATE CODE RED'.

Climate Rush was a success. Yet by making it to the door of Parliament, Omond had broken the conditions of the bail imposed on her for having previously made it on to the roof of that building. She spent the night of Climate Rush in a cell and was released the following day.

The eleven organizers went for a drink to celebrate the freedom of their Macher, and during the hours that followed they agreed to form a new association. It would be called Climate Rush, in honour of their founding event. There would be weekly meetings in a pub on Old Street and Creative Days once a month, in which they could make banners, sashes and yet more Suffragette-style dresses.

Less than a year after that rush on Parliament, Omond and her fellow Climate Rushettes embarked on a month-long walk through the West Country to raise awareness about climate change. They were accompanied throughout by a cart and three great barrel-chested Irish cobs.

I went to visit them several times and watched as they painted murals, organized workshops, gave talks, made potato-men and in other ways spread their message. Omond continued to play the part of the Macher and outline the vision behind the group to potential recruits, just as she co-ordinated and held together what was, on paper at least, 'an odd mixture of mankind'. It included a Californian actress, a mental health worker, an operatic librettist, several art students, a housewife, the truculent man in charge of the horses, an artist, a blogger, the heir to the Earl of Durham and an array of others who danced in and out of the penumbra of this group as it marched west. But it was the *way* Omond did all this that brings us to the third element of being a Macher.

Holding Back

One of the great challenges Omond faced when co-ordinating that rush on Parliament, as well as when leading her band of Climate Rushettes across the West Country, was knowing when to hold back. The success of each collective depended on the creative input of all involved, not just Omond. The group's original aims and demands, for example, were not hers. They emerged out of a group discussion. The same can be said of the look of the flyers for Climate Rush, the website design or the idea of wearing red sashes.

The third element to being a Macher is that you must not crowd out the others in the group, even if this means loosening your grip and allowing the association to become something slightly different to what you had in mind initially. A great Macher understands the Power of Giving. They know that any group is bound to last longer and achieve much more if everyone is giving gifts and the gift cycle is balanced. As we saw earlier, what made the Genesis Order work so well was the fact that Jeal did not do everything. It was a collaborative venture. In Laura's Book Group, the job of hosting each session was shared out between the members, so there was no danger of Wilkie doing too much.

Another skilful Macher is Faisal Al-Yafai. He runs a London-based discussion group, a Salon, in which about twenty to thirty people come together once a month for a debate. 'And quite early on it became clear that this wasn't going to work with everyone just speaking freely over each other,' he told me. 'To begin with, the discussion was quite small. It was easy for people to cut themselves off and ensure that they didn't interrupt. But with more people that changed. I realized that without a strong Chair, people just talked over each other. One or two would dominate the conversation – and that's not a Salon, it's a saloon! It's people yelling and throwing things around. I think the key to being the Chair is knowing when to step in and tell them they've had their say, but to do that without being overbearing. That's basically my job.'

As the great Sir Robert Megarry explained in court, when describing the role of the chairman of an association, 'above all, his duty is to act not as a dictator but as a servant of the members of the body, according to the law'. The best Machers know this. They will hold back and ensure that they do not become dictators. Like Omond, Al-Yafai is someone who has the mercurial ability to drive on a discussion without dominating it or making those involved feel inhibited.

Combining the first three qualities of a Macher is not easy, and some of us are much better at this than others. Recent research has shown that those who lead one group are far more likely to lead others. Clearly it is a skill, and something you get the hang of. There is an art to being a Macher, although it is not necessarily one we celebrate. I believe we should.

'Every child is an artist,' Picasso once said. 'The problem is how to remain an artist once we grow up.' Joseph Beuys went further. 'EVERY HUMAN BEING IS AN ARTIST', he loved to say. I think Beuys was right. We are all artists and artificers. We make things. The spirit of Daedalus is alive in us all, from the moment we wake up in the morning and decide what to wear or what to eat through to cooking a meal at night, the order in which we assemble the words that make up our sentences, the manner in which we deliver them, what we decide to buy in a shop, how to apply make-up, arrange our hair, move furniture, work out what colour to paint a wall – in even the most mundane activities we are artists and there is art.

In the same sense, for Omond, Wilkie, Locke King, Jeal, Tonson and Al-Yafai, playing the part of Macher was an art and each of these figures was a talented social artist. They *made* groups just as a painter makes paintings or a sculptor makes sculptures. Being able to make a group like this is a great skill, and one that we should set up on high.

Machers, Plural

I hope none of this implies that social artists always work alone. There is no need for the dreary stereotype of the solitary painter when it comes to the idea of a social artist. Just as great visual art has its roots in conversation, collaboration and competition, no matter how much we like to think of it as a lonely pilgrimage, so social artists will often work in pairs.

Think of a great rock band. The first face that comes to mind is bound to be the lead singer. Here is the figure-head, the conduit between the band and its audience. But the creative energy within most bands lies in a relationship between a pair of key characters. Look at the Rolling Stones, the Beatles, the Who, the Libertines, Oasis. Without getting into whether they are all great, let alone an order of great-ness, at the heart of each collective was a double act: think of Richards and Jagger, Lennon and McCartney, Daltrey and Townshend, Barat and Doherty, the Gallagher brothers. By the time the Climate Rushettes embarked on their month-long walk Omond was not the only Macher in that group. The other one playing this part was her friend Deborah Grayson. Although Omond was certainly the leader of the group, and the chief Macher, Grayson shared some of the burden.

In her survey of voluntary archaeology groups, Dr Suzie Thomas found 'that a group's level of activity is often dependent on the energies of one or two specific group members, often the Chair or Secretary, in "making things happen".' A recent survey of groups within the Transition Towns movement showed that while only 12 per cent of these voluntary associations were instigated by one person, 77 per cent were formed by more than one.

When the psychologist Robert Bales studied how groups choose their leaders, not only did he identify two different styles of leadership, but he found that these were usually co-present. Each one came to the fore according to the situation. Following thousands of laboratory observations, Bales identified a 'socio-emotional' leader, who made sure that everyone in the group was getting on, while the other leader was more political (and less popular) and became prominent in a time of crisis.

In the reality of life outside a laboratory the division is rarely this neat. But the point remains. Although most associations have one nominal chief – in my survey 92 per cent of the groups had a single formal leader – in groups that last there will often be a pair of prominent personalities driving the group on and sharing the responsibility of Macher.

Taking the Flak

There is just one other element that defines a Macher. During their trek from Heathrow to Totnes, the Climate Rushettes managed to find the country retreat of *Top Gear* presenter and renowned petrol-head Jeremy Clarkson. There they dumped a pile of horse manure, called in the press and were photographed next to it in their Edwardian outfits and a banner that read: 'THIS IS WHAT YOU'RE LANDING US IN'. It was their most successful stunt yet. The story appeared everywhere, from the *Daily Mail* to the *Guardian*, to local newspapers, Sky News and BBC News. Clarkson took it in his stride, laughing it off and referring to the Rushettes as 'silly little girls'. Others were less generous.

It soon became clear that the Rushettes had stirred up a hornet's nest of Clarkson devotees. The group began to be bombarded with abusive emails, text messages and phone calls. As Omond explained, 'every message was sexualized in some way. "You're all doing this because you're too ugly to have sex", or, "You should be in the kitchen having babies," that kind of thing. Or they were saying that after they'd done certain things to me, I was going to have hydrochloric acid poured on me and all that. But,' she paused, 'as Gandhi once said, "first they ignore you, then they laugh at you, then they get angry, then you win."'

There was one other quality that these messages shared. Not only were they all sexualized, but the majority were aimed at Omond. The fourth characteristic of a Macher is that you need a thick skin. As the lead Macher, you become the group figurehead, and often this will involve taking the flak.

Luckily for anyone playing the part of Macher, this is not a role that goes on in perpetuity. Instead the Macher tends to perform the opening act in the history of an association before stepping aside. In those groups that last for many years the Macher will be replaced by a different kind of leader once the group is firmly established.

One of the reasons why so few eighteenth-century associations lasted more than three or four years was that the Machers who started them did not loosen their grip. They would not step aside to let others take over. Figures such as Jacob Tonson or Thomas Britton were fantastic Machers in the sense that they created thriving groups. But they became so integral to their clubs that, like an arch without a keystone, when they left the group collapsed. If an association is to last for more than a generation, the Macher needs to be replaced by what I like to call a 'Maintainer'.

Maintainers

In 1963 the banker and clubman Sir Lionel Fraser published his memoirs, entitled *All to the Good*. At one point in the book Fraser cast his mind back to his days as Chairman of the now defunct St James's Club:

I am not sure I would recommend the job to my worst enemy. But it is a chore which somebody has to do. To be successful, a chairman of a club should have tact, firmness, a sense of humour, understanding of human relationships and at times a thick skin. . . . A chairman must be ready to appease disgruntled members and listen patiently to their complaints at all times. Subjects range from the suitability of prospective candidates, to too much water in the Brussels sprouts for yesterday's lunch; why there is a hole in the carpet, to why the strawberries were unripe at dinner last Sunday week. He is tackled whenever it suits the member, on the telephone, in his office or at home, when he is entertaining a guest in the club, or more frequently, for what in the eyes of the member appear to be really important matters, in the cloakroom when he is washing his hands.

Here we can see a very different style of leadership. Fraser was playing the part of a Maintainer. More of a steward than an impresario, a Maintainer is there to keep the association going without imposing their personality too much. Of course, to be a Maintainer you need something to maintain. The group must have an identity in the first place. Once this is established, and the group is not facing a crisis, then there usually is not the same need for the strong leadership of a Macher.

The idea that a group with a distinct identity does not need a Macher is echoed elsewhere. In hunter–gatherer societies, for example, those bands that develop religious behaviour have less need of a strong leader. They are more egalitarian. Their faith embodies the character of their group, and this lessens the need for a powerful Macher. Robert Axelrod's Co-operation Theory implies something very similar: that 'cooperation based on reciprocity can be self-policing', so within a group run like this 'no central authority is needed'. On that basis, any association with a coherent character, such as the St James's Club or the New Zealand Golf Club, is bound to have less need of a Macher at the helm.

Conclusion

The point of Part One has been to set out how associations work. This will help us get to grips with whether or not there was a resurgence of these groups in recent years. Looking at the Thursday Club and Thomas Britton's musical society, we saw that associations tend to start when a clump of individuals recognize a common cause or a shared interest, one that means a lot to them. This is more likely to happen among people with what George Homans called a 'capacity for membership'. We saw that nobody is forced to join one of these groups. Associations are voluntary and independent through and through. Groups that come about at the behest of a government initiative inspired by a fashionable think-tank, or a corporate scheme driven by a marketing agency, simply do not last in the way that a group run 'by some of us, for all of us' might. The spirit of an association derives from its autonomy, and this allows it to become an enclave apart from the state and the market.

Yet for an association to come about there must be at least one person who is prepared to play the part of Macher. It seems we coalesce around personalities as much as what George Orwell once called 'that un-English thing, an idea'.

Once the association is up and running, it will generally take on one of two shapes. Either it is centred on a room-sized cluster of men and women made up of anything between three and about thirty individuals – think of Laura's Book Group, the Genesis Order, the *Chevra Kadisha* or those Cardigan art protesters – or it expands beyond that to become much larger – this is true of the New Zealand Golf Club, the B. E. C. or F. C. United. In these types of associations you'll find less emphasis on coming together as one than on the identity of the group. This is where the New Zealand Tendency comes in. It is a reminder of just how important the identity of our associations can be, for those within and without, and the lengths we go to in order to keep these identities alive.

Alongside this need to belong is our love of escape and play. It seems that one of the things we treasure about our associations is the way they provide a short, sharp break from everyday life. Often the rules, roles and written constitutions can enhance that, as well as drawing us closer together.

Yet what really binds the members of any group to one another, more than sharing a playful escape, is the Power of Giving. When we give gifts to each other, no matter how large or small, a sense of camaraderie ensues. When this happens, associations become self-sustaining. Their members do not need to be paid with money, because they are compensated for their time with gifts and fellowship.

Soon you can see the Hothouse Effect. It means that within associations we take our interests much further. We pay less attention to the social background and age of our fellow enthusiasts and instead devote ourselves to the interest or cause that we have in common. Of course, if you combine this with a pronounced sense of detachment, something that may have happened to Anthony Blunt in the Apostles, group polarization can lead to more extreme or dangerous behaviour. But this is rare.

This has been a Beginners' Guide to Associations, and while there may have been moments when it seemed as though I was stating the obvious, I think it is important to come at these groups as though we know nothing about them, to retain a sense of wonder in spite of ourselves. That way it becomes possible to see these associations for what they are.

Now that we have a deeper understanding of how these groups work and what brings them about, we can move on to the main course. Is it possible that during the first decade of the twenty-first century, while some of us described growing levels of loneliness and bewailed the death of community, a growing number of Britons were actually coming together in small groups? Was there an unseen revival of associational activity that swept the nation, and if so, what is the evidence for this?

PART TWO
The Hidden Revival

8

The Evidence

Making the Case with Numbers

Father Brown laid down his cigar and said carefully:
'It isn't that they can't see the solution. It is that they
can't see the problem.'

G. K. Chesterton, 'The Point of a Pin'

This is not the book I set out to write. At the beginning, as
I began to map out the territory, I made several assumptions.
One of these was that, like a glacier in retreat, the mass of
clubs and societies in Britain was in decline in the sense that
fewer Britons were joining these groups. This was to be an
account of a vanishing world, a book about the last of these
associations. Forget about *Together*; what I had in mind was
Apart.

These assumptions were based on a number of things. There
were the reports I had read suggesting that levels of neighbourliness in Britain were on the wane and that a growing
proportion of us chose not to socialize with our neighbours.
There were others arguing that we were becoming lonelier,
and that increasingly we were living alone – two quite different
things. One study suggested that by 2016 as many as 35 per
cent of English households would be occupied by just one
person. Journalists, social scientists, politicians and commentators alike provided frequent reminders that British society
was apparently 'broken'. I had also read *Bowling Alone*, Robert
Putnam's grim account of the collapse of American civic

society which talks of Americans being slowly 'pulled apart from one another and from [their] communities over the last third of the century'. Seeing that most of the technological and social shifts responsible for this were at large in British society, I had assumed that a similar set of processes were at work on this side of the Atlantic.

If you look at the traditional British associations, these assumptions are borne out. During the first decade of the twenty-first century membership of trades unions slipped from 7.8 million to 6.5 million; the number of women who came together within WIs fell from 250,000 to 205,000; the membership of British and Irish Rotary Clubs fell from 59,000 to 55,000. Although there were 350,000 Freemasons in 1999, by 2009 that figure was down to 240,000. The number of Working Men's Clubs and Institutes fell from around 3,000 to 2,150. As far as I could tell, we really were losing our appetite for coming together in small groups. The only question left was, how long before British associations disappeared altogether?

Changing UK

But all was not as it seemed. Early on in my research I took a closer look at one of the studies explaining how and why we were becoming increasingly lonely. I wanted to understand the mechanics of it, and just how bad things were going to become.

Changing UK came out in late 2008. It was the work of an interdisciplinary research group at the University of Sheffield and had been commissioned by the BBC.

In the weeks that followed its publication, *Changing UK* generated a string of gloomy headlines. BBC News began with 'Life in UK "has become lonelier"'. The *Daily Telegraph* announced that 'Britain has become "much lonelier" over past 30 years, says report'. 'Britain has become a "lonelier" place over the past 30 years, where even your neighbour's a stranger', warned the *Daily Mail*. 'New research [. . .] has revealed that the UK has become a nation of lonely hearts, with traditional community life disappearing', went another source. 'Life in the UK has become lonelier, as neighbourhoods have got more fragmented and community life has substantially weakened.' The New Economics Foundation cited this report as evidence that Britons were negative about their 'sense of trust and belonging with people in general'. News of *Changing UK* even made it to the United States, where a blog linked to Putnam's *Bowling Alone* announced, very simply, 'Brits increasingly "Bowling Alone"'.

End of story, you might think. Here was a report that confirmed what most of us already knew. One of *Changing UK*'s conclusions was that between 1971 and 2001 levels of 'loneliness' in Britain may have risen from 18.7 per cent to 26.2 per cent. This sounded precise in an impressive, scientific way, especially with those decimal points. But how did they come up with these numbers? This is where it got interesting.

The study's 'loneliness indices' were calculated using a method employed earlier by Professor Peter Congdon, in a study published back in 1996. But he was not examining loneliness. He was analysing suicide and attempted suicide, and not in the country as a whole but in a handful of London boroughs.

Congdon wanted to see if there was a relationship between the number of suicides and attempted suicides in these areas and the social and demographic breakdown of their populations. He set out to measure the correlation between the two. To do this, he combined four sets of data, measuring the number of people in these boroughs who lived alone, rented their property, had moved to their home in the last year, or were unmarried. Then he applied a suitable scale and weightings to give what he called a 'total anomie score'. This he compared to the levels of suicide and attempted suicide.

The results were mixed. While suicide and attempted suicide were 'both positively correlated with anomic and deprivation variables', the impact of these different criteria was by no means uniform. In some places deprivation played a more significant role, and it's fair to say that Congdon's 'total anomie score' did not anticipate with striking accuracy the suicidal tendencies of the people living in these London boroughs.

So the authors of *Changing UK* got it wrong on two counts. First, they used a technique designed to anticipate levels of suicide or attempted suicide in pockets of London to measure loneliness in Britain as a whole. This was never going to work. Even if they had been looking at the national suicide rate, this approach was doomed. Using Congdon's method, they projected a nationwide rise from 18.7 per cent to 26.2 per cent over the thirty-year period from 1971. In reality, by 2003 adult suicide rates in the UK had actually reached a thirty-year low. By 2007 suicide rates in Britain had dropped to a new sixteen-year low. Effectively the authors of this report described a slump as a growth.

Of course they were not talking about suicide rates. They wanted to see how lonely we had become. So they came up with a semantic fudge. They suggested that 'anomie' is 'the sociological term to describe, according to some interpretations, the feeling of "not belonging"'. They renamed Congdon's anomie indices 'loneliness indices'. This is nonsense. Anomie and loneliness are not the same thing. Anomie comes from the Greek *anomia*, meaning 'lawlessness', and was used first in 1893 by Émile Durkheim to describe a kind of urban isolation that was so acute that it could induce or exaggerate suicidal tendencies.

Loneliness is quite different. It is neither a disease nor a condition but a behavioural response to what John Cacioppo, author of *Loneliness*, has called 'social pain'. It registers in our dorsal cingulate, the same part of the brain that picks up physical pain. Loneliness was an evolutionary adaptation to life as prehistoric hunter-gatherers, when being separated from the group meant being in trouble. The pang of loneliness any one of us feels today is a relic of that. Like so many parts of our anatomy or behavioural make-up, it may not be ideally suited to life in the twenty-first century. Realizing that you are alone in Britain today rarely means you are in serious danger. Nonetheless, we carry it around within us.

Experiencing loneliness like this is quite different from feeling a suicidal sense of anomie. You can be clinically depressed but not at all lonely, just as you can be lonely without being clinically depressed. 'Loneliness' is not a substitute for 'anomie', just as 'pain' is not the same as 'cancer'.

But even if you set aside the wonky methodology and ignore its semantic fudge, the findings of this report still do not add up. To gauge loneliness in Britain it brought together estimates of how many unmarried adults there were in Britain, how many Britons were living alone, the proportion of the population that had moved house in the last year, and the number of people living in privately rented homes. The problem with this is simple: being alone is not the same as feeling lonely. As Cacioppo explained, the effects of the latter are, at their very worst, 'comparable to the effect of high blood pressure, lack of exercise, obesity, or smoking'. A sense of crippling loneliness can accelerate ageing and limit one's immune and cardiovascular functions. It can do all these things, but, as he also makes clear, feeling lonely is not the inevitable result of living alone or being single. Our perception of isolation is quite different from the reality of it. As a married man you could feel hopelessly lonely and adrift in the house that you have owned for decades, and as a single woman living alone in a rented flat that you have just moved into you could be having the time of your life and experience not one jot of loneliness.

Yet the idea that we were becoming lonelier with every passing decade made sense to the authors of this report. It complemented the other conclusions in *Changing UK* and confirmed a broader long-term trend towards social atomization and segregation. So they went with it.

If this was the most convincing evidence that a team of five academics could produce to argue that we were becoming lonelier, then perhaps something was amiss. In my mind those headlines about loneliness no longer meant so much. Seeing this 'statistic' about loneliness fall apart forced me to rethink certain elements of the book I was beginning to write. It confirmed an idea that I had come across elsewhere – that there was in Britain a surprising 'level of incomprehension' about how and why we come together, as the editor of a collection of essays on community put it.

If the evidence for our rising levels of national loneliness was thin to the point of being non-existent, then perhaps the idea that our clubs, societies and voluntary associations were in a state of decline was also a house built on sand? Certainly the groups I was starting to spend time with showed no signs of being in recession. Slowly, and at first reluctantly, I began to realize where I had gone wrong.

Some Numbers

There is a different way of thinking about how we come together in Britain today, and it involves focusing on small voluntary groups. Towards the end of what the authors of *Changing UK* describe as a thirty-year hike in loneliness, the educationalist Konrad Elsdon, working with John Reynolds and Susan Stewart, estimated the existence in Britain of 'at least 1.3 million small democracies'. By 'small democracy' he meant an organization that 'draws its membership from a limited area, is based on the principle of personal membership, is self-governing, and pursues objectives which are internal to itself'. In other words: associations. Elsdon thought there could be as many as 1.5 million of these in Britain, adding that, had they been able 'to track down not just every church group, every local political party and all their daughter organisations, every cub scout group, first aid or rugby team', that total 'would certainly be exceeded substantially'. They showed no signs of being in decline.

Two years later, in 1997, a report argued that 4.4 million people used community buildings in England and Wales *each week*. Community buildings tend to attract clubs and societies more than anything else.

In 1999 the political scientist Peter Hall looked into whether Putnam's 'bowling alone' thesis applied to British society, as many (including me) assumed it would. Hall concluded that there had been 'no equivalent erosion' of social capital on these islands during the late twentieth century, and that the average number of associational memberships had actually increased since 1959 by 44 per cent. Back then it was 0.73; by 1990 it was 1.12. At the close of the twentieth century, Hall continued, 'even a conservative interpretation would suggest that there has been some expansion in informal sociability over the past forty years.'

Two years after Hall's report the New Economics Foundation produced a study that estimated the existence of between 600,000 and 900,000 'micro social enterprises' involving up to 5.4 million people. Although they gave no indication as to whether this field was in decline or on the rise, the authors argued that these 'low-flying heroes', many of them small community-based groups without either offices, staff or formal charitable status, were essentially unknown to social policy-makers and to the state. They were invisible. Hence the title of the report. Clearly there was much more to the world of associations than the more traditional Working Men's Clubs, trades unions, Rotary Clubs, Women's Institutes and Freemasons.

During the run-up to the Queen's Golden Jubilee in 2002, Buckingham Palace contacted the Community Development Foundation to send a message from the Queen to every 'community group' in Britain. Chris Church was working there at the time. As he explained, 'at that point, in 2002, we had contact with 280,000 community groups. But as a rule of thumb, when it comes to how many groups there actually are, you can assume two associations for every one that you know about. So we began to talk about there being about 750,000 of these groups.'

Four years later, in 2006, the National Council for Voluntary Organisations estimated the existence of 865,000 civil society organizations. Not *members* of groups, but actual associations. By 2008 that figure had grown to 900,000.

In 2002 the General Household Survey estimated that the percentage of Britons who belonged to clubs had risen between 1996 and 2002 from 34 per cent to 38 per cent. Of those who took part in the British Social Attitudes Survey of 1998, 21 per cent said they belonged to community groups, while 26 per cent were involved in sports and cultural groups. Few belonged to both. In 2007 a similar question was asked in the same survey about whether participants had been involved with '"associations or groups", ranging from sports and cultural groups to civic or political organisations'. Some 57 per cent replied that they had, indicating a steady increase.

These figures all point towards the same thing: sustained associational growth. But they are not conclusive. For the most part these data are based on estimates, extrapolations and comparisons that are rarely like-for-like. It's only when you look more carefully at particular fields that the overall picture becomes clear.

In Detail

First, let's take the arts. In 2008 the Department of Culture, Media and Sport and Arts Council England commissioned a survey of the voluntary arts called *Our Creative Talent*. This report concluded that by 2008 there were 49,140 artistic associations in England alone, and that between them they involved up to 9.4 million people.

Crucially, and this is the figure that matters, the report found that between 2003 and 2008, as many as 85 per cent of these associations experienced either a growth or stasis in their membership figures. This is a startling statistic. Narrow your focus, and the pattern of sustained growth is repeated throughout this part of our associational landscape.

Between 2005 and 2010 the number of groups within the National Federation of Music Societies grew from 2,331 to more than 2,800. The total number of musicians involved grew by at least 18 per cent. The number of choirs affiliated to the National Association of Choirs grew by 34 per cent between 2000 and 2010. It's also possible that the number of unsigned bands may have grown over this period, and although there will never be any precise figures, one estimate suggested that there were more than 30,000 bands in Britain by 2010.

Book groups also appear to have flourished during the first decade of the twenty-first century. Again there are no precise figures, but a study published in 2001 argued that 'reading groups are the success story of the past few years'. In 2008 the co-director of the reading group website bookgroup.info, Claire Chandler, estimated the existence of some 50,000 reading groups in Britain, adding that they were 'fantastically diverse – village groups, prison groups, school groups; all different ages, with different reasons for getting together', and, crucially, that their numbers were growing.

Move away from books and music, and the picture remains

the same. A nationwide study of natural history societies, commissioned by the Natural History Museum and Open Air Laboratories (OPAL), found that by 2009, although

> there is a popular view that natural history societies are somewhat under threat from declining and ageing membership, however, the conclusions of this survey create a different picture. Many Societies do work hard to keep going, but the general picture is one of a thriving community, with many Societies experiencing significant growth. [. . .] Despite anecdotal evidence for the decline of society membership, the results of this survey show a relatively healthy situation with 8/10 responding groups maintaining or increasing membership.

The number of people on waiting lists to join allotment associations shot up during the first decade of the twenty-first century. According to the Council for British Archaeology, although there were only 408 voluntary archaeological groups in Britain by the end of 1986, that figure had rocketed to 2,030 by 2009. These involved as many as 215,000 individuals. The number of beekeepers affiliated to the British Beekeepers' Association rose from just under 9,000 to 17,300 by the end of the decade (even though the poor bees themselves were in decline). The Federation of Family History Societies also reported a growth in the number of family history groups.

In even more specific and niche fields this pattern of overall growth was repeated. There were some groups whose numbers were static – the membership of the British Astronomical Association, for example, remained at about 3,000, and the National Association of Flower Arranging Societies had a constant 75,000 members between 2005 and 2010 – but elsewhere there was growth. The number of clubs affiliated to the Federation of British Historic Vehicle Clubs grew from 385 to well over 500 between 2004 and 2010. The membership of the Radio Society of Great Britain was 'increasing constantly' during that same period, with over 500 amateur radio clubs linked to the society by 2010. Even morris dancing may have experienced some kind of growth, and by 2010 there were at least 800 morris teams nationwide.

In the other major field of associational activity, sport, again there was steady growth throughout the country. In 2003 Paul Haezewindt wrote that 'there has also been a boom in the formation of new sports clubs'. Participation in every type of sport surveyed by the General Household Survey increased between 1977 and 1997. A survey conducted by Sport England between 2005 and 2006 found that '25.1 per cent of the adult population (10.2 million) are members of a club where they take part in sport – an increase from 17 per cent in 2002'. That figure remained more or less stable over the following five years, so that by 2010 there were thought to be 10.1 million members of different sporting clubs in Britain, representing a major increase during the first decade of the twenty-first century.

You can see this more clearly in the membership of specific federations of sports clubs. Again there were one or two sports in which the number of registered teams, clubs and groups fell or remained static. So the number of rugby clubs affiliated to the Rugby Football Union did not budge between 2002 and 2010. The same can be said of hockey clubs linked to England Hockey, and of swimming clubs within the Amateur Swimming Association. And although there were 165,543 members of clubs affiliated to either the English Bowling Association or the English Women's Bowling Association in 2001, eight years later that number had dropped to 129,143. And the membership of golf clubs within the English Golf Union fell slightly from 736,000 to about 690,000 between 2000 and 2009, even if the quantity of clubs grew from 1,889 to 1,951.

Elsewhere, however, the picture was rosier. The number of clubs belonging to the English Football Association (FA) grew by 23 per cent during the 1980s and 1990s, and while there are no precise figures for what followed, we know that by 2010 there were 125,000 teams affiliated to the FA, and according to one representative this figure had grown over the last decade. In Scotland the number of teams linked to the SFA remained roughly the same. The number of rowing clubs linked to British Rowing grew from 449 to 543 between 2000 and 2010, while their total membership rose from about 16,500 to 25,500. The total membership of clubs affiliated to the Lawn Tennis Association grew from 291,640 to 358,161 between 2007 and 2010, with an equivalent increase among junior members. Between 2006 and 2010 the number of badminton clubs affiliated to Badminton England grew from 2,200 to 2,425; the membership of these groups grew from 51,000 to 51,496 over the same period. There may have been an equivalent increase among clubs linked to Badminton Scotland. During the first decade of the twenty-first century the number of clubs linked to the Rugby Football League grew from 400 to 557, with participation up from 43,000 to 60,000. While there was a drop in the volume of canoe clubs affiliated to Canoe England, from 442 to 425, the total membership (the figure that matters) increased from 12,400 to 35,000. A similar thing is believed to have happened in Canoe Scotland and in Northern Ireland, where participation more than tripled between 1995 and 2008. Membership of archery clubs affiliated to the Grand National Archery Society shot up from 21,418 to 31,744 between 2003 and 2009.

In 2007 there were 1,072 clubs affiliated to England Athletics. By 2009 that figure had grown to 1,156. The number of athletes registered to these clubs grew from 96,000 to 110,000 during those years. In Scotland the number of people belonging to athletics clubs linked to Scottish Athletics grew from about 5,000 to 8,500, while the number of clubs rose from 120 to 138. For Welsh Athletics the number of people affiliated to their clubs doubled during this period.

This pattern of overall growth is repeated on a less dramatic scale in the world of civic groups. While some declined slightly – the membership of the National Women's Register dropped from 7,357 to 7,276 – others experienced growth. In 2000 the National Neighbourhood Watch Association estimated the existence of 155,000 schemes nationwide. By 2010 that figure was up to 170,000. In 2001 there were 22,000 members of Young Farmers' Clubs around the country. Eight years later there were 25,000 involved. The number of user groups made up of those with an experience of having been treated for mental health problems has also grown since the late 1990s. By 2009 there were at least 1,000 Civic Society groups, with over 250,000 members. By the end of the same year some 100 Transition Towns, Villages, Cities and Islands were in existence. The number of groups advertising themselves on the website Meetup.com grew substantially during this period. Again, exact figures are hard to come by, but in London alone there were nearly 2,000 of these groups active by 2010, ranging from those that brought together expats from a particular country to film clubs, book clubs, groups dedicated to hula-hooping, French poodles, crochet, vampirism or even social anxiety.

In need of more data, I began my own nationwide online survey of associations. Rather than take a narrow sample and ask about their associational habits or hunt down all the groups in a specific area, I chose to promote it as widely as possible, in the hope that a great variety of people would learn about the survey and pass it on. The range of associations that completed the questionnaire was stunning, with responses from all over the country. Although the results should be treated with caution, as they provide no more than a snapshot of our associational landscape, one finding stood out.

To the question about whether their numbers were growing, declining or remaining static, only 8 per cent of the groups reported that their numbers were falling. The remaining 92 per cent indicated that their numbers were either on the rise or remained stable.

The message was consistent and clear. If you look beyond the traditional forms of association, such as WIs, and Working Men's Clubs, all of which reported a small decline during the first decade of the twenty-first century, there is a clear pattern of overall associational growth.

And it appeared to easily outstrip population growth. During the first decade of the twenty-first century the British population grew by about 5 per cent, with just over 3 million more inhabitants in mid-2009 than in 2001. The majority of increases in clubs and members of clubs exceeded that figure.

But this mass of numbers gives us only one part of the picture. These statistics either describe groups that belong to national federations or they are estimates extrapolated from surveys that rarely involve more than a few thousand participants. The point here is that most of the groups we are interested in fly beneath the radar. Within every sport, for example, there will be countless clubs that choose not to join the national governing body. They are the sporting equivalent of what the New Economics Foundation called 'low-flying heroes'. We simply do not have the numbers to describe with absolute, unflinching accuracy the total number of Britons involved in associations. This limits what we can do using nothing but statistics.

But why is this? We have data describing so many aspects of our life. Why should associations be any different? The answer takes us to the dawn of our associational past and tells us something important about these groups.

Beneath the Radar

Most rulers of ancient Rome shared Trajan's gut feeling that, when 'people assemble for a common purpose, whatever name we give them and for whatever reason, they soon turn into a political club'. These were thought to be mischievous and divisive, the kind of group that should be treated with caution. In Rome, a typical response to political unrest was to disable such clubs, or just abolish them. This is what happened during the dying days of the Roman Republic, when the *collegia sodalica* were accused of corruption, vote-rigging and meddling with the *comitia*. They were swiftly shut down.

An identical prejudice emerged in England as soon as guilds and fraternities became a significant force. Until then the idea of belonging to an independent association was known to only a fraction of the population. During the Middle Ages this changed. In 1388 a writ was delivered to Richard II's Cambridge Parliament proposing the suppression of almost all these bodies. At the time there may have been as many as 30,000 fraternities and an unknown, although probably similar, number of guilds.

While this came to naught, the sentiment lingered like a terrible grudge. Over a century later it resurfaced. In 1534 the Tudors' assault on the nation's monasteries, fraternities, chantries and guilds began with Henry VIII's Act of Supremacy. It ended in 1547, with a Chantries Act passed in the name of his son, Edward VI. This act alone abolished several thousand fraternities by name and forced many more, including colleges and hospitals, to close or be incorporated into the state.

The battle lines were drawn. Small, independent associations were anathema to a strong, centralized state. During the century that followed our associational landscape became barren. It was only in the wake of the English Civil War that it came back to life, and this time it was bigger, bushier and more virulent than ever before.

Soon afterwards, a growing number of Britons began to agree that what they got up to with others in the privacy of their homes or in private taverns or coffee houses should have nothing to do with the state. As the poet and later MP Andrew Marvell warned in 1675, when Charles II tried to shut down the nation's coffee houses, 'They who conquered the father won't be slaves to the son.'

This was a harbinger of what Isaiah Berlin would later call 'negative liberty', and it was during the late seventeenth and early eighteenth centuries that the social and political independence of these clubs and societies became bound up in the notion of liberty. Attempts to limit or control these associations threatened this implicitly. Freedom of association came to be seen as a moral right.

Over the centuries that followed, associations in Britain flourished as never before. *The Times* in 1785 suggested that 'we have numberless assemblies, clubs and societies in this kingdom'. Although there were intermittent attempts to limit the activities of radical groups – namely, the various Combination Acts, the Unlawful Oaths Act of 1797, the Unlawful Societies Act of 1799 and the Seditious Meetings Act of 1817 – for the most part associational growth was unfettered.

Our associational landscape grew and grew, and by the start of the twentieth century it was as if it had been designated a national park. As the *Encyclopaedia Britannica* put it in 1902, 'a wise and strong Government usually protects and encourages [clubs] as a most important condition of human progress.'

By the death of Queen Victoria, these associations had become a cherished part of our national culture. Any attempt to monitor or control them would have been threatening from a libertarian point of view as well as impractical, owing to the vast number of groups.

This begins to explain why there were no systems in place to tell us how many of these bodies there were at the start of the twenty-first century. It can also shed some light on why most associations in Britain today have no legal personality and are not required to register with a central authority or adhere to specific associational laws.* They are fundamentally independent, and that independence is born of liberty. Although there are isolated examples of British courts becoming involved in disputes concerning the 'membership, expulsion and dissolution' of small associations, generally they steer clear of these groups unless property or criminality is involved, or they are registered charities.

By their nature then, associations shy away from central authority and the world of national statistics. In the DNA of most small groups you find a sliver of independence. The sociologist Robert Nisbet once called them 'the greatest single barrier to the conversion of democracy from its liberal form to its totalitarian form'. These groups have an inbuilt resistance to unnecessary contact with the state, and this is something that dominates their history. It is an attitude I got a taste of myself when conducting my survey. One of the questions I was asked repeatedly was whether I was part of a government initiative. The reply that I was not, would always be met with a sigh of relief, a loosening of the voice or a more responsive email.

This is why so many small voluntary groups are invisible to the state and its statisticians. Seeing that we can only get so far with numbers, it is time for Plan B. Earlier I suggested that there were two approaches to any question. One involves evidence, statistics and observation. The other relies on calculation. We have looked at the data, and while they clearly

*For more on this see Appendix B.

indicate that there probably was a revival of associational activity during the first decade of the twenty-first century, one that exceeded population growth, this is not conclusive. In that case, when we set aside statistics, what other arguments can be made for the idea of an unexpected surge of associational activity?

9

The Internet

Catapulting Associations into the Twenty-First Century

Their passionate common exchange and endeavour was
of a type that would not be possible again – until today,
with the fast, collaborative intimacy of the Internet.

Jenny Uglow, *The Lunar Men*

In Birmingham in the late eighteenth century there was a
small group called the Lunar Society. Its members were bound
by what one member, Joseph Priestley, called their 'common
love of science'. As Jenny Uglow explained in her superb
account of this group, *The Lunar Men*, the society's members
were 'at the leading edge of almost every movement of its
time in science, in industry and in the arts, even in agricul-
ture'. Yet 'their passionate common exchange and endeavour
was of a type that would not be possible again – until today,
with the fast, collaborative intimacy of the Internet.'

What Uglow was referring to was the way the members
of the Lunar Society communicated during that lull between
meetings. As most of them lived very close together, they
would do this using handwritten notes, and they could meet
individually and send each other printed material. Their
communication was speedy, frequent and cheap. But it was
a shadow of what was to come.

For as long as we have come together in associations we
have worked out ways of staying in touch between meetings.
Once this would have involved verbal messages passed between

members, handwritten notes or letters, notices and signs; church bells also played a part, along with bellmen and town criers. Perhaps you wanted to send a reminder to the members of your group that a meeting is about to start or let them know about a change of venue, or it could be that you want to continue a conversation that began during a meeting. It might also be that you hoped to advertise the existence of your association in an attempt to recruit new members.

All of these involve the use of communicative media. Being able to do this enriches the life of any association, and you would think that our ability to communicate between meetings improves as the technology of communication evolves. With each breakthrough it becomes easier to send a message to the group, to share news and to recruit, surely?

But it doesn't work like that. While some media have improved the way members of associations can communicate when apart; others have not. Johannes Gutenberg's invention of a printing press with movable type, the advent of cheap paper and the introduction of more reliable postage – all of these fuelled the associational surge that followed the Restoration. They made communication between meetings faster, easier and cheaper, and this allowed Britons to take their interests that little bit further, faster.

'Newspapers make associations, and associations make newspapers', wrote de Tocqueville, for whom it was essential that the members of an association could 'converse every day without seeing each other, and [. . .] take steps in common without having met. Thus hardly any democratic association can do without newspapers.' During the nineteenth century the cost of doing all this was driven down further as the production of paper and printing became steam-powered. Postage become cheaper and faster.

At around the same time there was another, more startling breakthrough in the history of communication. In 1837 Sir Charles Wheatstone designed the first telegraph system, and less than forty years later Alexander Graham Bell invented the telephone. Between them they had pioneered telecommunications. But this had almost no effect on associations. 'One does not meet new friends on the telephone', as one survey helpfully pointed out. Neither the telegraph nor the telephone was an effective recruitment tool. Nor did they allow group communiqués to pass among the members of a group. Instead, both were geared towards dyadic communication, and although this made it easier for pairs of members to stay in touch between meetings, neither medium did anything to enhance group communication. That was the problem.

Other forms of telecommunication, such as radio and television, were equally useless from an associational point of view. For the most part these were intransitive mass media and were far too expensive for small bands of enthusiasts to use. Like two people who don't quite see eye to eye and probably never will, telecommunications and associations did not get on. It was hard to see how this would ever change.

In 1991 the physicist Tim Berners-Lee launched the World Wide Web. Although there had been computer networks in the United States since the 1950s and these had become steadily more inter-connected over the following decades, nobody had thought to combine these with the idea of a hypertext.

Human communication would never be the same again. By 2009 almost three-quarters of British households had access to what had become known as the internet. During those first eighteen years Berners-Lee's form of telecommunication improved the speed and ease with which billions of humans could communicate with each other; it broadened their access to information and their ability to express themselves before a vast audience. It also had a remarkable effect on the experience of belonging to an association in Britain.

The Wonder of Email

The internet, and specifically email, was faster than anything the Lunar Men had access to, it could be more frequent and it was almost certainly cheaper. The Lunar Society's 'fast, collaborative intimacy' was a shadow of what its members would have experienced had they been able to send emails. Nor would their communication have been constrained by geography. If one Lunar man had travelled to London for a few weeks, he could have kept up easily with developments back in Birmingham had the group had access to emails.

Yet there is one element of email that I think the Lunar men would have relished above all others – the idea of sending a *group* email. By 2010 the members of most associations in Britain could communicate at a stroke with the others in the group. Although this kind of communication had been possible before, with printed newsletters, the beauty of a group email is that anyone in the association can respond, and they can do so instantly. What's more, it is infinitely cheaper to do so.

Group email comes closer than any other communicative medium to recreating at almost no cost the kind of shared, multi-part discussion that you find within the meeting of an association. It does this in an undemanding way. You do not have to be at your computer at a certain moment to participate in this drawn-out, collaborative dialogue, nor is it particularly rude to observe a succession of group emails and wait until the next meeting to join in.

Email has changed for ever the way associations fill that hiatus between gatherings, from the very oldest to the youngest.

'Although we are considered to be an old, private and stuffy club,' explained Roger Marrett of the New Zealand Golf Club, 'we now have only six or seven members out of several hundred who don't use the internet. Ninety-nine per cent of our communication is done by email nowadays.'

'What has the internet changed for us?' began Phil Ainsworth, Treasurer of the Blackburn and East Lancashire Beekeepers Association. 'Well it's transformed the way our members stay in touch with each other. That's one thing. Most of them are online now. So we send out a group email before each meeting to remind them it's coming up. We still print out a card with a list of all the year's meetings, but the email certainly helps.'

'And what you've got to understand about bees,' added fellow beekeeper Bill Ainsworth (no relation), 'is that there's no definite way of keeping them. You're always learning. Every year the bees present you with something interesting to work out. You'll always find yourself scratching your head, going, "Why the heck have they done that?" That's why you need a group, and that's where the emails come into it. You can't always wait till the meeting to ask someone else for their advice.'

It goes on. For the Colchester Natural History Society, emails have 'enabled people who have moved away from the area to keep in touch with what we are doing'. Just as the Lunar men would have done, the Young Georgians found that email 'saves a lot of money as less postage [is] needed'. In the Rotary Club of Stirling 'email has saved the office-bearers and committee convenors a lot of time and expense.' For the Welford School Association, 'meetings, agendas and minutes are all sorted online.' The South Wales Caving Club found that email has 'made communication easier and quicker to those who are connected' as well as making 'committee business easier'. The Herefordshire Goat Club felt that email allowed 'quicker and easier communication due to members living in very rural parts of the county', and for members of Subterranea Britannica, a group dedicated to exploring and mapping abandoned man-made underground sites throughout Britain, email had 'increased dialogue between members'.

Email seems to have three distinct effects on associations. First, it allows the group to *simmer* between meetings. Think of an association as a stew. When the group is in session it is on the boil, and in the days before the internet that lull between meetings was a bit like taking the pot off the heat. The effect of group email is that you merely reduce the heat, leaving the dish to simmer away at a low temperature. When it is time to bring it back to the boil, it does so rapidly – when the group comes together again after a month of group emails things get going again in no time. This enhances the Hothouse Effect and allows the members of any association to take their interest further, faster.

Second, emails add to the feeling of fellowship within a group. The messages that are sent might contain advice, tips and other shards of information. In this sense each is a gift. Not a particularly generous gift, but a gift, and often one given to the group rather than an individual. We know from the Power of Giving that as more gifts are given within any group its gift cycle is bolstered, bringing its members closer and generating a greater sense of camaraderie.

Finally, group emails accelerate the development of a group character. They make for a richer history between members. Jokes and stories are thrown about, and people learn what they have in common. The New Zealand Tendency shows that this strengthens collective identity. Members understand more about what sets their group apart. Although it may be taking that cooking analogy too far, if you leave a dish to simmer, the flavours blend faster and become more intense. In the same sense, emails sent between meetings as the group simmers allow the character of the association to become richer.

These are the principal effects of email on life within an association, but there's a good deal more to the internet than email.

A Virtual Clubhouse

'I'm pleased to say membership is up from 52 last year to 68 this year.' So began one section of the January meeting of the Blackburn and East Lancashire Beekeepers Association in 2010. 'And that's 68 *before* we get in touch with the 30 or so people who have not yet renewed.' Numbers were up in part because of the worldwide decline in the number of bees. Nobody was quite sure why this was happening, and news of this was inspiring more people to take up beekeeping. But how would anyone newly interested in bees find the Blackburn and East Lancashire Beekeepers Association?

While some new recruits heard about the group through a friend, or they knew an existing member, most came to it via the internet. Like so many associations in Britain, by 2010 this band of enthusiasts had developed an online presence. In this case, it was a beige-coloured website whose home page showed a hive and one or two animated bees buzzing merrily about. It provided information about the association such as where it meets and when, and an email address to which you could direct your queries.

Online search engines have made it extremely easy to find a specialist association like this one. Enter the words 'Lancashire', 'association' and 'beekeeping', press 'Search' and before you the details of almost every beekeeping association in Lancashire will appear. This takes seconds. The internet has enhanced dramatically the ability of associations to attract new members, just as it has transformed the way an individual can find those who share their specialist interests.

If you belonged to a small club that was looking to expand in the 1750s, you'd have tried to spread the word among your friends and acquaintances, as you would now; you might have bought a small advertisement in a periodical or written a letter to one of these that mentioned your group. Perhaps you would have invited a journalist to one of your meetings or pulled a publicity stunt in the hope that it would be covered. The idea was to put a single thought 'before a thousand readers', as de Tocqueville explained, in the hope that some of these readers were the *right* readers and would then come to join your group.

The internet has changed this entirely. It allows a small group without any financial backing to transmit the equivalent of an elaborate advertisement at very little cost. On a personal web page the members of an association can describe themselves exactly as they want to be seen. The people who find these pages will be those who have a specialist interest in that subject already. They are the *right* readers.

For someone living in Britain as recently as the 1970s who had an interest in the American Civil War, for example, the prospect of finding those who shared your interest, if they existed, was daunting. You might not get around to it. With the internet it takes no more than a few seconds to find your nearest group of American Civil War enthusiasts and when their next meeting is.

For the American Civil War Society, based in Yorkshire, 'the internet boosted overall numbers, as more and more like-minded people became switched on to re-enacting.' The Apperley Cricket Club, although it found that being online 'has not had too many benefits in attracting new members', nevertheless did 'acquire the services of one Aussie thru' advertising on the internet'. The Greater London Dutch Rabbit Club 'received interest from members of the public who have found us through the internet, a couple of whom have joined the club and become part of the fancy'. The Sevenoaks Allotment Holder Association found that having an online presence made it easier 'to recruit many younger adult members'.

Not only does the internet make recruitment easier, it can lead to more interest in your group as well. Thanks to their website and Facebook page, a Welsh belly-dancing group called the Desert Divas 'have had requests to perform from all over south Wales and parts of the West Country'. And yet a website is about much more than recruitment. It can also become a repository of virtual keepsakes, and will usually contain sections on the club's past and how it came about. Perhaps there will be photos from past events, as well as an insignia or logo.

These are the elements that flesh out the identity of any association. An online presence allows a group's character to become more defined. A website can become a virtual clubhouse that anyone can visit. It contains mementoes of the club's past, an account of its history and a sense of what makes it different, what defines it.

We know from the New Zealand Tendency that this is how we construct identities for our groups and that, as our ability to do this improves, so does the sense of belonging we feel within these associations. So the internet makes it simpler, cheaper and easier for any association to strengthen its identity.

A Hotter Hothouse

There is another way in which the internet has enriched our twenty-first-century experience of associations. For the Birkbeck Early Modern Society, 'the Internet has allowed us to organise effectively. The committee, for example, arranges events using e-mail. The Facebook page has brought in members from all over the world.' So far, so normal. But as they go on to add, the internet also allows their long-distance members to 'take advantage of the links on the page', while 'our Twitter account helps the website live up to its purpose as an "Intelligencer" in the early modern sense of the word.'

An intelligencer was originally a conveyor of information and news, a medium, although the word also had a connotation of spying and some kind of subterfuge. Not only did the internet allow these historians to run their group more efficiently and recruit more members, but it also meant that when one of them spotted something interesting she or he could share it with the rest of the group. They had become internet spies, with the website as their spymaster.

The internet meant that they could take their interest further, and that the Hothouse Effect was ratcheted up by one or two degrees. Sharing relevant articles and news at very little cost enabled the members of this group to improve their understanding of the subject that drew them together.

Other groups experienced a very similar thing. For the Denmead Operatic Society, the internet provided access to 'more and better information on stage work'. The Stoke-on-Trent Reading Group used it to read more book recommendations and reviews. For the Dulwich Quilters, having access to specialist information on a computer screen 'saved us money on photocopying'.

Yet there is one potential drawback. While the internet meant that the National Fancy Rat Society could attract new members, there were 'a lot of people who've decided there is so much information now available online that they don't need to be a member of a club'. This appears to have been an exception to the rule.

Overall the internet has invigorated the experience of belonging to a club, society or any other small voluntary association in twenty-first-century Britain. It made it easier to find those who share your interests. Recruitment became more efficient and effective. Locating information about your subject was faster and cheaper. The identity of your group could become more defined. Crucially, the internet transformed the way in which we could continue group conversations between meetings – and this is what most groups are, really. They are discussions. They are communicative, and as such they depend on the media of communication. If the telephone transformed the way pairs of people stayed in touch, the internet has revolutionized our ability to do this as a group.

However, there are some associations for whom the internet has had no impact. They simply do not need it. They have enough members, and they know when to meet. This is an important point. While the internet has enhanced for many groups the communication that goes on between meetings, it has not replaced those actual meetings.

Back in the late 1990s, when most internet users were young, unmarried men and less than one British household in ten was connected, this was the fear. The internet was portrayed as a weapon of social atomization. It seemed to herald a world in which we no longer needed to communicate in person. There were academic studies that warned against 'time-space distanciation'. Some predicted a brave new world of 'post-social' communication, in which face-to-face meetings might become a thing of the past.

This was grist to the mill for anyone worried about a more lonely Britain, a 'Broken Britain' in which our relationships were to be played out vicariously through online avatars. More and more of us appeared to be joining 'virtual' communities. It was as if meeting up online was removing our need to come together in the flesh.

But the internet has actually had the opposite effect. In Britain it has helped to bring more of us together face to face by enriching the experience of belonging to an association. Virtual communion turned out to be a shoddy and inadequate substitute for the real thing. There was something about meeting in person that the internet was unable to replicate.

The Beekeepers

Picture yourself in a village hall in east Lancashire. It's a bright, double-glazed affair, lit by halogen strips. Out of its south-facing windows lies Pendle Hill, protuberant and steep, its upper reaches dusted with snow. The stone around here is the colour of rain. Sheep are scattered over the fields like melting ice floes.

It is a wintry afternoon, and the members of the Blackburn and East Lancashire Beekeepers Association have come together for one of their monthly meetings. You are surrounded by at least fifty beekeepers. A man in a collared T-shirt bearing the club insignia bangs the handle of a pair of scissors on a table, *crack-crack-crack-crack*. For a moment he looks bewildered by the strength of the sound.

'Right, right, can I have your attention please!' There are a few 'oh, rights' and 'here he goes'. 'Now, before we get going, do all the new members have one of these?' He waves a handful of envelopes back and forth. They make a buzzing sound at the peak of each arc. 'I don't,' says an elderly man several rows back. Everyone laughs.

These are welcome packs, and Bill has been a member for forty years, or 'longer than I can remember'. How long has the club been going, Bill? 'Haven't a clue. Longer than me and I'm about a hundred and a fifty,' he says, grabbing your shoulder with a quick, conspiratorial 'I'm only joking, kid.'

'Which reminds me,' the man at the front continues, 'a little later we're going to have a silent auction for some beekeeping kit. But before we get on to that or how to make candles' – he glances down at a magician's array of pots, stoves, moulds and lumps of beeswax on the table – 'there's a bit of housekeeping to deal with.'

'Er, before we get on to that,' Bill interrupts, getting to his feet with great care (he is a tall, elderly man with a definite manner), 'I want to say a few words about balsam.' There is a communal sigh from the audience. A few of them look around at each other, silent registers of the fact that they know what's coming. 'Now, as you are all aware, bees love balsam, really, they can't get enough of the stuff. However, recently there has been . . .' Bill goes on like this for a while, his delivery smooth and unhurried, the Lancastrian vowels soft and easy on the ear. 'Well, there are some people out there who want to get rid of this balsam outright. I'll not mention any names, but . . .'

By now the woman in front of you is tutting to great effect, until this bubbles over into an interruption. 'It's just not as simple as that, Bill,' she exclaims. 'I've been working at a nature reserve recently and as the people there tell me, balsam is a weed. It gets everywhere. No matter how hard you cut it back it will always . . .'

Back and forth it goes, with others giving their views on balsam and what to do about it, until the conversation moves on to other beekeeping issues, such as the correct levels of oxalic acid required to kill off the varroa mite to which bees are so susceptible. There are many opinions on this, each one minutely different from the last.

One couple confesses that they have used what appears to have been the wrong mixture of oxalic acid. Their bees have since died – all of them. Husband and wife wear a drawn, plaintive look. There is a silent flood of sympathy from those seated around them. At last, the man at the front begins to describe the art of making candles out of beeswax.

The meeting goes on for two hours in all, and there's no need for a blow-by-blow account of what was said or the minutiae of how to make a candle out of beeswax. The reason for the description here is that during this gathering something strange and to my mind wonderful took place that none of these beekeepers was aware of. Roughly the same thing will happen during the meeting of any small group, now and always. When we come together like this in person, we perform an extraordinary and microscopic dance that cannot be replicated using the technology of communication. This is why virtual communion can never become a meaningful substitute for the real thing.

The Beekeepers' Dance

As far as we know, there are only two types of animal that communicate symbolically: humans and bees. When a foraging bee finds a source of nectar, it heads back to the hive and passes on what it has found, using a combination of smell and dance. This is called a 'round dance' or 'waggle dance'. Karl von Frisch was the first to analyse it in detail (although Aristotle had observed something similar). The foraging bee starts by

> whirling around in a narrow circle, constantly changing her direction, turning now right, now left, dancing clockwise and anti-clockwise in quick succession, describing between one and two circles in each direction. The dance is performed among the thickest bustle of the hive. What makes it so particu-larly striking is the way it infects the surrounding bees; those sitting next to the dancer start tripping after her [. . .] so that the dancer herself, in her madly wheeling movements, appears to carry behind her a perpetual comet's tail of bees.

By watching this dance, other bees learn the direction of the food source in relation to the sun, and roughly how far away it is. The dancing bee will even adjust the angle of its dance during the day to accommodate the changing position of the sun.

But what does this have to do with the meeting of the beekeepers? Surely the way bees communicate has nothing to do with how an association of beekeepers goes about this? One set of animals had the facility of speech. You'd think there would be no useful comparison.

In the early 1970s the psychologist Albert Mehrabian examined the way we communicate our likes and dislikes to each other. He broke it down into three parts: the actual words we use to express our feelings, our intonation, and our facial or bodily expression. Mehrabian found that only 7 per cent of what we feel about the person delivering a message relates to the words they use. An astonishing 93 per cent concerns non-verbal cues such as intonation and body language (38 per cent for the former, 55 per cent for the latter). As Mehrabian explained, these non-verbal cues are 'so important that when our words contradict the silent messages contained within them others mistrust what we say – they rely almost completely on what we do'.

In my brief description of the beekeepers you would have noticed that Bill got to his feet 'with great care'. After making a joke he gave you a friendly pat on the shoulder. When he spoke, his delivery was 'smooth and unhurried'. He had a 'definite manner'. His voice was 'easy on the ear'. I was trying to convey a sense of what Bill was like. To do this I relied as much on what he said as the way he said it and one or two non-verbal cues. Picture that passage purged of any mention of Bill's body language, what he looked like or his intonation. He disappears.

When someone begins to speak to us, we do not just observe their gestures and movements but we respond to them as well. Without necessarily meaning to, we display signs of engagement, disbelief or boredom. When delivering a speech, most of us can register these cues. We may even adjust the direction of a sentence before it finishes, according to our perception of how the audience is reacting.

Yet there's more to this than meets the eye, and by 'eye' I mean the conscious brain. In the 1960s William S. Condon examined precisely what happens when we communicate face to face. With a team of fellow psychologists he began to study film clips of various people communicating with each other. Initially Condon 'had the naive view that all you have to do is look at a sound film and see how people behave, and lo and behold you'll understand communication. But the people in the film refused to co-operate.'

Condon had the idea of slowing down each clip in order to study it frame by frame. Amazingly, he studied one 4½-second clip 100,000 times. His copy of that clip then wore out. He got another one. A hundred thousand viewings later this too was no longer watchable. In total he worked through 130 copies of the same clip and spent up to a year and a half studying it. Only then was he confident of what was happening.

What Condon argued was this: as we speak, we make thousands of minute gestures and bodily movements, involving our facial muscles, limbs, torso and hands, and we synchronize these movements to the rhythm of our speech. As he put it, we 'self-synchronize'. These tiny expressions and movements are so rapid, so micro, that we do not consciously observe them in ourselves or others. Nor can we switch them off. 'You can't break out of this,' Condon insisted, 'no matter what you do.'

Perhaps the most extraordinary part of what Condon found concerns what happens to us when we listen to someone else speak. When engaging with a foreign sound, whether animate or inanimate, Condon found that between 10 to 50 milliseconds after perceiving the sound we begin to synchronize our micro-expressions and movements to its rhythm.

The participants in a face-to-face conversation start to synchronize their micro-expressions not only to the sound of whoever is speaking, but to the rhythm of their own speech as well. In other words, when we communicate with each other in the flesh, we are actually performing an intricate and microscopic dance, a miniature version of the bees' waggle dance. Only this one is far more interactive: we are not just spectators; we are dancing to the sound of the voices we hear as well as that of our own speech.

There is a Zimbabwean proverb that goes: if you can talk you can sing, if you can walk you can dance. Well, according to Condon, if you can talk you can dance. Had it been slowed down and analysed in meticulous detail, the discussion among those Lancastrian beekeepers would have been a sumptuous display of exceptionally rapid non-verbal gestures and communication between some fifty different participants. It was fiendishly intricate and detailed.

An equally miraculous performance goes on when any group of people come together in person. I like to think of this as the Beekeepers' Dance, and it is particularly important in the context of associations and the internet. The Beekeepers' Dance explains why the emails sent between meetings, the newsletters and telephone calls cannot replicate what happens when we come together in the flesh. Instead they fill the gap between these dances.

Although the internet has encouraged 'an explosion in a distinctive kind of relationship, one formed *without* or *before* initial face-to-face contact', it has not replaced this. Either it encourages it, or it strengthens the relations between individuals who have already met in the flesh and plan do so again. The fact that it cannot reproduce the staggering intricacy of the Beekeepers' Dance is one of the reasons why the internet did not bring about a collapse in associational activity.

It seems clear that we *need* to perform the Beekeepers' Dance, and that this is at the heart of any association. The constitution of a group – its titles, character, clubhouse, artefacts – all of these are no more than scaffolding there to support the main event within an association: the Beekeepers' Dance. This is one of the things we relish about coming together. It is as old as we are and dates back to our earliest imaginings as sub-Saharan hunter-gatherers sharing what we had to eat or as prehistoric villagers. It stood for being alive, for being fed and the possibility of projecting our existence meaningfully into the future. 'Let us eat and drink; for tomorrow we die', as the book of Isaiah has it.

This kind of communion is essentially human. Although our levels of general intelligence are broadly similar to those of orang-utans and chimpanzees, research has shown that our social cognition is far superior. As primates go, we are ultrasocial and the Beekeepers' Dance is testament to this.

So, contrary to earlier reports, the internet has been a boon for associations in early twenty-first-century Britain. It has made it easier to get one of these groups going, and to find one that matches your interests. Administration has become simpler and faster. Conversations are more likely to continue when the members of a group are apart. Groups can simmer between meetings, and the internet has not replaced the Beekeepers' Dance. Instead it has made it easier for us to take part in one. More than any other development in British society, the internet appears to have fuelled a surge in associational activity during the first decade of the twenty-first century.

10

The Decline of
Traditional Community, 1
Religion

And who or what shall fill his place?

Thomas Hardy, 'God's Funeral'

As well as being a Soviet spy and an eminent art historian, Anthony Blunt was the son of an Anglican vicar. Born in 1907, by the time Blunt died in 1983 the extent and nature of religious belief in Britain had changed almost beyond recognition. It is hard to imagine what his father would have made of it. The evolution of religious activity in twentieth-century Britain was dramatic and fast, and this has had a major impact on our associational landscape.

In the decade before Blunt was born, Christianity was at its acme. Blunt's father would have addressed heaving congregations. Religion had not been brushed aside by Darwin's discoveries, and God was certainly not dead. Instead deism was enriched by the possibility of non-belief. For many Britons going to church had become more of a choice than an inheritance, one that you kept with a degree of reactionary pride.

By the time Blunt was born, religious attendances had begun to slide. The Revd Blunt would have addressed slightly smaller congregations during the years leading up to the First World War, and as the numbers continued to fall the character of the Church of England changed as a result. Fire-and-brimstone sermons were out. In came a more avuncular and friendly approach, one that many of us would recognize today.

There was also a shift in the way churches were being used. Increasingly they became centres for leisure and recreation. Across the country there was a wave of new clubs, societies and associations whose activities were focused on their local parish church. Take Reading, where the

> Church of England Men's Society was matched by the dissenters' Christian Endeavour Society. The Boy's Brigade was countered by the Church Lads' Brigade. Book clubs and discussion societies came and went. Each winter different groups turned towards the various needs they perceived amongst the poor. Ladies' Visiting Associations, Dorcas Societies, Soup Kitchens, Provident Funds, Coal and Clothing Clubs, Penny Banks and Poor Stewards met around the Methodist chapels.

This kind of thing had not been seen in parish churches since the Reformation. If the emphasis had been previously on a calendar of feasts, mysteries and saint's days, when attendance was pretty much obligatory, now it was focused on the activities of a mass of voluntary associations. This was a reflection of the extent to which these kinds of groups had become a mainstay of our social culture.

Yet by the time Blunt went up to Cambridge in the 1920s, church attendances were again in decline, a trend that would continue into the 1930s. 'And who or what shall fill his place?' Thomas Hardy asked in 'God's Funeral'. 'Whither will wanderers turn distracted eyes / For some fixed star to stimulate their pace?'

For many that 'fixed star' was political. It was a proto-religious ideology such as Fascism or Communism that promised salvation. These belief systems were at once modern and Positivist. They were rooted in a Judaeo-Christian worldview that saw history as a teleological drama in which the final act was forever about to take place.

Blunt was not immune to this. Here was a theotropic creature living in a more godless age than the one in which he had grown up. Marxism was an ideology that appealed not only to the modern ideals he had acquired but also to the religious sentiment that he had inherited.

At one point Blunt actually described the allure of left-wing ideals as 'almost religious in quality'. He remained the son of an Anglican vicar, someone who knew by heart the sound made by a church door as it heaves shut, the echo of footsteps down the nave, the slam of hymnal, scratch of pew, the play of opalescent light through stained-glass windows, or the sight of candles as they are extinguished at the end of a service before lines of smoke begin to hurry heavenwards like streams of watery handwriting.

Looking back in 1944, George Orwell insisted that 'one cannot have any worthwhile picture of the future, unless one realises how much we have lost by the decay of Christianity.' Throughout the 1920s and 1930s an unprecedented number of Britons turned away from the Church. At the same time there was a surge of interest in political ideologies such as Communism and Fascism. This much we know. But what happened during this period was about much more than millions of souls looking for a new 'fixed star'. They were not just filling the 'God-shaped hole' in their heads, there was also a church-shaped hole in their hearts that needed to be addressed.

Losing your faith and deciding not to go to church was much more than an intellectual decision. It was an act of social masochism as well. To do this was to divorce yourself from the religious community that you had grown up within or around, the one to which your parents probably belonged as well as your neighbours, acquaintances, people you had known as a child, local figures of authority and standing.

Religion in its earliest form was social. It was geared less towards resolving arcane metaphysical quandaries as to providing a shared moral code and a sense of justice. As Durkheim put it, 'originally [religion] extended to everything, everything social was religious – the two words were synonymous.'

The drift away from Christianity between the wars was for many Britons a social loss as much as a spiritual one. Those people who left the Church did not just acquire new beliefs; they looked for new communities as well. They became members of political associations, and in these they came together with others and performed the Beekeepers' Dance.

By the time Blunt began to work for the Soviet Union, the Communist Party of Great Britain and Mosley's British Union of Fascists were both flourishing. Each had local associations all over the country. There were more than a thousand Co-operative Societies nationwide at the time. During the previous three decades a spate of Clarion clubs had appeared, each linked to the socialist newspaper of the same name and dedicated to rambling, cycling, handicrafts, drama, singing, and there were the Clarion Cinderella clubs for impoverished children. The avowedly non-religious and non-political Women's Institutes were also flourishing: by 1927 there were nearly 4,000 of these associations, with 250,000 members.

I think this is important. It suggests that for many of us our response to a life without church is not to sit at home and sulk but to try and assuage that lack. We look to fill that church-shaped hole, and often this involves joining or starting an association.

To the Margins

As the Second World War reached its conclusion, the decline of Christianity in Britain seemed set to pick up from where it had left off before the conflict began. But this is not what happened. In the fifteen years following VE Day, Britain experienced a surge of Christian sentiment. Church attendances shot up, as did the number of church weddings and Sunday school attendees. In 1954 some 2 million people went to see the American evangelical preacher Billy Graham as he toured the country. For a moment the Church of England was in the ascendant once again. Things appeared to be back to normal.

During the 1960s this revival came to an abrupt end. According to the historian Callum Brown, in that decade alone British society 'experienced more secularisation than in all the four [preceding] centuries put together'. From 1963, Philip Larkin's *annus mirabilis*, the year that 'sexual intercourse began', Christianity entered 'a downward spiral' that took it to 'the margins of social significance'. Over the following decades the number of baptisms and church weddings halved. By 2005 fewer than 1 million people attended church each Sunday, and of these a record number were temporary migrants from Eastern Europe and almost a third were older than sixty-five. By 2040 the proportion of elderly Christian congregants looks set to double.

The decline of Christianity in Britain during the late twentieth century was epic and rapid, and it was about much more than 'bums on pews'. Although many of us today continue to believe in the possibility of a higher godly force, far fewer think of Jesus Christ as a god-human composite with the superhuman ability to rise from the dead and perform miracles.

A MORI poll conducted in 2003 found that 45 per cent of Britons could not name a single Christian gospel. Only

18 per cent knew the name of the Archbishop of Canterbury. Although our morality and cultural references retain elements of this shared Christian heritage, you will find far fewer Christian narratives, idioms or references in twenty-first-century novels, plays, films and obituaries than you would have done half a century earlier.

Contrary to earlier projections of a dystopic, irreligious future – think of *Nineteen Eighty-Four* or *Brave New World* – the decline of Christianity in Britain was not the work of the state. Nor was the Church of England the victim of a sustained atheistic campaign or the emergence of a rival belief-system. Many Britons simply lost their faith and did not pass it on to their offspring. So a growing number of children failed to acquire it in the first place. Of course, they may become religious of their own accord, but when faith is rooted in a form of rebellion like this it is often harder to sustain.

Waiting for God No More

By 2010 only a small proportion of British adults experienced a regular sense of community in their local church. And yet, as we know, staying away from church does not mean that we cauterize our need for communion, for the Beekeepers' Dance. We simply look for it elsewhere.

As they did during the 1920s and 1930s, it seems that during the first decade of the twenty-first century Britons who might have experienced a sense of community in their local church found it in associations instead. Part of the reason is to do with the age at which we tend to join clubs.

In the United States age 'is second only to education as a predictor of virtually all forms of civic engagement'. In Britain as well it seems that one's 'joining' years begin with middle age. Of course, all adults form associations, but we are statistic-ally more likely to do so later on in life. In my survey of associations the average age was only a shade under fifty. Not only do we become more likely to join an association after our fiftieth birthday, but traditionally this is the stage in our lives when we turn to religion. If before we were too busy, or just not particularly worried about death, as we near the end of our lives we gravitate towards religion. At least, that's the idea. It is certainly what happens in most parts of the world today, as millions of elderly men and women settle down to wait for their God.

During the early twenty-first century in Britain this did not happen on anything like the scale of the 1950s. In the 2000s, the generation of Britons who grew up during the 1960s and had experienced at first hand the genesis of Christianity's rapid decline reached their associational and religious prime. Rather than go to church once a week, a growing number of these elderly Britons apparently chose to get involved in knitting circles or reading groups; they banded together to form walking groups, or to play bowls, bridge or bingo.

As we saw during the 1920s and 1930s, it seems that when people turn away from religion they look for something to fill that church-shaped hole. During the early twenty-first century, with church attendances in many parts of the country at record lows, this appears to have involved a major shift towards associations.

11

The Decline of
Traditional Community, 2
Neighbourhoods

And now you live dispersed on ribbon roads,
And no man knows or cares who is his neighbour
Unless his neighbour makes too much disturbance,
But all dash to and fro in motor cars,
Familiar with the roads and settled nowhere.

T. S. Eliot, Choruses from The Rock

Some statistics, to begin with: by 2003 more than 10 per cent of the British working-age population changed their address *every year*. By the start of the twenty-first century a typical Briton would make four moves during his or her lifetime. The first took them away from home, possibly for higher education; the next was as they moved into an urban centre to look for work. On having children, the trend was to move away from these centres into the suburbs or the country, and finally, towards the end of their lives, many Britons migrated towards coastal areas. In 2005 less than half of British dwellings had been lived in by the same people for more than ten years. In the history of the last few thousand years, we have never been so nomadic.

These figures would have been inconceivable during the 1950s. Not only were we more god-fearing back then, but many of us were happy to 'spend all [our] lives in [our] home town or village'. At that time T. S. Eliot's feeling that it was 'for the best that the great majority of human beings should go on living in the place in which they were born' was neither peculiar nor reactionary.

During the second half of the twentieth century that changed, and it did so extravagantly. Not only did we start to move house much more, but by the start of the twenty-first century a growing proportion of Britons owned more than one home: between 1994 and 2008 second-home ownership may have risen by 20 per cent.

This was just one of the factors that changed the way we connected to our local neighbourhoods and the people who lived in them. What may have had a much greater impact was the effect of technological advance. This continued to transform our spatial mobility. By 2009 at least one car was registered to almost 80 per cent of British households, and most Britons had access to an extensive public transport network. If it took three to four days to get from Manchester to London in the late eighteenth century, the same journey took only a few hours at the start of the twenty-first. The average distance travelled by a Briton is thought to have increased over this period by a factor of more than a thousand.

Technology also reduced the dependency we would have once had our neighbours. It slashed the number of times our paths were likely to cross. Fridges meant that we shopped for food as little as once a week. No longer did we need to gather at communal pumps to collect our water. We did not head to the same shared loo. Fuel to warm our homes was pumped in, so there was no need to schlep about with sacks of coal and wood. We were generally impervious to the weather and rarely needed to club together in the face of a coming storm or drought.

By the dawn of the twenty-first century the average Briton had far fewer opportunities to bump into his or her neighbours than ever before. This is perhaps why half of us 'would rather drive to the shops than ask a neighbour for a cup of sugar', as one recent survey suggested. Roughly three-quarters of us do not know the names of our next-door neighbours, and one in ten will 'admit we've never helped a neighbour as we don't know them or would not feel comfortable doing so'.

The situation six centuries ago could not have been more different. The arrival or departure of a new family in most neighbourhoods was celebrated with a 'welcoming' or 'foy'. These were among 'the most drunken feasts in this country'. With less mobility there was a much stronger sense of local community based purely on the fact that you lived near each other. As the historian Peter Clark has shown, 'neighbours came together at different stages of the agricultural and liturgical year: at ploughing time and sheep-shearing, at Rogationtide, Candlemas, Shrovetide, mid-Lent, Easter, Maytime, Whitsuntide, midsummer, and St Peter's Eve' – and don't forget Lent, Hocktide, Palm Sunday, St George's Day, May Day and Ascension, as well as the host of festivals and events specific to different areas. We know that 'rush-bearing ceremonies flourished in Lancashire and Yorkshire, and Robin Hood plays in Devon (probably linked to church ales), while the West Midlands had its Abbot of Marham games at Maytide.'

By 2010, a typical Briton was highly unlikely to experience the modern-day equivalent of these. There was a much weaker sense of community based only on where you lived, but this was not because we had become a nation of curmudgeons. The problem was that we no longer had as many excuses to get to know the people who lived next to us. But what was the effect of this on our associational landscape?

Putting Down Roots

In the wake of the Norman Conquest in the eleventh century, travel and trade became safer and faster. Towns and villages expanded, and between 1086 and 1300 the number of English urban centres may have quadrupled. At the same time, the number of guilds and fraternities rocketed.

These bodies were essentially associations. They were independent organizations with their own rules and officers, whose members met periodically for a Beekeepers' Dance. Fraternities and guilds were also extremely active in their local neighbourhoods or villages. They paid for repairs to religious buildings as well as town walls and bridges. They gave alms to beggars and took care of the salaries of local preachers or schoolmasters. They organized processions near where they met, along with plays, pageants, anniversary feasts, elaborate funerals for their brethren and ceremonies marking the anniversaries of their death.

One reason why so many of these guilds and fraternities appeared during the Middle Ages was economic. By the fifteenth and sixteenth centuries most guilds in the British Isles had exclusive trading rights in particular industries. If you wanted to work in one of these trades, you had to join the requisite guild. For instance, there was a charter drawn up in 1163 in the name of Henry II listing those guilds that could produce dyed and striped cloth in Yorkshire. To be on that list, each guild paid £10 a year. This meant that many of them were only 'quasi-voluntary associations'.

One of the other reasons why so many fraternities appeared during the fourteenth century in particular had to do with the Black Death. This was seen as a punishment from God. Belonging to a fraternity or guild was a small act of piety, and if you saw the disease as a punishment from God then this was the kind of thing that might keep you alive a little longer. Living through this disease also created a binding sense of solidarity among the survivors, another potential spur to associational activity.

But one of the key reasons why these associations flourished during this period – the one that I am interested in – has to do with moving house and our need for community. As the country became more stable politically, not only did levels of migration increase but the population also grew. This changed the atmosphere and society in many neighbourhoods and villages. It began to threaten some of the informal social networks that had been in place for generations.

It is now thought that one of the reasons why so many fraternities and guilds appeared during this period was in response to the fact that these traditional social networks began to fall away. Fraternities and guilds provided a way of recreating in a bustling town the small-scale trust you would have once found in a village.

Here's an example of how this works. If you lived in a typical twelfth-century village and you needed a loan to buy some sheep, you might ask one of your neighbours. This is reasonable. The pair of you have grown up around each other, and neither of you is in the habit of moving house every few years. So there is a good deal of trust built into your relationship. Had you moved to a nearby town, that kind of trust between neighbours would no longer be guaranteed. If you had asked your new neighbours for a loan, they may have been less inclined to help. Because of the increased mobility and fluidity, living next to someone was no longer a mark of trust and community.

Guilds and fraternities filled that gap. They offered their members loans and financial support, and in this way they recreated an element of village life in the busier and more fluid setting of a town. Yet these associations were about more than providing loans. 'Man's economy, as a rule, is submerged in his social relationships', as the economic historian Karl Polanyi put it. 'He does not act so as to safeguard his individual interest in the possession of material goods; he acts so as to safeguard his social standing, his social claims, his social assets.'

It seems that one of our principal responses to moving to a new setting, the kind of place that does not have informal social networks that we can easily slot into, is to look for more formal versions of these. We seek out associations, and if they don't exist then we start them up. This is what happened during the Middle Ages, just as it occurred on a colossal scale throughout Britain during the second half of the nineteenth century. As urban centres all over the country expanded like a series of pricked yolks in response to industrialization, villagers poured into these suburban slums. Millions proceeded to join or form Friendly Societies as well as trades unions. By the start of the twentieth century some 6 million men belonged to Friendly Societies across Britain. As with the medieval guilds and fraternities, these bodies allowed them to recreate the small-scale sociability of a village in the far more fluid and uncertain setting of a town. Each one was a response to the dislocation and lack of local community that some people feel on moving to a new urban setting.

It is tempting to surmise that if we move house more often, we are bound to join more associations and that these groups are a response to migration. But that's not quite how it works. What defined these moves, whether they occurred in the Middle Ages or during the nineteenth century, was a degree of permanence. The people who made them planned to stay in the places they moved to, and it was only when they could see themselves being there for some time that they joined or formed associations.

Earlier we saw the Thursday Club of Leicester in action. It was made up of South Asians who migrated to Britain in the 1970s, but the club did not start until 1984, almost a decade after many of its members arrived. This was because in the early days few of these men saw themselves living in Leicester for the rest of their lives. Starting an association was a way of putting down roots. It was an expression of permanence, and the idea that 'this is my home, this is where I will stay.'

You could say something very similar about the thousands of Britons who moved to India during the nineteenth century, including those who took to Uganda the ancestors of those Gujaratis, Pakistanis and Bangladeshis later expelled by Idi Amin. They formed hundreds of clubs, societies and other associations. By 1930 there were 1,090 Masonic lodges across the empire. For Leonard Woolf, the colonial club was 'the centre and symbol of British imperialism', while a British policeman in Australia in 1827 described 'the *necessity* of being' a Mason for any Briton who moved abroad. Again, this was a response to moving to a new place in which people could see themselves remaining for many years, but finding that there were no informal social networks that they could easily join.

During the research for this book I spent a day with the 2nd Battalion, 95th Rifles Re-enactment Group, a superb illustration of just how geographically diverse an association can be – their members hailed from Gosport, Kent, London, Bristol, Norfolk, Derbyshire, Gloucestershire and Oldham. They were a friendly, lively bunch, and towards the end of the day I asked a man called Bob, a lecturer in sociology, why he had joined. 'Well, I'd just moved down from Yorkshire, where I grew up, and to be honest I didn't really know anyone in London. I wanted to meet people and become a part of something. So I got on the internet and that's how I found this lot,' he said, jerking his head upwards.

By the start of the twenty-first century the experience of moving to a new town in Britain could be very lonely, unless you knew people living there already or were happy to spend your spare time with work colleagues. Otherwise it could be hard to meet new people. Knocking on your neighbour's door and inviting yourself in for a drink had become frightening rather than friendly.

Associations provide a solution to this problem. Not only do you meet new people but you do so in a relaxed way. You are coming together not *to be friends* but to play a particular sport, discuss a shared interest or a cause that you have in common.

To sum up, our spatial mobility has increased dramatically, and an array of technological advances mean that we now see much less of our neighbours. Together these developments have eroded the sense of local community that you might expect to find in a typical British neighbourhood. Historically, one of the responses to situations like this has been to look for associations to join, as these can provide a ready-made social network. This certainly explains why 93 per cent of the groups featured in my survey knew the people who belonged to their associations better than they knew their neighbours. A survey conducted in 2000 also argued that most hobbyists felt a stronger connection to their co-hobbyists than to their neighbours.

As we saw with the decline of Christianity during the 1920s and 1930s, when a traditional source of community disintegrates, we do not slide into a well of insularity and sit around at home by ourselves. Instead we tend to look for new social networks. It seems to me that, along with the advent of the internet and the decline of Christianity, the fact that our sense of local community continued to evaporate was the third great spur to renewed associational activity in the first decade of the twenty-first century.

12

The Elevation of Interest
From Coffee Houses to Universities

> If two Englishmen were to be cast aside on an uninhabited island, their first consideration would be the formation of a club.
>
> Edmond and Jules de Goncourt

Pretend you left London on the eve of the English Civil War and returned late in 1659. Why did you leave? Up to you. Perhaps you were on the run, accused of a crime you didn't commit, you were a spy, a revolutionary, you fell in love with a Sicilian prince or princess (delete as appropriate) and have spent the last seventeen years in a tempestuous relationship that has now run its course. Maybe you were bored with London.

It doesn't matter. In your absence a generation of Englishmen and -women have come closer than any previous one to effecting a lasting, wholesale revision of their political system. But what has actually changed since you were last in town? On stepping off the ship that brings you back, what would you notice as you begin to renegotiate the streets, markets and thoroughfares of this enormous, muddling metropolis? Strange as it may sound, one of the answers to this question gives us yet another factor that I think drove the surge of associational activity in early twenty-first-century Britain.

You disembark near the Tower of London and wander up Cheapside towards Smithfield. The air is thick with sulphur and smoke. London is pungent. Everywhere you look, there are people and animals. Occasionally a sedan chair moves past, or there is a carriage curtained with velvet. Elsewhere you see drunkards, bands of apprentices, men in liveries, African slaves, aldermen, sailors, mountebanks, one-eyed soldiers and beggars, many of whom have also lost an arm, a leg or a finger or two over the last seventeen years.

One of the first changes you spot is an unsightly eleven-mile wall that now snakes clumsily around the heart of the city. London was not sacked while you were away, and although some of the buildings you expected to see are no longer there, lost to fire or structural collapse, the streets are pretty much as you left them. They remain what John Evelyn called 'a congestion of mis-shapen and extravagant houses' bunched together around narrow, pock-marked streets. A stream of manure and litter runs down the centre of each, like a trail leading you on.

Still no *major* changes. London continues to be at least twenty times bigger than any other British town; it is the third largest city in the known world, and it attracts migrants faster than it can kill them – so it grows and grows.

You carry on towards the heart of things, down the Strand, past Somerset House and the Savoy, keeping close to the river at all times, until you reach Parliament House. It is a journey Charles II would make soon afterwards, yet it would take him four hours to move through a crescendo of celebration, pennants, trumpets and church bells.

Near Parliament you spot something you have never seen before. In New Palace Yard there is a shop that has a sign bearing the outline of a Turk's head and the words 'Miles's Coffee House'.

Coffee? Coffee, yes, you've heard of it. Coffee comes from Central America, doesn't it? No, that's the other one, 'chocolate'. Coffee comes from the East: it is the Ottomans who have given us coffee, hence the Turk's Head. You've heard about both drinks and the miraculous effect one of them has on conversation: it sharpens the mind and can turn even the most stumbling lunkhead into a great wit. Or so you have heard.

You head towards the door of this coffee house, cross the threshold and scan the room like a deer about to break cover. You take a seat at a long table. It is unadorned but for one or two candles set in simple pitchers. Outside, dusk begins. The sound in here is full of exclamation and point-making, and in the background the kitchen clanks and steams. Coffee drinkers settle down on either side of you. The smell is a blend of what you assume to be coffee and the more familiar puff of powdered periwigs, wood smoke, soot and, beneath it all, an occasional stab of tobacco. They combine to mask, more or less, the hum of men on either side of you who have not bathed in days.

A cup of dark, viscous liquid is set before you. At last! You consider the cup for a moment and pick it up as if to test its weight. You bring it towards you. Your nose snarls involuntarily. A sip. Ech! It is bitter and piping hot. Coffee may not be for you. You try again, but no, best to leave it for now.

No longer so intrigued by the miraculous properties of coffee, your attention turns to the room and its occupants. At first it looks like a teetotal tavern. You are surrounded by what you presume to be a gathering of locals who have come to their neighbourhood coffee house to drink coffee rather than ale or beer. But there's much more to it than that. On one side of the room is a mass of papers heaped up like kindling – pamphlets, periodicals, newspapers, broadsheets, single-sheet screeds and learned tracts, mostly with a political flavour. As we know, the bounds of what can be put in print have transformed since you left, so it's exciting to see these. You admire the pages, each frail and knotted like a sliver of ivory. Here and there a word has been obscured by a smudged kiss of coffee, or there are parts where the print is too faint to be legible.

You pick out one to read. It is an angry (although quite funny) attack on a recent proposal suggesting that England would be better off without property rights. Rubbish, says the author. You are about half-way through when something very unusual happens. The man on your left asks what you think of that pamphlet. You suggest he has mistaken you for someone else. No, he says, not yet offended, he wants to know what you think.

This is strange. Not because you are a snob or a recluse, but you are unaccustomed to this kind of thing happening in a tavern or an alehouse – and these remain your points of reference. Where is an introduction, an excuse or any other stamp of formality with which an exchange like this should begin?

You begin to talk to this man and his friends, and as you learn about them and their jobs and where they come from you realize that you got it quite wrong earlier. This is not a gathering of locals. Nor are these men birds of a feather in that they do not share the same social background. As *The Rules and Orders of the Coffee House* put it some years later, in a London coffee house 'gentry, tradesmen, all are welcome./[. . .] Pre-eminence of place none here should mind,/But take the next fit seat that he can find.' Indeed 'each man seems a Leveller [. . .] so that oft you may see a silly *Fop*, and a worshipful *Justice*, a griping *Rock*, and a grave *Citizen*, a worthy *Lawyer*, and an errant *Pickpocket*, a Reverend *Nonconformist*, and a Canting *Mountebank*; all blended together.'

Not only do these coffee drinkers hail from different backgrounds, and nor do they work together, but only a handful live within a hundred yards of the coffee house. You had assumed that these people came here because it was their local coffee house. Not a bit of it. These men have travelled to be here, and they have done so in order to talk politics. That's why anyone – apart from you – goes to Miles's.

This marks a critical shift. Over the coming decades coffee houses all over this city became linked like this to particular subjects. In Restoration London, if you were interested in natural philosophy, you would head to Garraway's coffee house. Lawyers in their Mechlin ruffles and lace coats generally went to the Grecian or Nando's coffee house. Writers and booksellers patronized the Chapter coffee house in Paternoster Row. Lloyd's of London is so called because shipping men used to meet in Lloyd's coffee house. Truby's was where parsons caught up on academic gossip; Forrest's was full of Scots; Giles's and Old Slaughter's were meeting points for Frenchmen and -women living in London; and for political debate the best place to go was the one in which you find yourself now, Miles's.

These coffee houses were famed for the quality of their debate. It was certainly sharper and more imaginative than what you could expect to find in a leading university at the time. The atmosphere in a coffee house was a world apart from the staid and more religious feel of Oxford or Cambridge.

Indeed when Isaac Newton presented the first outline of his 'Theory on Light and Colour' at Trinity College, Cambridge, one of the great breakthroughs in the history of what would later be called science, the room was almost empty. When he returned for the follow-up lecture, not a soul was there. He is thought to have addressed an empty room. By contrast, the letters, visits and conversations involving Newton, Hooke and others that inspired the great man to write his *Principia Mathematica*, now thought to be 'probably the greatest single work of science ever written', are thought to have begun in a London coffee house – probably Garraway's.

By late 1659 a small but growing number of Britons – and it really was a small proportion, so we mustn't think of this as a sudden revolution – were travelling short distances in order to attend particular coffee houses where they would be with others who shared the same secular interest. They made regular journeys away from their homes or places of work to indulge their common enthusiasm. Today this may not sound like much. It is utterly ordinary. At the time, though, it was unusual, and in the history of associations it was momentous.

It suggested that one's interests could be elevated above the identities you inherited in life. In the right circumstances your intellectual enthusiasms could become marginally more significant than the neighbourhood you lived in, your family or your social background. Without this, Thomas Britton's society of music lovers could not have come about. Nor would Laura's Book Group many years later, the Dulwich Quilters, the historical re-enactors I mentioned a few pages ago or any one of the hundreds of thousands of associations today whose members come together around nothing more than a shared interest.

This kind of association is possible only in a society in which interests can trump inherited identities. When this happens on a wider scale, associations flourish. They appear in larger numbers, and more of us join them. But how does a growing emphasis on the interests we have actually translate into more of us joining small groups?

Rota

Back in the coffee house you continue to chat away to your new acquaintances, and after an hour or so there is a pause in the conversation, an interregnum, a gap that is as unplanned as it is sudden. In the way that these things work, one or two other conversations come to a halt at the same instant. This aural lacuna lasts for no more than a few seconds, if that, but it is enough for you to hear a noise from upstairs.

It is a single sound – an 'arl', perhaps the 'arli-' from

'Parliament' – it is hard to say. You are intrigued. You make an excuse and head towards the far end of the room. A door gives on to a slender set of stairs. Each ripples under your weight, making a questioning 'eeyore' sound as you ascend. On the landing is an open door, and beyond it you can see a clutch of men gathered around an oval table with a cavity in the centre – a piece of furniture later described as a 'machine for debate' and 'a stunningly original piece of political technology'.

The room is ribcaged by a regularity of low, sleepy beams. One man is in full flight, speaking and hammering his right arm in rhythm to his speech as he denounces the political state of the nation. The others remain silent or stand around the edge of the room and fidget. This is the Rota Club. It is one of the first associations anywhere in the world to be described in print as a 'club', or 'clubbe',* and was founded only a few months earlier by the essayist and republican James Harrington. In here, Harrington is Macher. Not only was the idea for the club his, but he has since steered the group through its first few months.

The Rota is dedicated to political debate, and like so many associations since, it came about when a series of people chose to act on a shared interest. These men understood that for real intellectual adventure you need a scintilla of exclusion and organization. Rather than gather informally in the maelstrom of Miles's, they chose to meet in private up above. The Rota had limited membership, rules, officers and a subscription to cover the cost of printing accounts of their debates. All of this was geared towards one thing: taking their interest further. They formed an association to improve the quality of their debate, and clearly it worked. John Aubrey described the conversation in the Rota as 'the most inge-

*For more on how the word club may have come to mean a small group of people, see Appendix A.

niose, and smart, that ever I heard, or expect to heare, [. . .] Arguments in the Parliament howse were but flatt to it.' Even if drinking coffee did not agree with his digestion, a young Samuel Pepys was also a member and thought the discussion was 'very good'.

When we elevate our interests like this, it is only a matter of time before associations appear. Although there were barely any of these voluntary interest groups before the English Civil War, by the time of the Glorious Revolution in 1688 things had changed. There were now loyalist clubs, Catholic clubs, Anglican societies such as the Sons of Clergy, and alumni associations at schools like St Paul's, Charterhouse and Eton; there were at least seventy-seven Friendly Societies, county societies, patronymic societies of men with surnames such as Smith, Adam, Lloyd or King (Charles II was said to have been an honorary member); there were Whig political clubs including the Green Ribbon Club (renowned then for its mass demonstrations) or the Royal Society (famous today for introducing the concept of peer-reviewed articles and repeatable experimentation as the basis for all scientific laws). We know about musical societies, literary groups such as John Dryden's Witty Club, which met at Will's coffee house, and hundreds of drinking societies. Bellringing societies were popular; by 1666 there was a cricket club in St Albans; archery societies were appearing; there were associations of florists and benefit societies known as 'boxes'; then there were the once persecuted communities of religious Nonconformists including Quakers, Baptists, Levellers, Winstanley's Diggers, Muggletonians and Grindletonians.

The surge of associational activity that began in the late seventeenth century would not have been possible without an elevation of interest. But is this what also happened in the early twenty-first century? What is the evidence to suggest that during the first decade of this century we experienced an equivalent elevation of interest?

Universities, Spare Time and the Associational Time Bomb

For a young working-class man in Britain during the 1960s the statistical likelihood of going to university was roughly the same as being treated in a mental health facility. Over the next fifty years the scale and nature of higher education in this country were transformed. By 2010 a much wider range of Britons had begun to attend university, and the number of people doing so mushroomed. In 1900 there were 25,000 full-time students in British universities. By the close of the twentieth century that figure had grown to over a million. If you include part-time and mature students, there were almost 5 million men and women in tertiary education by the start of the twenty-first century, and ten times as many eighteen- and nineteen-year-olds going to university in 2008 as there had been in 1968.

University is the very embodiment of what we have been looking at – the elevation of one's interests over one's traditional and inherited identities. It involves individuals travelling away from where they were born in order to pursue a secular enthusiasm or passion. They come together with others who share these interests, and together they take their understanding to a new level.

Of course, class, geography and ethnicity do not suddenly become invisible any more than they do within an association, but they cease to stand in the way of you taking your interest further in the company of others. University in Britain during the early twenty-first century was, really, an extreme extrapolation of Miles's coffee house in 1659.

It is also an ideal apprenticeship for starting or joining an association later on in life. Going to university during the late twentieth and early twenty-first centuries meant becoming more accustomed to research and to what it is to take part in collaborative discussion. Again, these skills lend themselves to life in an association. These are some of the reasons why, as Peter Hall has explained, 'it is well-established that each additional year of education increases the propensity of an individual to become involved in community affairs, whether by joining an association or providing voluntary work for the community.' By 1990 the average number of associational memberships for a university graduate was 2.18, while the national average was only 1.12. The fact that so many more of us went to university during the late twentieth century encouraged an elevation of interest, and I have no doubt that this fuelled a surge of associational activity.

This may be merely the start of it. Beyond our fiftieth birthday it seems that we become more inclined to join associations, and by 2004 less than 10 per cent of men under the age of thirty had no educational qualifications. And yet, more than half of those older than sixty-five had none. In that case we are sitting on an associational time bomb. Soon we may have a generation of university-educated Britons with access to the internet and little or no interest in organized religion, living in neighbourhoods that contain barely any local community spirit. If this happens, the number of people starting and joining associations will surely experience another surge.

Then there is the changing nature of our spare time. We have much more of it than our great-grandparents did. A man in full-time employment in 1938 worked an average of 47.7 hours per week, while his counterpart in 1997 would work for only 42.8 hours. For women the drop was from 49.3 hours to 39.2. By 2005 the average adult British male had almost five and a half hours of leisure time every day, while a woman had a little under five hours.

If you were of a gloomy disposition, you might say that this is immaterial as we seem to spend this extra time watching television. Yet by 2005 a typical Briton spent only two hours and forty minutes a day watching television and listening to music or the radio. To put this in perspective, in the United

States an equivalent adult would watch between three and four hours of television each day.

Moreover, the way we watch television and listen to the radio is changing. Increasingly we have become 'selective' users rather than 'habitual' ones. Instead of slumping passively in front of the television each night, by 2010 we experienced much greater choice and could watch programmes that went out weeks ago. As Donna, a member of Laura's Book Group, explained, 'it certainly means you'd never consider missing book group to watch something on television. Not that I would anyway! But having it all on Freeview or the internet means that you wouldn't consider it. Television tends to play a smaller part in my life now.'

The fact that so many more of us are going to university, that we have more spare time and increasingly we are in control of it appears to have fuelled an elevation of interest in Britain during the early twenty-first century. As we saw in the late seventeenth century, this is a spur to associational activity. There is just one other development to consider.

Subcultures

'I think we live in a relentlessly sub-cultural world,' said the novelist Hari Kunzru back in 2008. 'To invoke the great I-word – the internet – it's very possible for all sorts of scenes to run in parallel. They may be more or less difficult, they may be more or less formally experimental, they may feed into things that are commercially successful, they may not. But participation in subcultures is one of the defining facts of people's cultural lives these days.'

First of all, what did Kunzru mean by a subculture? A sub-culture is essentially a scene that develops around a specialist interest. Sometimes you'll hear these referred to as 'tribes'. You could say that historical re-enactment is a subculture of sorts, as is pedigree dog breeding, stamp collecting, non-league football or contemporary art.

A subculture is about more than one's knowledge of certain texts and attitudes; it may also involve ownership of particular products. Bikers in a biking subculture are known by their choice of bike. Dedicated football or music fans earn acceptance by the clothing they wear and other purchases they make.

Subcultures matter to us for several reasons. Not only do you find a nucleus of associations at the heart of each, but a subculture can only come about when a large number of people begin to take their interest more seriously. In other words, they elevate it above the other parts of their life.

Within each subculture in Britain today you will find thousands of people who have elevated their interest to such an extent that they may even define themselves by it. Rather than be known by their profession or where they come from, they will think of themselves first and foremost as 'a historical re-enactor', 'a biker', 'a Chelsea fan' or 'a breeder of Tibetan Terriers'. That is their thing, their interest, and the existence of a subculture makes that identity more concrete.

There is ample evidence to suggest that subcultures flourished during the late twentieth and early twenty-first centuries. As Charles Leadbeater and Paul Miller explained in *The Pro-Am Revolution*, during the 1990s there was an 'explosion of specialist magazines, catering to specialist tastes and interests'. During that same period 'the number of television channels rose from four to more than 60; commercial radio stations went from 60 to 188 and CD-ROM titles from 390 to 16,762.' This continued throughout the following decade, and thanks to what Kunzru called 'the great I-word' these specialist subcultures became more defined. There was greater access to specialist material and equipment, contributing to what is now known as the 'long tail effect'.

During the early twenty-first century subcultures in Britain became more detailed, more communicative and more coherent. If they weren't there already, then national federations were formed to represent the associations within each. These federations provided groups with support and advice, and in most cases extended their life-expectancy.

The combination of many, many more Britons going to university, increased leisure time – over which we seem to be gaining control – and the growing definition of our subcultures indicate that there was certainly an elevation of interest in British society during the early twenty-first century. What had once happened mainly in London during the late seventeenth century now occurred nationwide. Millions of Britons, rather than thousands, were travelling away from their neighbourhoods, their families and their places of work to pursue their interests for a few hours once a month or once a week. When they got home, they would continue to do this online.

The idea of behaving like this became more normal. The internet, dwindling church attendances and the shifts that led to the decline of local community also played a part in this. They have helped to cement the idea that in the context of a small group one's interests can be more important than one's inherited identity. For reasons I will get on to in Part Three, I think this is something to celebrate.

And Finally

There are one or two other factors that have helped to bring about an associational revival. One of these is the fact that we now live a lot longer. An Englishman in the first decade of the twentieth century could expect to live to the not very ripe old age of forty-eight. His great-grandson in 1995 could realistically hope to celebrate his seventy-fourth birthday, while this man's wife would be confident of making it to seventy-nine. By the start of the twenty-first century, 18 per cent of the British population was over sixty-five, and that figure looks set to increase to 25 per cent by 2031 – in 1900 only 7 per cent of Britons were that old. Earlier we saw that, as we age, we may become more inclined to join associations, so as the proportion of Britons enjoying a long retirement grows it follows that the number of us involved in associations will increase.

Another factor that contributed to this surge of associational activity concerns the way we work. By the start of the twenty-first century the idea of a job-for-life that you would start in your early twenties and leave four decades later with a party and perhaps a personalized set of golf clubs or a gold watch has become something of a relic. Britons change jobs far more frequently than they did in the 1950s, and a larger proportion of us work part-time or are self-employed. The number of self-employed Britons rose from 3 million in 2002 to nearly 4 million by the end of 2008, while there were four times as many men working part-time in 1991 as there were in 1961 – by 2002 over 7 million Britons were in part-time employment.

This has meant that a growing number of us are less likely to find a meaningful sense of community in a workplace. If we do work in an office, the relationships we have with our colleagues may not have the same innate longevity. You do not have the camaraderie of castaways. You can say the same of the relationship between any two neighbours – both our workplaces and our neighbourhoods have become more fluid and nomadic. As such they are no longer reliable sources of identity and community.

Another source of belonging is the family. The shape and size of British families has also changed during the late twentieth century. Three generations of one family are less likely to live under the same roof. Our homes are emptier than before – the average household size was 2.37 in 2008, having been 2.91 in 1971. We are less likely to live near our parents, and the number of families led by a lone parent grew from 8 per cent in 1971 to 23 per cent in 2008. Here we can see yet another traditional source of community that has attenuated. When that happens, all the evidence suggests that we look for alternative social networks – we get involved in associations.

Finally, we saw at the very beginning of this book that to join an association you will often need a 'capacity for membership'. This is something you acquire, and as traditional forms of community fall into decline, one after the other, you might think that we would be in danger of losing this. Strangely, this hasn't happened. New Labour, in particular, had a penchant for schemes encouraging volunteering and civic participation. They backed charities such as V, an organization that aimed to 'create a culture where volunteering comes naturally', and orchestrated what they believed to be 'the biggest youth action scheme England has ever seen'. There was Volunteering Day, Volunteering Week and a Volunteering Year. By the end of the twentieth century roughly 1.3 million children belonged either to the Scouts or the Girl Guides, up from 115,000 in 1910, while three-quarters of a million were involved in schemes such as the Duke of Edinburgh's Award, the Combined Cadet Force or Youth Clubs UK.

So by the start of the twenty-first century we continued to acquire a 'capacity for membership' as children. Again this points towards the overwhelming possibility of a growth in the number of Britons involved in associations. But there is another side to all this.

13

The Case Against

Fashion, Hubs and the State

> Voluntary effort, unaided, is quite incapable of meeting the
> needs for social and recreational facilities.
> *Community Centres*, Ministry of Education publication, 1944

'I thought about hosting the group in my home,' said Faisal
Al-Yafai of his monthly discussion group, 'but I realized it
wouldn't work. It's so important for the room you use to
be a neutral space, a place in which everyone can bypass
their instinctive response to hospitality. If it had been in my
home, people might have thought, "Well, he's chairing the
discussion, he's invited us to it, and he's our host. I can't
exactly tell him to shut up." That would change the discussion, it would limit it. In a neutral space people feel as
though they can argue with anyone and that they own it as
much as anyone else. For me, that's when it gets interesting.'

Most associations need somewhere to meet, a place in which
they can perform a Beekeepers' Dance. A handful are lucky
enough to have a clubhouse of their own. There are Working
Men's Clubs or British Legion clubhouses just as there are
the gentlemen's clubs of St James's, 'each possessing a well-
appointed mansion'. But most associations like Al-Yafai's
cannot afford their own premises. In that case, where do they
go?

Rather than meet in Al-Yafai's home, the group convened
in a bar in Soho, London. Not in the main area, but in a

room set aside in the basement, just as the Rota Club met in a private room on the first floor of Miles's. Both the coffee house and that bar in Soho were 'mixed' spaces in the sense that, while the building was privately owned, parts of it were open to the public. What has allowed associations to flourish since the English Civil War has been an abundance of mixed spaces like these. Without these spaces, these Hubs, as I like to call them, associations suffer.

Over the past three and a half centuries these associational Hubs have included taverns, inns, pubs, bars and ale-houses as well as community centres, village halls, churches, church halls, assembly rooms, town halls, sports centres, theatres and other religious centres such as mosques and Friends' Meeting Houses. An associational Hub might easily be a university lecture hall or a school classroom, a coffee house, chocolate house, café, hotel or perhaps a conference centre. The beauty of these Hubs is that each can sustain an array of associations, and in theory they do not cost the groups themselves very much to use.

To take two wildly different examples of Hubs in action, had you gone to the Hanwell Community Centre in Acton during the early 1970s you would have found Deep Purple rehearsing in one room and next door Uriah Heep. At the time both metal bands were associations. Move back to the eighteenth century, and in the Thatched House tavern on St James's Street at different times you could find: the Catch Club, Johnson's Club, the Cornish Club, the Dilettanti Society, the Farmers' Club, the Geographical Club, the Geological Club, the Linnaean Club, the Literary Society, the Navy Club, the Philosophical Club, the College of Physicians Club, the Political Economy Club, the Royal Academy Club, the Royal Astronomical Club, the Royal Institution Club, the Royal London Yacht Club, the Royal Naval Club, the Royal Society Club, St Albans Medical Club, St Bartholomew's Contemporaries, the Star Club, the Statistical

Club, the Sussex Club and St James's Union Society – as well as nine different Masonic lodges.

Hubs are essential to the country's associational health. But were there enough of them during the first decade of the twenty-first century to sustain a surge of associational activity? Obviously it's hard to know how many 'enough' might be, but we can at least look at the long-term trends.

A good place to start is the pub. In the 1690s there were about 64,000 inns and ale-houses to service a population of just under 6 million people. Although the population of Britain today is more than ten times what it was then, there were actually fewer licensed drinking houses by 2010 – their numbers fell from 61,000 at the start of the twenty-first century to 54,000 by 2010.

This drop becomes more ominous when you consider the kinds of pubs that closed. Often they were local and rural. By 2009 over half of Britain's small villages were pub-less, and a growing proportion of the pubs that remained were controlled by 'Pubcos' that needed to demonstrate to their shareholders a growing profit margin. Their owners may refer to punters as 'traffic' and remove chairs on the grounds that standing 'traffic' drinks faster. Of course, Hubs like these are less inclined to encourage a knitting circle, for example, to meet in one of their back rooms.

Perhaps this does not matter. Pubs are by no means the only associational Hubs in twenty-first-century Britain. In his survey of community buildings conducted during the late 1990s Paul Marriott estimated the existence of nearly 19,000 community centres and village halls, both twentieth-century additions to the Hub canon, as well as church halls and other religious centres in England and Wales.

Then there are our actual places of worship. Although these are no longer the thriving associational centres they were in the early twentieth century, they continue to have great potential as Hubs, particularly when you bear in mind how little some of them are used. By 2005 there were 47,600 churches in Britain, and although the need to find extra funding to maintain them 'is escalating at an alarming rate', and as many as 4,000 may close by 2020, our churches remain a valuable associational resource that is largely untapped.

Combine these figures, and you can get a rough idea of how many Hubs there may have been by 2010. Marriott's survey suggested a ratio of 1:2,157 for community buildings to adults in England and Wales. The figure for churches and church buildings comes out as about 1:1,054 adults, and for pubs it is closer to 1:944 adults. Combine these and you get one Hub for every 405 adults.

By the close of the seventeenth century the ratio of Britons of all ages to ale-houses and inns was approximately 1:100. The modern figure appears to be a long way off. Yet when you factor in cafés and sports centres as well as other religious buildings, that projection of 1:405 improves considerably.

The problem many associations faced in the early twenty-first century, however, was not just to do with their access to Hubs but also the cost of using them. The 2008 government survey of amateur arts groups stressed that 'access to good-quality venues, at a reasonable cost that is suitable for the artform, is a key issue.' In that year alone, voluntary arts groups such as amateur dramatic societies and choirs spent an estimated £93 million on renting premises. The report went on to say that among these groups 'there is widespread concern about the rising cost of venue hire.'

Although there are some associations that do not need a Hub in which to meet, such as walking groups, and a handful will have their own clubhouses, for most small groups this would appear to present a problem. However, a growing number of associations were able to meet in a member's home instead, even if this was not ideal. Think of Laura's Book Group, the Cardigan art protesters or the *Chevra Kadisha*. Yet for many Britons this would not have been possible several centuries ago.

Once described by John Ruskin as 'the place of Peace; the shelter, not only from all injury, but from all terror, doubt, and division', by the start of the twenty-first century the average British home had become a well-appointed citadel. We spent almost £7 billion a year on DIY. With its slogan 'Home is the most important place in the world', IKEA welcomed just short of 40 million Britons to their stores in 2008. Never before had our homes been so secure, so comfortable or so capacious, nor had what we got up to within these cocoons ever been quite so sequestered from the world beyond, thanks to curtains, sound-proofed walls, insulation and double-glazing.

And yet Al-Yafai's point still stands. While some groups are happy to meet in a member's house, it is rarely preferable to using a neutral, mixed space. Hubs are essential to the associational health of this country, and during the first decade of the twenty-first century their numbers appear to have dropped while many of those that remained became more expensive.

So what can be done to keep our Hubs affordable or, better still, how can we inspire the creation of new ones? Interestingly, much of the answer lies in the way we think about our associations and in our failure to adjust to the reality of the more secular society in which we live. By the start of the twenty-first century the Church no longer had a monopoly on bringing groups of people together in their spare time. There were many other ways to commune with others, yet by 2010 our legal system and political attitudes failed to reflect this.

Two Ideas For How We Can Reduce the Bias against Non-Religious Groups with Private Aims

Pretend there's a derelict building at the end of your street, and that one day workmen arrive and surround it with a chrysalis of scaffolding and tarpaulin. A year later an evangelical church emerges out of this. You go in to have a look around. All is as you might expect. There is a prayer hall and a small shop selling religious trinkets, prayer guides and other devotional ephemera, as well as posters describing the power of prayer. On your way out you spot a noticeboard advertising weekend retreats run by the church.

Yet because of the religious nature of what appears to be going on in this building, the people running it will enjoy a series of exemptions and subsidies. For example, as a religious institution they are not required to pay non-domestic rates to the local authority. British law guarantees this privilege to any building associated with a religious structure. In one instance a school located in the grounds of a mosque was exempted from non-domestic rates. When it comes to VAT, again, the evangelical church will get preferential treatment largely on account of its religious ends. It will not be considered a business and as such will not be required to charge VAT on any items thought to be incidental to the provision of 'spiritual welfare' – i.e., everything in the shop or those retreats you saw advertised.

Had the new occupants of this building been bound by a shared interest in something else – a non-religious enthusiasm such as, say, caving – their experience would have been quite different. Let's imagine that out of that cocoon of scaffolding came the New Belfry. For the sake of argument, pretend that those cavers of the Bristol Exploration Club, the ones we met earlier on the Mendips, have located a system of caves beneath your street. This building is to be their new clubhouse.

We know a certain amount about this club already. Under their stewardship the building will host regular congregations of people bound by a common interest. These meetings would probably be larger than those of most English churches, and there will be cohesion and fellowship among the members of this community of cavers thanks to the

Power of Giving. Though they have a limited membership, any member of the public with an interest in caves is welcome to apply for membership and you do not have to be a member to use the clubhouse. These caving enthusiasts will help each other out, they have a shared identity, and without any paid leaders the bond between these people is bound to be stronger than it would be in the evangelical church. They will also memorialize their dead, thus adding to the sense of community within the group.

Yet the B. E. C. would be required to pay full non-domestic rates, unless they tried to do something about it. The Local Government Finance Act of 1988 allows any local rating authority to grant relief to small independent groups that are not geared towards profit and 'whose main objects are charitable or are otherwise philanthropic or religious or concerned with education, social welfare, science, literature or the fine arts'. So the B. E. C. may qualify for this. Just. But there is no guarantee that they would receive this relief, which is entirely at the discretion of the local authority.

Perhaps the B. E. C. could apply for charitable status? One of the rewards would be a mandatory 80 per cent reduction in non-domestic rates, and if they were lucky this could become a complete exemption. But as a registered charity they would be subject to charity law. They'd need to appoint trustees and submit an annual report and a copy of their accounts if their turnover rose above a certain threshold. So they would lose some of their independence and it would become harder to alter their constitution.

Realizing that they were still in need of some extra cash, an enterprising Belfryite might establish a kiosk near the entrance to the New Belfry to sell caving key rings and mugs. She offers guided trips down some of the local caves as well. Unlike the evangelical church, however, this activity is unlikely to be exempt from VAT. This is to do with who appears to benefit. If the group's objectives are thought to be in the public domain, then from a VAT point of view this unincorporated association is not a business, even if there are annual subscriptions involved. But the problem here is the definition of 'the public domain'. It remains something of a grey area, yet most of the groups in this book would probably not qualify. Their aims appear to be private. So they become liable for VAT once the value of their taxable supplies exceeds £45,000 (unless they are youth clubs).

By contrast, when voluntary organizations are 'in the public domain and are of a political, religious, philanthropic, philosophical or patriotic nature', they are not considered to be businesses and need not worry about VAT. In the majority of rulings and legislation directed towards voluntary groups you will find a similar bias against groups that appear to have private aims. The paradox here is that while the members of, say, the B.E.C. belong to 'the public', and will benefit from the group's activities, the group's activities will not be seen as benefiting 'the public'.

Rate-relief and VAT exemptions are just two examples of ways in which the law can be prejudiced against organizations, societies and associations with 'private' and secular aims. Several hundred years ago this would have made more sense. Parish churches brought together local communities of believers in the name of social and educational improvement, and they did so without seeking to generate a profit. There was no welfare state and so they needed all the help they could get. The case for public subsidies was straightforward. But as we have seen, most twenty-first-century Britons no longer look to the Church for social and educational improvement in the way that their Georgian or Victorian predecessors did. Christianity was becoming a minority interest. Yet by the time Gordon Brown left office as Prime Minister the law did not reflect this.

In his report published in the late 1990s Paul Marriott argued that secular community buildings 'should be seen as key agents in any policy attempt to maintain or develop social cohesion', adding that we need 'a concerted effort to ensure that policy makers at central and local government level, funders and social housing providers realise the strategic importance and potential of what is a vast network'.

We must look beyond community centres and village halls to other kinds of Hubs as well. These too need our support. In 2001 the Prince of Wales launched 'The Pub is the Hub' scheme, a charity aimed at keeping local pubs afloat by offering advice on how to diversify by providing services such as laundry collection, deposit services and, ironically enough, hosting religious ceremonies.

This is more like it. Since then a 'Community Right to Buy' scheme has been proposed, whereby not-for-profit local organizations would have the right to take over struggling pubs, parks, post offices and other Hubs. 'Asset transfer' is another way of securing these Hubs for the future, involving the transfer of some of the estimated £250 billion of council-owned assets into private ownership. As Phillip Blond has argued, 'central government should impose a legally binding duty on local authorities reasonably to consider asset transfer to social enterprises by emphasizing the social rather than the monetary return.'

Blond's idea of a 'social return' is hugely important. We must not think of these Hubs purely in terms of their religiosity, or whether they are geared towards making a profit. What matters is their *social* value. The social return of a local pub, a British Legion social club or even a bingo hall, for example, is immense and easily comparable to that of a parish church.

Many bingo halls closed in Scotland and the north of England following the smoking ban of 2006–7, and just as local pubs are about much more than drinking and the sale of food and drink, so 'the Bingo club does not only act as a venue for a Bingo game, but moreover enables a unique social support network for both members and club employees', as one report explained.

The drive to play Bingo regularly is largely orientated around a need for social interaction and belonging. [. . .] The closure of Bingo clubs, especially those in the small, rural venues and deprived urban locations, has meant not only the loss of a pastime and form of entertainment but the disappearance of a unique social support network, relied upon especially by retired women.

We must do more to preserve Hubs like these. One of the ways to achieve this would be to offer mandatory relief from non-domestic rates to any Hub that can demonstrate it is being used by an association, society or club with legal ends. Or a grant scheme could be established, allowing the proprietor of any Hub to reclaim the VAT charged on repair work to his or her premises.

When it comes to Hubs run by local authorities, such as sports centres or community centres, there is a good economic argument for transferring power to the associations that use these venues. Ninety per cent of the community buildings surveyed by Marriott were run by voluntary management committees, and the average annual turnover of each was £14,000. Their state-run equivalents, meanwhile, cost an average of £39,900 per year to operate.

In a similar sense, the upkeep of England's Anglican churches is largely the responsibility of thousands of parochial church councils, each one of which is a voluntary association. The cost of running these groups is minimal, and we know precisely why. They are fuelled not by cash but by religious devotion and the Power of Giving. If we accept that Hubs become more cost-efficient when run by the independent associations that use them, rather than as an arm of the state, they stand a much better chance of long term survival.

More than anything else, we must recognize the part played by Hubs in generating social capital. Churches do not have a monopoly on this. It is only by accepting the role of secular

Hubs that we can edge towards a legal and social reality in which an evangelical church and a clubhouse full of cavers are seen in the same terms. There should be no difference in the eyes of the law or society between a group that comes together to talk about God and one that gathers to discuss caves. What matters is the 'social return' of each.

Big State

Between 1997 and 2010 the British government and its agencies became more powerful, more centralized and more obsessed with surveillance than at any other point during the post-war era. By 2009 the NHS had become the largest employer in Europe. The Civil Service employed 492,000 staff – more than the population of Iceland – and over a fifth of all employed Britons worked for the public sector. In 1913 government expenditure was just 13 per cent of GDP. By 2010 it exceeded 52 per cent.

Such a swollen state militates against associational growth. In the 1850s the idea of a British government that looked after the needs of *every* citizen was the stuff of obscure, radical screeds. Relief and moral reform were provided not by the state but by a vast network of voluntary associations, charities and mutual aid societies. Most of these worked in tandem with the government.

By the start of the First World War this had started to change. The government employed twice as many bureaucrats and knew much more about the levels of degradation and poverty in which some Britons lived. The war that followed necessitated an epic expansion of the state's power. For Winston Churchill it was 'the greatest argument for State Socialism that has ever been produced'. It was also 'a kick in the teeth to the traditional relationship between the state and the individual', as the historian Ben Wilson has put it.

Following the advent of universal suffrage, the idea that the state *should* look after the needs of every citizen became a realistic and reasonable expectation. There was a stronger belief in the possibilities of science and a world without want. The emergence of Communism and Fascism lent credence to the idea that you needed a powerful and centralized state to face the future.

During the Second World War the government expanded further than ever before. The Emergency Powers Act of 1939 granted it authority over almost every aspect of its citizens' lives, and the traditional and more negative role of the state as arbiter and protector was set to one side. In the midst of this, in 1942, a document appeared that would enable a series of politicians and civil servants to take the power and reach of a peacetime British government into a land of Wellsian fantasy. Though it was not their main aim, this would have a devastating effect on thousands of associations nationwide.

The history of associations in this country is one of gradual, overlapping shifts that have swept across a languid land-scape. Every now and again this is upset by an earthquake. The Tudor assault on monasteries was one of these, the English Civil War another. The creation of the welfare state represents the third great rupture in our associational past.

The author of this explosive document was Sir William Beveridge. Awkward and talented, Beveridge had been at different times a statistician, academic, radio broadcaster, newspaper columnist, MP, social worker and civil servant. In 1941 he was asked to produce a report on social insurance and allied services. What followed was a publishing phenom-enon. A hundred thousand copies were sold in the first month. Thousands were dropped over Nazi-occupied Europe. Analyses of Beveridge's proposals even made their way into Hitler's bunker – each offering begrudging approval.

What made this report so compelling was its ambition. Beveridge set out to slay the five social ills of his day: disease, ignorance, squalor, idleness and want – i.e., poverty – an approach that owed a great deal to Positivist thinkers such as Henri Saint-Simon and Auguste Comte. Beveridge proposed a Keynesian commitment to full employment, stringent taxation of inherited wealth, the nationalization of the major manufacturing industries and the Bank of England, and – the line everyone latched on to – he argued that a centralized state should be responsible for the welfare of all citizens from the cradle to the grave.

Until then social welfare had been local, amateur and infused with the spirit of voluntarism. It was consistently inconsistent. No more. Beveridge's report contained the blueprint for 'a British Revolution', and the nation was behind it. In a survey at the time only 6 per cent of those polled opposed these proposals.

Yet very few could have predicted the disastrous effect on our associations. Worst hit were the Friendly Societies. The National Insurance Acts of 1946 meant that, contrary to Beveridge's proposals, these voluntary bodies were no longer responsible for the distribution of sickness benefits. Their numbers dropped from 18,923 just after the war to 1,307 in 1995. The creation of the NHS at around the same time nationalized as many as 1,000 hospitals that had been run previously as voluntary organizations. Butler's Education Act of 1944 ensured that 9,000 voluntary religious schools run largely on donations of time and money lost their independence and began to exist under the aegis of the state. Housing Associations also suffered as Nye Bevan's restriction on the number of 'private' houses that could be built led to 'the extinction of all but the richest and longest established associations'.

What happened to Britain's community centres gives us a pretty good insight into the thinking behind this. In the fifteen years that followed the Second World War the number of paid staff in these associational Hubs quadrupled. Previously they had been run largely by volunteers. A Ministry of Education publication in 1944 insisted that 'voluntary effort, unaided, is quite incapable of meeting the needs for social and recreational facilities.' The tutting tone is unmistakable. It was no longer sensible to 'depend upon the voluntary part-time leadership of enthusiasts as was so often done in the early days'. Running a community centre was, they insisted, 'a skilled and difficult job needing men and women who not only have natural gifts but considerable experience and training'.

The enthusiasm and energy of small-scale voluntary endeavour was no longer an asset but a liability. It was old hat, the kind of thing that had happened in the 'early days'. The labour movement – labour with a small 'l' – was sidelined. Unlike Beveridge, the post-war British government saw little or no intrinsic value in associational networks such as the Co-operative movement, the holiday fellowships or any other voluntary working-class organizations based on the principle of mutual aid. From now on, democracy would be about the relationship between the state and the individual. This didn't leave much room for associations.

It would be naive to mourn the disappearance of each voluntary body. Thanks to the reforms of the post-war Labour government and the shift away from voluntarism, the distribution of material welfare became far more efficient. The creation of the NHS was a remarkable and inspiring achievement. Gone were the disputes within Friendly Societies over who had paid what and to whom, and many, if not most, of the egregious geographic variations in healthcare, welfare, housing and education were elided.

But there were at least two elements of amateur voluntarism that the welfare state could not match: reciprocity and personality. To put it in the terms of this book, within the new system both the Power of Giving and the New Zealand Tendency were denied.

Take the Friendly Societies. Until the National Insurance Acts of 1946 these bodies did not just meet the financial needs of their members but also fulfilled some of their social requirements. Over many years the members of each Friendly Society helped each other out. They gave gifts within the group, and as we know from the Power of Giving, this creates a sense of fellowship. A Friendly Society provided a burr of camaraderie that the welfare state simply could not.

The New Zealand Tendency suggests that belonging to one of these Friendly Societies also provided a sense of identity. The same applies to other pre-war voluntary bodies run largely on gifts, charity and payment in kind. Each had a more intimate and fraternal character than any state-run successor.

When the state expands, associations suffer. This is as true for the early sixteenth century as it is for today. For any government that becomes remote from its people, whether by ideology, geography or just the size of the population it is trying to serve, numbers and measures come to the fore. The Achilles heel of any association in a situation like this is that you cannot describe its value using numbers. It is impossible to put fellowship or identity into a graph. There are no targets that can be set. And yet, as before, we must not fall for the idea that if it can't be measured then it doesn't exist.

An enlarged state can also stifle the activities of small groups by creating a carapace of regulation and procedural bureaucracy. For an amateur dramatic society it might become too expensive to stage a performance because of the cost of public liability insurance, ensuring the health and safety of all those involved and carrying out risk assessments. In 2009 the Vetting and Barring Scheme was introduced, making it impossible for an individual to ferry a group of children to a school football match, for example, unless they had been formally vetted by the Criminal Records Bureau, an executive agency of the Home Office.

An overgrown state also narrows our notions of personal and civic responsibility. Rather than come together with others to get something done, we fall into the habit of turning to the state or, worse, we no longer turn to it, do nothing and assume that the state will provide in due course.

As Durkheim argued, when the state recedes, the individual 'feels, and he is in reality, much less *acted upon*; he becomes more a source of spontaneous activity'. A swollen state can impede our ability to associate just as it may numb the desire to do so. This is why the expansion of the state under New Labour may have slowed the revival of associational activity during the early twenty-first century.

On Trend

Is that it for the 'against' column? Not quite. There is just one other development that may have weakened this surge of associational activity – although really it is the *lack* of a particular development that I want to look at.

By the time Thomas Britton's musical society came to an end in the early eighteenth century there were thousands of clubs and societies popping up in urban centres all over Britain. Not only was it easier than ever before to start one of these but it had become fashionable to do so.

This was unexpected. In the aftermath of the English Civil War these groups were often caricatured as hotbeds of political intrigue. And yet by the early eighteenth century joining a club had become a mark of civilized refinement. There was nothing unusual about the Earl of Shaftesbury explaining that belonging to an association allows us to 'polish one another and rub off our corners and rough sides by a sort of amicable collision'. In 1711 Joseph Addison explained in the *Spectator* that:

When men are thus knit together, by a love of society, not a spirit of faction, and do not meet to censure or annoy those that are absent, but to enjoy one another; when they are thus combined for their own improvement, or for the good of others, or at least to relax themselves from the business of the day, by an innocent and cheerful conversation, there may be something very useful in these little institutions and establishments.

The *Spectator* played a key part in making clubs and societies fashionable. As well as talking up the virtues of belonging to a club, its authors, Addison and Steele, employed the fictional device of the 'Spectator Club', an imaginary group whose members corresponded roughly to the nation's social types. You could also argue that the written style of the *Spectator* was that of a club conversation. One moment Mr Spectator would be telling jokes and silly stories, the next he was making serious points about the state of society. It was like being gathered round a table with a series of different characters contributing to the discussion. Finally, the *Spectator* was very good at making the reader feel as though he or she belonged to an imaginary club with its frequent references to past issues and correspondence, both real and imagined.

There's no doubt that during the eighteenth century clubs and societies were fashionable in a way that they were not during the first decade of the twenty-first century. Although you might have read a half-hearted snippet at the beginning of a Sunday supplement describing the popularity of knitting circles, or a piece in a local newspaper praising the efforts of a local voluntary charitable group, there was no pervasive sense during the first decade of the twenty-first century that getting involved in one of these groups was a trendy thing to do. Perhaps this was for the best?

Some years ago a group called Utrophia began to organize 'mobile clubbing' events. To get involved, you joined an email list and were then sent details of where to meet and when. Invariably it was a railway station concourse. There was no money involved. You would turn up and at the agreed time start 'dancing like you've never danced before'. Just as you began to do this, so would several hundred other people. It was a 'flash-mob'. But you were not moving to a sound system that had been set up; instead you'd jump around to the music in your iPod.

Sometimes these mobile clubbing events would carry on for up to an hour, with bemused passers-by often joining in. It was not an experiment, and it looked shambolic, with everyone dancing to their own drum in every sense. But it was a lot of fun and they became popular.

'What I loved about it,' said Ben Cummins, who came up with the idea, 'was that you got to dance in a huge, well-lit space. That was it. It made such a change from being bunched up in a dingy club. There you were with all this light and space. Of course there were other things to it, like challenging the use of a public space, and bringing joy to a place that you might otherwise associate with waiting, commuting and work. But at the heart of it was just the fun of dancing around in a big space.'

These mobile clubbing events became more frequent. The police no longer tried to break them up, seeing them as harmless. Then a large mobile phone company got wind of them. They trained up a team of more than a hundred professional dancers and created an advertisement in one of these railway stations. It was made to look like a mobile clubbing event – only it was a scrubbed-up, choreographed version of what really went on. This became part of a successful nationwide advertising campaign.

I remember meeting Cummins several weeks after those advertisements began to run. He looked drained. 'It's more or less gone now,' he had said, slowly and without bitterness. 'If we do it again people will just think we're working for a mobile phone company. Of course I never *owned* that idea. You can't feel proprietorial over something like dancing together in a train station to your iPod. I guess we'll just have to think of something else. And, I mean, it was amazing seeing that ad. It looked fantastic! But it is now well and truly theirs. It's gone.'

It is rare today to find a trend that is genuinely unusual, home-grown and popular which has not been appropriated by the worlds of advertising or fashion. Both are primed to mine the irreverent and alternative margins of our culture. They use that patina of non-commercial authenticity in order to sell more units, and during the late twentieth century a string of countercultural events or movements were targeted like this.

As we have seen, the surge of clubs and associations during the early twenty-first century went largely unnoticed. This meant that these groups were generally left alone by advertisers and fashionistas, with very few exceptions, such as mobile clubbing. So perhaps this was a blessing. If joining an association had become trendy in a mainstream sense, there would have been advertisements exploiting, say, the intimate charm of a book group in order to sell a brand of wine, or the laddish camaraderie of a five-a-side football team to promote male skincare products.

Either way, the idea of joining a small voluntary group was not fashionable during the early twenty-first century in the way that it was during the eighteenth. This may have slowed our associational growth.

A Global Associational Revolution?

According to the statistics we have, there was probably a surge in the number of Britons involved in associations during the first decade of this century, one that exceeded population growth. When we look beyond the numbers and approach this question using a deeper understanding of how associations work, this trend is confirmed emphatically.

The advent of the internet, the continued decline of Christianity, our increased spatial mobility, the fact that we move house more often, the hollowing-out of local community, the increase in leisure time, the massive shift in the number of Britons going to university, subculturization, and the fact that we live longer and are more likely to join associations the older we get – these form the vital elements of a compelling argument to suggest that there was indeed a surge of associational activity during the early twenty-first century, one that looks set to continue.

Although there were mitigating factors – such as the expansion of the state, the rising cost of venue hire, the closure of some associational Hubs and the fact that joining these groups did not become fashionable (although the effect of this is unclear) – it is unlikely that these did anything more than slow the rate of growth.

Perhaps we Britons were not the only ones. In 1999 Lester Salamon, the Director of the Institute for Policy Studies at Johns Hopkins University, suggested that 'a global "associational revolution" appears to be underway' and that there was 'a striking upsurge of organized private, voluntary activity in virtually every corner of the globe'. He also argued that

> from the developed countries of North America, Europe and Asia to the developing societies of Africa, Latin America and the former Soviet bloc, people are forming associations, foundations and similar institutions to deliver human services, promote grass-roots economic development, prevent environmental degradation, protect civil rights and pursue a thousand other objectives formerly unattended or left to the state. The scope and scale of this phenomenon are immense.

'Immense' is the right word. But if this book has established anything, it is the difficulty of identifying associational growth in just one country. Taking on the entire planet is daunting, to say the least. While it is tempting, wonderfully tempting – I can feel my eyes turn to pound signs as I think of the potential market for such a book – to agree with Salamon that there may well be a worldwide 'associational revolution' under way, I do not begin to have the evidence or the arguments to back this up. Nor, I suspect, does he.

To do that would also run counter to the spirit in which I've tried to approach this subject. Where possible, I have steered clear of a universal assertion where a nationally specific one would do. There is a constant danger when writing a book like this that your argument can slide into a proto-Positivist mush in which humans are all essentially the same and our cultural inheritance is singular. Unless you're careful the history of the world becomes little more than an endless supply of anecdotes there to support your various theories – the intellectual equivalent of a nodding dog.

Our actions cannot be explained by a pantheon of 'truths' that reflect the results of late twentieth-century psychological studies carried out in the United States or Europe. Looking at the world like this only reduces the precision and power of what it is you are trying to say. Phenomena such as the Power of Giving, the New Zealand Tendency or the Hothouse Effect are not unique to Britain. Yet there are many elements of this story – such as the decline of Christianity, what has happened to our local neighbourhoods and the fact that we have such a long and unique tradition of forming associations – that are not at all universal.

Whether or not there was a global associational revolution, it is fair to say that a significantly larger proportion of British society was involved in some kind of small voluntary group in 2010 than had been the case in 2000. Instead of celebrating this, we spent the second half of the 2000s moaning about

'Broken Britain', the increased levels of 'loneliness' in society and the death of community.

So what are the implications of this? A discovery is only as good as its use. What can we actually do with this idea? Suggesting that a growing number of us joined associations during the 2000s is interesting in its own right, as it is to understand the terrific power of association. But how can either change the way we see the world around us? For me, this is where it gets really interesting.

I believe these findings can lead to a fresh understanding of 'community'. They can also highlight the role of an ancient suspicion in a mass of recent government policies, strategies and initiatives. More than that, I think they give us a new and far more persuasive answer to the age-old question: what is the good life? In Part Three I want to explore what happens when we start to look at the world in a different way, if we think of it in light of what we know about the power of association and just how many of us are joining these small groups.

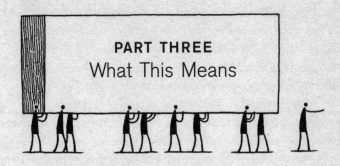

PART THREE
What This Means

14

The Community Agenda
How New Labour Came to See Community

When the Stranger says: 'What is the meaning of this city?
Do you huddle close together because you love each other?'
What will you answer? 'We all dwell together
To make money from each other'? or 'This is a community'?
And the Stranger will depart and return to the desert.

T. S. Eliot, *Choruses from The Rock*

Not long ago I went to a discussion at the Royal Society of Arts in London about community. It began with an excellent speech by Amitai Etzioni, an ageing sociologist who had once been Senior Advisor to the White House and was famous for having set up the Communitarian Network.

From the start Etzioni was magnetic and irreverent. He knew what he was talking about, he spoke with passion and he held his audience well. Towards the end of his speech Etzioni arrived at something of a full stop.

'We need a conversation about what is the good life,' he said, scanning the room.

Usually when I hear the words 'we need a conversation about . . .', I tend to switch off. Like a clinician saying, 'there is a need for more research', this can be an intelligent-sounding way of saying, 'I haven't a clue, and what's more, I won't be looking into this. But I think someone else should.'

This was different, and Etzioni had several answers lined up. He felt that 'for too long, we measured the good life by how much money we make and the goods we buy'. But as countless studies have shown, beyond a certain threshold it seems that buying more 'stuff' does not make us happier. Etzioni was not urging us to turn against this, to embrace frugality, he wanted us to address what it was that we should aspire to, as a society, once we have worked our way out of poverty.

He gave two answers. On the one hand, he suggested that the good life involved personal 'transcendental pursuits' such as listening to music, reading, prayer, reflection and other solitary activities. On the other, it was about 'community'. 'We find it richly rewarding', he said, 'when we have stable relationships with other people.'

Yet what exactly did he mean by 'community'? Here was a word that was rarely picked apart, and I, for one, was not sure which communities Etzioni had in mind.

Annoyingly, he did not go into this and instead made way for the other speaker that night, Liam Byrne MP, then Chief Secretary to the Treasury. Before us was a man in his political prime. Addressing the room in a polished, Blairite diction – all well-heeled vowels finessed by artful glottal stops and a smattering of 'y'knows' – Byrne described his vision of community in Britain. He told us about an initiative he had launched in his Birmingham constituency designed to improve 'social cohesion'. Byrne had begun by 'looking around my community for community leaders to come forward and begin leading a kind of community-led regeneration. [. . .] We didn't get very far,' he added. 'There weren't many people who had that kind of self-confidence to actually come forward and say, "Yes, y'know, I will help lead this community forward."' To begin with, members of this community were 'not actually coming out to begin the job of recreating a local commonwealth'.

This was interesting stuff. But what was the community Byrne referred to? I wasn't sure, so I sent an email to his office, where it was confirmed that the community their boss had described was made up of the 108,000 men, women and children living in the section of Birmingham described on some maps (not all) as Hodge Hill. This was also Byrne's electoral constituency.

The Meaning of Community

The question I want to ask is simple: was Byrne right to call his constituency a 'community'? That may sound like nit-picking, but it's important.

The word 'community' generally refers to one of two things: either it is a quality, or it describes an actual group. If a series of people club together to buy a book, you could say that they owned it *in community*. As someone who likes to sleep on my stomach – bad for you, I know – I am *in community* with anyone else in the world who sleeps like this. Preferring to sleep on our front is a quality that we share. But this does not mean that I and all of the world's stomach-sleepers can be usefully described as a community. That would be silly.

So what does it take for a group of individuals to become an actual community? There is no *ex cathedra* definition, but for reasons that will become clear, I think Aristotle's understanding of the ward is a good place to start. Aristotle wrote that each of us was a *zôon koinônikon*, a communal animal, and he gave examples of various communities in fifth-century BC Athens. These included religious associations, dining clubs and tribal groups; he went on to describe Athens as *koinônia teleios* – the ultimate product of community.

This tells us several things. First, a community is more than an abstract grouping of people who share a given quality. To belong to a community you must acknowledge both that the group exists and that you belong to it. Membership is self-determined, so it is not an identity that you can foist on an unsuspecting set of individuals.

Second, a community needs some kind of collective identity that distinguishes it from the rest of the world. This is where the New Zealand Tendency comes in. Just as we give our associations identities based on comparison and go out of our way to preserve these, so the members of a community will do the same. In a community you need an understanding of your past, and doubtless there will be stories that illustrate this and certain objects or landmarks that bring that shared history to life. There may be norms and traditions as well. All of these combine to give any community its own unique identity.

The third characteristic of the communities Aristotle described is a degree of self-government. It seems that communities make at least some decisions for themselves. Often this requires some kind of hierarchy or a set of rules. Again, this mirrors the associations we have been looking at.

Finally, the members of an Aristotelian community are able to come together. In other words, they experience the Beekeepers' Dance. Our understanding of this particular element of community has widened since Aristotle's time to include groups that do not actually gather as one – 'imagined communities', as Benedict Anderson called them in his book of the same name. An early example of an imagined community was that of the thousands of Christians scattered around the Mediterranean in the third century. Here was an imagined community whose members would not 'know most of their fellow-members, meet them, or even hear of them, yet in the minds of each lives the image of their communion'.

What made it possible to think of this group of co-religionists as an imagined community was that it met the other criteria of community – these Christians recognized that they belonged to the same group, there was a shared sense of identity and there were countless stories and traditions that set this group apart, as well as objects and landmarks. There was also an element of self-government.

So it is easy to see what a community is *not*. Take the stomach-sleepers of the world. I do not long for the day when all of us can congregate as one. Nor do we come together in real life. At least, I haven't been invited. We have no shared history, no self-determined identity that sets us apart, no objects or artefacts that have special meaning and no hint of self-government. So the stomach-sleepers of the world are not a community.

How about the community Byrne referred to? Amazingly, it fulfilled almost none of the criteria of community that we have just looked at. The 108,000 people living within the boundaries of Hodge Hill had not constructed for themselves a shared history that set them apart from the rest of Birmingham or the wider world. A resident of Hodge Hill would not grow up learning a series of traditions and stories that were unique to Hodge Hill. Nor was there a Hodge Hill way of doing things. You wouldn't hear anyone saying, 'oh, that's so Hodge Hill.' Or, 'what a typical Hodge Hiller!'

The boundaries of this so-called community had been decided not by the members of this group but by a centralized authority in response to population growth. The electoral constituency of Hodge Hill only came into existence in 1983. Finally, the residents of Hodge Hill did not meet up as one, and as far as we know the image of their communion was not alive in their minds either.

The only thing to suggest that these people were an actual community, in the original sense of the word, was that they enjoyed a degree of self-government. They elected their councillors and their representative in parliament – Liam Byrne, an outsider who felt at one point that his constituents lacked the self-confidence to lead themselves.

The group Byrne referred to was in fact an 'aggregate', a

series of individuals living in some kind of proximity to one another but who do not enjoy a shared, self-determined identity. It's hardly surprising that when Byrne launched his cohesion initiative there were no 'community leaders' willing to 'step up'. There was no community to lead! It was a phantom community. Drawing a line on a map does not a community make. It was regrettable on Byrne's part that he interpreted this reluctance as a collective lack of 'self-confidence'.

'Real communities are found in villages or estates rarely, if ever, conforming to administrative boundaries', as one body within the Gloucestershire County Council put it. In the eighteenth century it might have been accurate for a politician to refer to his constituency as a single community, but by the twenty-first century generally it was not. With very few exceptions, electoral boundaries no longer reflected those of actual communities.

What makes this frustrating is that within Hodge Hill at that time there were plenty of active, lively communities – communities with elected leaders, communities whose members communicated with each other regularly and constructively, cohesive communities. Byrne was unaware of them. It was like watching a man with his back to a taxi rank stuffed with taxis as he tries in vain to hail a passing cab, before finally settling for an unlicensed mini-cab.

I believe that some of the most dynamic and vibrant communities in Hodge Hill, as well as those neighbourhoods or estates that considered themselves to be communities, were its associations – the kinds of small voluntary groups we have looked at throughout this book. By these I mean the cricket teams, the football clubs, the organized community groups, residents' associations, book groups, walking groups, prayer groups and many, many others, from the Raven Bowling Club or the Friends of Project Kingfisher to the Bromford Bridge Members Club, the Bond Owners Club, the Bordesley Green Leisure Gardens Residents Association or the Ward End and Hodge Hill Local History Society. These were just some of the real communities in Hodge Hill at that moment.

Think of Laura's Book Group, the Thursday Club, the B. E. C., the Cardigan art protesters, F. C. United, the Farnley Estate Women's Institute. Based on an original understanding of the word, I would argue that each of these groups is a community in its own right. They certainly fulfil all the criteria. Their members recognize that they belong to these groups. They have a shared history – one that emerges in the stories they tell or the objects they keep – and this gives them a shared identity. They are self-governing, and most have their own hierarchies and rules. Finally, if they do not come together in person for a Beekeepers' Dance, then they are imagined communities and in the minds of their members is the image of their communion.

We saw in Part Two that during the first decade of the twenty-first century a growing number of Britons became involved in associations. One reason for this was that so many of us ceased to experience a sense of local community in our neighbourhoods. Traditional forms of community were on the wane.

If we recognize these associations, clubs and societies as communities in their own right, as I think we should, then we can begin to see what has happened to community in Britain. Having once been dominated by place and faith, the focus has broadened to include groups bound by a common interest or cause that are not rooted to one spot. Community is beginning to reflect the choices we make in life as much as our inheritances, such as where we live, our ethnicity or indeed our faith.

Of course, during the early twenty-first century there were still plenty of streets, neighbourhoods and estates that could be described as local communities in their own right. But increasingly these did not and could not inspire the same level of commitment, fellowship or identity that you might find within, say, a thriving book group, a five-a-side football team, a residents' association or a band of historical re-enactors.

We know why this is: the people living in the same neighbourhood rarely have a shared set of values or rules, there are far fewer excuses for them to bump into each other and they don't give as many gifts to one another as the members of an association would do. Then there is the issue of choice. You choose to become a part of a voluntary group, yet many of us do not choose exactly where we live, nor our faith.

Add to this the elevation of interest that occurred during the late twentieth and early twenty-first centuries, and you can begin to see what has happened. A growing number of Britons experienced community in voluntary associations as well as or instead of the neighbourhoods in which they lived or their local place of worship. It's worth repeating that 93 per cent of the respondents in my survey felt they knew the members of their associations better than their neighbours.

I think this marks one of the most significant shifts in British society during the early twenty-first century. It was nationwide, it involved millions of Britons and by 2010 it showed no signs of letting up. Yet for the most part we have been oblivious. The problem was that many of us continued to think of community in very narrow terms. We were happy to address phantom communities like that of Hodge Hill. But why was this? What stood in the way of a new understanding of community?

Communitybuilders

During the first decade of the twenty-first century the British government unleashed a landslide of legislation, strategies and initiatives aimed at promoting a very particular and limited vision of community. Although some of the communities they addressed were 'communities of interest', such as those bound by a shared experience of disability or refugee status or a minority ethnicity, most were 'communities of place'. They were administrative divisions to be found on maps such as electoral wards, villages, parishes, towns, boroughs or constituencies like Hodge Hill.

It began in earnest in 2002. The Home Secretary, David Blunkett, argued in no uncertain terms that 'the strongest defence of democracy resides in the engagement of every citizen with the community'. 'Communities' were to be afforded the kind of moral emphasis and protection that had once been aimed at the individual. This was new. 'Patriotism in its most decent, deeply expressed sense', Blunkett went on, was about 'a commitment to one's community, its values and institutions.'

The floodgates soon opened. From 2002 our streets began to be policed by Community Support Officers. There followed Community Justice Centres, in which 'the community' designed 'community sentences' for low-level offenders, such as cleaning the streets in bibs that read 'Community Payback'. In 2006 the Communities and Local Government Department came into existence, and with it a new Cabinet position: Secretary of State for Communities and Local Government. There were White Papers with titles such as *Strong and Prosperous Communities* or *Communities in Control: Real People, Real Power*. The new Communities Secretary launched initiatives including 'Confident Communities', 'Community Anchors' and a £70m fund to 'empower communities' called 'Communitybuilders'. Otherwise the Communities Secretary could be heard unveiling 'a ten-point action plan to promote cohesion and tackle community tensions' (set to cost £50 million), including national indicators on 'community cohesion' and 'a cohesion web-based "one-stop shop"' to help develop 'cohesion policies or respond to cohesion issues' and serve as 'a useful tool for "cohesion proofing" policies'.

There was the Community Empowerment agenda, the Community Engagement initiative and a new emphasis on Community Capacity Building. In 2008, at the cost of £2 billion, the government launched a programme called 'New Deal for Communities'. By this stage the sector known as 'Communities Development' was booming. In 2006 there were thought to be 20,000 community practitioners, ably assisted and represented by bodies such as Community Development XChange, the Community Development Foundation and the Federation for Community Development Learning. In 2005 the Department of Trade and Industry created Community Interest Companies (CICs) for social enterprises that provided a clear benefit for 'the community' or 'a community'.

Elsewhere the allocation of public resources acquired a new emphasis on 'community'. Whether you belonged to an independent arts body or a charity for stray dogs, it became funding suicide to submit an application that did not include the C-word. When historians come to look at the first decade of the twenty-first century, they will be struck by the pronounced surge in the number of community colleges, community schools, community stadiums, community gardens and even community cafés that appeared during this period. In 2002, the Charity Shield match that marks the start of the new football season was renamed Community Shield. Non-governmental initiatives such as Community Action for Energy, the Community Recycling Network or the Community Composting Network echoed this new sense that charity and governmental support should be directed at communities as much as individuals.

'Community' even made its way into the language of town planning. New public spaces were no longer there to look good, encourage trade and allow people to get about more easily. They should foster 'community interactions'. It was felt that the shape of these spaces could engineer a heightened sensation of 'community' among those passing through.

Like so much of the rhetoric and legislation inspired by community, this was based on a fuzzy understanding of what a community really was. 'Our desire for public space', as one expert later argued, and 'our desire for community [. . .] are only loosely connected, if at all.' Something strange was happening here. It seemed as though the government's community agenda was based more on an ideal than on a rigorous understanding of how community works or what it was.

In 2009 *Private Eye* began to have fun with this and launched a 'Communities' section, a compilation of some of the silliest uses of the word. One of the first offerings came from a police officer appealing 'to anyone in the community that has any information about this burglary to come forward and contact the police, including those from the criminal community'. Not only did the officer assume that the individuals living in a given neighbourhood must also constitute a community, he also imagined that being *in community* with a series of others means that you are an actual community.

But if the government's community agenda was inspired by an ideal, what was it, and why did they go to such lengths to promote it?

A Patchwork of Communities

Part of the impetus for this sudden emphasis on community lay in the events of 2001. During the summer of that year a series of riots broke out across the north of England. Each involved a confrontation between a minority Asian population and their white neighbours. Soon after, in September, the United States suffered a day of attacks by militants claiming Islam as their justification.

In the wake of this, it was thought that disaffected British Muslims, the kind of people who might have been involved in these riots, could become radicalized and launch similar attacks against the United Kingdom. The government wanted to engage these people in the political process, to make them feel that their voice was being heard and that they were having their say in the delivery of local services.

But how to go about this? Most of those potentially disaffected young men belonged to tightly knit geographic communities dominated by a single ethnicity. The government called them 'ethnic communities', and according to the Parekh Report of 2000 that focused on the future of multi-ethnic Britain, it was essential to maintain their autonomy and integrity. Therefore any attempt to engage these young men must be channelled through the ethnic community to which they appeared to belong.

In a quite different sense – and it was the confluence of the two that provided the push – there were those in the government who had become worried about what opinion polls, well-being surveys and tabloid headlines seemed to confirm: that in recent years there had been a woeful drop in neighbourliness, social trust and local community spirit in Britain. Although nobody could accuse the government of having done nothing to address this since they came to power in 1997, it had not been a top priority. From 2001 this changed and there was a new desire to do something about the perceived lack of neighbourliness.

Their answer was to try to engineer feelings of local community, not 'neighbourliness'. 'Neighbourliness' was a bit of a mouthful, and besides, 'community' sounded better. There was something wholesome about it, and from that moment the word 'neighbourhood' was replaced by 'community'.

The nostrum for what followed was simple: Britain was to be re-imagined as a vast patchwork of some 20,000 local communities (not neighbourhoods). Resources would then be poured into each of these 'communities' to bolster its identity and sense of cohesion.

In Whitehall this must have sounded great. The idea of community had become politically fashionable. It went hand-in-hand with other buzzy concepts such as social capital, social cohesion, stakeholding and the Third Way. Yet beneath this community agenda was an ideal that could hardly have been more archaic.

At the heart of the government's vision of community was the desire to engineer a stronger attachment to place. Byrne had said that he wanted his constituents 'to begin the job of recreating a local commonwealth', and in his choice of words you can begin to see the medieval and pre-industrial root of what was going on here. At a certain level, the idea was to engineer a society made up of village-like communities in which people knew their neighbours and experienced renewed local community spirit. Our streets were to become miniature versions of Ambridge in *The Archers*, only without the drama.

But why was this attachment to place so important? What was wrong with a community defined by an interest in caves or reading books? The answer to this takes us initially to the late nineteenth century and the work of the likes of Comte, Mill, Spencer, Hegel, Kropotkin, William Morris and in particular Ferdinand Tönnies. As these men articulated their various responses to the shock of urbanization, mass-industrialization, the nation-state and the supremacy of machines, each began to hark back to an earlier existence. In different ways they pined after the idea of a medieval village. It became something of an ideal. The pre-industrial European village seemed to be everything that their late nineteenth-century urban existence was not, and soon this romanticized historic idyll began to be associated with the word 'community'.

The clearest example of this was Tönnies's *Gemeinschaft und Gesellschaft* (Community and Society), published in 1887. Tönnies set out a polarity between Community and Society.

He saw Society as urban, mechanical and rational, a way of being that was defined by one's lack of connection to where you lived and a subservience to the state. Community, by contrast, was natural, local, organic and far more sociable. Community was about face-to-face relations and an authentic connection to what you produced. There was no division of labour, and in a Community you could influence the political direction of your social unit.

Community was essentially rural, and it was also pre-industrial. It was the medieval European village. 'All praise of rural life has pointed out that the *Gemeinschaft* [Community] among people is stronger there and more alive; it is the lasting and genuine form of living together', wrote Tönnies. This idealization of life in a medieval village should not matter to us, but for the fact that Tönnies's work became hugely influential during the twentieth century. Part of his legacy can be found in the meaning most of us attach to the word 'community' today. Although Aristotle thought a community could be a religious association or a dining club – groups that were not at all village-like in their attachment to place – for Tönnies a community had to be local. It should be rooted to one spot and permanent. To talk about a club as a community would have sounded like a mistake to him.

I am not trying to suggest that either meaning of 'community' is more correct in purely etymological terms. Words do not have fixed, absolute meanings. Instead I want to argue that one of these meanings was infinitely better suited to life in twenty-first-century Britain than the other.

There were three major problems with the idea of applying Tönnies's vision of community to British society in the early twenty-first-century. These problems really only become apparent in light of what we now know about associations.

First, Tönnies's vision was at odds with the social reality of most people in Britain. As we have seen, by 2010 it was no longer practical to think of people living in proximity to each other as perforce a community. A growing number of Britons were experiencing a sense of cohesion, trust and fellowship elsewhere. They were joining small voluntary groups based on their shared interests and concerns. Pouring billions of pounds into bolstering communities of place, many of which did not exist, was a waste of money – money that could have been usefully redirected towards failing local pubs and other associational Hubs.

The second problem with New Labour's community agenda was broader. It was based on a misunderstanding of how community works. You cannot engineer from above a sense of geographic community – unless, that is, you lie to the residents of a particular street and tell them that they are in danger of being wiped out by a meteor in the exact shape of their street. Then, perhaps, these people would feel a genuine sense of solidarity and cohesion. Otherwise, as David Willetts MP has pointed out, we must remember that 'politics [. . .] is not about pouring social cement over atomised citizens to stick them together so they co-operate'. If we experience a sense of local community, it is indigenous. If it is to be authentic and lasting it comes from within. Being told to feel a greater sense of community by a series of public sector employees is unlikely to have much effect. This is one of the most elementary principles in group psychology.

The third problem with New Labour's community agenda was altogether different: it was that in some places it might actually work. I don't mean that it would create cohesive communities where before there were none. But in those areas where there were real geographic communities already in existence, such as those ethnic communities that the government was keen to address, this community agenda might encourage the mentality of a medieval village. It turns out that the pre-industrial idyll once idealized by Tönnies and others was not quite as bucolic as they made out.

15

Witches and the Problem with Localism
The Reality of Life in a Closed Community

When the individual feels, the community reels.
Aldous Huxley, *Brave New World*

In my last book I described Krentoma, a man living in Nansepotiti, a village in the heart of the Amazon. It was surrounded on all sides by a stew of vegetation, a wealth of greens that spread for thousands of miles in all directions. Krentoma belonged to the Panará, a tribe of indigenous people that had had no formal contact with Western civilization until the 1970s.

At one point I explained that Krentoma had slit the throat of a fellow tribesman, although I did not go into the details. It did not seem relevant. Now it does. Not because of what it tells us about Krentoma, but what it tells us about the small community to which he belonged.

His victim was a fellow tribesman called Pôpôa, someone Krentoma had known all his life. By most accounts Pôpôa was an overweight man and would sweat profusely. He was a marginal figure among the Panará. But so was Krentoma. Here were two fringe characters, yet the difference between them was that Krentoma seemed to make people laugh. He was more of an amiable eccentric and was loved. Pôpôa was not. This may have been because of his size. Among the Panará obesity is seen not only as ugly but also an indication that you may have some involvement with witchcraft.

One day a tribesman claimed to have seen Pôpôa sneak off into the forest and pull jaguar spirits out of his anus – a sure sign of being a witch. This was shocking news, as you can imagine, yet Pôpôa was not confronted. Perhaps it was a one-off. However, not long after, Krentoma reported that he too had seen Pôpôa pull sinister animal spirits out of his bottom.

It was decided that Pôpôa must be a witch. A handful of villagers, including Krentoma, stole into Pôpôa's hut and strangled him. He did not die. It was at this point that Krentoma cut his throat. At his funeral, as one villager recalled, 'nobody cried for him, not even his widow.'

In some tribes of Brazilian indigenous people any incident of illness, disability or non-violent death is attributed to witchcraft. When a man or woman is dying of an unseen illness, the elders will crowd around them asking 'who did this to you?' If a villager is accused of being involved, they are in mortal danger. Often they will run away. Invariably the people accused of witchcraft are marginal characters like Pôpôa. They are the subversive figures, the fat ones, or those who are ugly, peculiar, handicapped or in any other way atypical. In other words, the members of these small, closed communities are suspicious of those who they consider to be the odd ones out. They will persecute them when things go wrong. They will banish them or have them killed.

This is not unique to the Amazon. All over the world and throughout history in societies that are small and closed there are instances of local communities ganging up to expel, murder or punish the black sheep, the newcomer or the outsider. It is more likely to happen if the group is in peril, as the French historian and philosopher René Girard describes in *The Scapegoat*, his analysis of why we do this, but even the slightest mishap can induce this kind of behaviour.

Just as it occurs in the Amazon today, this is what happened throughout Europe during the Middle Ages. It was then that thousands of men and women who were slightly unusual and did not fully conform to the norms of their communities were executed on suspicion of witchcraft. When Tönnies and so many other nineteenth-century writers lusted after the idea of life in a medieval village, they turned a blind eye to this.

Earlier I mentioned Amitai Etzioni, the sociologist who spoke about community at the Royal Society of Arts. Early in his speech Etzioni described life in the United States during the 1950s. 'Its norms were clear,' he said, 'crime was very low, drug abuse was very low, people didn't have to lock their homes or their cars, people knew what was expected of them, people took responsibility.' He paused for effect. 'And it was a God-awful society – because it discriminated against minorities, it discriminated against women, it discriminated against the handicapped, it discriminated against gay people. It was a very authoritarian society.'

There are telling similarities between life in an Amazonian tribe, a medieval European village and an American suburb during the 1950s. In each case you have a community that is small, closed and rooted to one spot. Generally speaking there are four things we can say about what happens to us when we end up in a society like this.

First, our attitude towards those who inhabit the margins of society will change ever so slightly. We become fractionally more suspicious of outsiders, and more worried by non-conformity. Steadily, we start to prefer things that do not threaten what we understand to be the norm, and when something goes wrong, we tend to direct our anger, or at least our suspicion, towards the margins of our group. We blame the outsider, the newcomer or the odd one out. In other words, we look for witches or scapegoats. That witch could be someone who is excessively fat and sweats too much like Pôpôa, just as it might be the new arrival, the eccentric or someone who is gay, handicapped or unusual in any way.

This is one of the things that can happen to us within small, closed communities. But we also begin to frown upon private space. Life becomes more public. Wandering off by yourself to be alone and indulge in solitary or transcendental pursuits becomes more suspect. After all, what have you got to hide? Why not do it in public? Remember that when Pôpôa got up to his 'witchcraft', he took himself away from the group and was alone in the forest.

Third, when grouped together in small communities that are anchored to one place, our perspective often becomes more authoritarian or patriarchal. We begin to see the world in a more conservative and masculine light. Traditions matter more. We defer to our male elders more readily.

Finally, belonging to a small, closed society like the one that Krentoma was a part of, or the medieval villages that once made up much of this country, invariably brings out a defensive attachment to where we live. We become territorial. One idea about the etymology of 'territory' is that it stems from *terrere*, meaning 'to frighten'. Originally a territory was the kind of place you were frightened away from. The political scientist Robert Pape has argued that most instances of modern-day terrorism can be traced not to religious extremism but some kind of territorialism. Whether in the heart of the Amazon, 1950s America or the medieval villages of Europe, belonging to a society like this allows us to forget the prehistoric spirit of nomadism. We become manacled to the land. The world beyond becomes sinister and a place to avoid. Within Pôpôa's tribe the word for 'stranger' was the same as 'enemy'. The first time they saw a white man they killed him.*

---

* This was Richard Mason, one of three Englishmen on the ill-fated Iriri River expedition of 1961. The other two were Kit Lambert, who went on to manage The Who, and John Hemming (my father), who later wrote a three-volume history of the Brazilian Amerindians and helped set up the charity Survival International.

The history of British society over the last three and a half centuries can be seen as a flight from the medieval village and many of the things it stood for. It has been driven by the idea of liberty. The quintessence of liberty in this country has been and remains freedom from social conformity. Successive generations of Britons have helped to fashion a society in which it has been possible to be a religious Nonconformist, a political rebel, a petitioner, a dandy, a hobbyist, a virtuoso, a misanthrope or an eccentric, just as you could be fat, thin, weird, colourful, gregarious, introverted, gay and in any other sense the odd one out. In many cases it was not only possible to stand out like this but actually celebrated, and over the last three centuries we have developed a strange and powerful affinity for people who inhabit the colourful margins of our society, the eccentrics.

Without this welcome shift away from the medieval notion of a village, the explosion of associational activity that began in the seventeenth century would not have happened. These groups flourished partly because Britons had become more mobile and were able to travel away from their neighbourhoods to spend an evening with those who shared a particular interest or concern.

The success of associations in Britain has been predicated on mobility and the idea of a short, playful escape from everyday life. This is anathema to the experience of a small, closed village in which you are anchored to your territory. Tönnies's vision of a medieval village was skewed. Of course, there were positive things to say about life in one of these communities, and he said them. There certainly was greater trust, individuals probably felt more grounded than they would do elsewhere and they had a stronger connection to what they made. If you wanted to live in a community that placed great emphasis on tradition and a more conservative outlook, where life was more public, then the medieval village was surely the place for you. But Tönnies ignored the more troubling aspects of life in one of these small closed communities. He did not describe our capacity to look for witches, nor the stifling reality of social conformity and the extent to which this was at odds with the modern notion of liberty.

Nevertheless it was essentially Tönnies's vision of a medieval village that underpinned New Labour's community agenda in the 2000s. So what was the effect of all this?

'Honour'

In many parts of Britain the community agenda fell on stony ground. The money was used to build more affordable homes, renovate playgrounds or smarten up derelict areas; it may have gone into public initiatives aimed at raising community awareness and cohesion. These are all perfectly commendable, but they simply did not induce a strong or lasting sense of community where before there was none.

Yet there were certain parts of Britain where the residents of a particular estate or neighbourhood could already be thought of as a community, a real community, and it was here that you could see the worrying implications of what happens when you apply the idea of a medieval village to twenty-first-century British society.

First, it was decided in Whitehall that these local communities should have chiefs, or 'community leaders'. You'll remember Byrne placing great emphasis on the need to find 'community leaders'. Yet within an ethnic community, for example, these unelected pontiffs were invariably 'male and from religious groups, but also from the business classes', as Women Against Fundamentalism and Southall Black Sisters fumed. 'Needless to say, such leaders have little or no interest in promoting social justice or women's equality.' Instead, 'most have vested interests in representing only the dominant and often orthodox versions of culture and religion.'

This echoes what we have seen elsewhere. If you treat a neighbourhood or estate as though it is a medieval village, then this is how people may start to behave. They become more authoritarian and patriarchal. Inadvertently, the government's vision of community clearly discriminated against women, younger people and non-conformists.

Re-imagining our neighbourhoods according to the ideal of a medieval village also denies some of our individuality. It encourages what Nobel prizewinner Amartya Sen once called 'plural monoculturalism'. A monoculture is a group of people thought of purely in terms of a single characteristic they share, such as their ethnicity, faith or social background. So to talk about an ethnic community is to see a series of individuals purely in terms of their ethnicity. Doing this, Sen has rightly argued, 'can be a good way of misunderstanding nearly everyone in the world'. In a monocultural world our inherited identities become more important than the choices we make in life – our intellectual or sporting interests, the careers we pursue, our education, tastes, friends, sexuality and politics. It is the very opposite of the elevation of interest that allows associations to flourish. The idea of 'ethnic communities' was rooted in this kind of monoculturalism.

Something else that happens if you apply a village-like vision of community to twenty-first-century Britain: we become more inclined to look for witches in our midst. In 2002 a sixteen-year-old girl called Heshu Yones was stabbed to death by her father in London. In 2006 Banaz Mahmod, a nineteen-year-old living in Surrey, was murdered by her family after falling in love with a man they did not approve of. In 2005 a twenty-five-year-old recruitment consultant called Samaira Nazir was summoned to her home, whereupon she was murdered as her family watched.

By 2009 there had been in Britain over the past decade what the *Evening Standard* called a 'massive rise in "honour" violence cases'. A quarter of these victims were under the age of eighteen. The figures were described as 'shocking'. A representative of the Iranian and Kurdish Women's Rights Organisation confirmed that this kind of violence was on the rise in Britain. The founder of a charity aimed at overcoming cultural and linguistic barriers in Britain added, 'I know from personal experience, and from working with victims, that such "honour" crimes are a huge social problem in this country.'

You might think that this is to do with religious sentiment. But these crimes had nothing at all to do with religion. There is certainly no passage in the Qur'an that condones 'honour killing' as we know it. I think that if we are to understand these 'honour' crimes, we must see them in terms of the small, closed communities in which they took place. These crimes were motivated not by religion but by a patriarchal and conservative desire to punish non-conformity. In a sociological sense there is very little to separate these 'honour' crimes from the murder of Pôpôa in the Amazon or the execution of witches in medieval Europe.

In 2002, after Nuziat Khan was murdered by her husband in yet another 'honour' killing, Khan's family explained that her husband acted like this to maintain his standing in the community. When Mohammed Merheban murdered his brother-in-law in the late 1990s, a member of Merheban's family claimed that, if he had not done this, he 'would not be allowed to live within that society', meaning the community to which he belonged.

As one police officer explained, when it comes to 'honour crimes', 'it's rare for [one person] to take unilateral action, it's all done in consultation and there is logistical support and collusion in the extended community'. What makes this even more worrying is the idea that we know about only a fraction of the murders, suicides, rapes, expulsions and other instances of unreported violence that have occurred within these tightly knit communities. In 2000 a Bradford police community officer reported that in one year he had received roughly 300 requests for help from survivors of this kind of abuse, and that this probably represented less than 1 per cent of the actual incidents.

Whether or not the government's decision to pour vast sums into promoting a village-like understanding of community played any part in this is hard to tell. Yet there is a clear correlation between the sense of local community they wanted to encourage and the kinds of communities that became more prone to orchestrating 'honour' crimes. As the Home Secretary, David Blunkett, put it in 2002, they wanted to build a society in which 'a commitment to one's community, its values and institutions' was paramount. I don't think the architects of this community agenda considered fully the implications of that.

None of this is to say that whenever we find ourselves rooted to one spot in a small community we immediately start looking for witches in our midst. Of course not. But our attitudes towards non-conformity, subversion and outsiders certainly begin to shift, at times imperceptibly. So this is not a problem confined to ethnic communities. There are plenty of examples of eccentric, disabled or atypical personalities living in tightly knit white neighbourhoods who have been bullied or abused and in some cases killed on account of being the odd ones out.

Think of Brent Martin, a young man with learning difficulties living on a small estate in Sunderland, who was targeted for years by a series of local youths. In 2007 he was murdered when two of them had a £5 bet on who could knock him out.

For ten years Fiona Pilkington and her daughter Francecca Hardwick, who had learning difficulties, were tormented by a series of local boys near their home in Barwell, Leicestershire. In 2007 Pilkington drove her car to a lay-by and set fire to it with both herself and her daughter inside.

David Raymond Atherton was an alcoholic with learning

difficulties living in Warrington. He too was targeted for years by local teenagers, who would pour bleach over him, cover his face with make-up and ink, burn his hair, urinate on him and vandalize his flat. In May 2006 they beat him until he died before dumping his body in the River Mersey.

Elsewhere there are tales of innocent men being hounded like witches, such as Steve Hoskin, in Cornwall, another man with learning difficulties. In 2006 Hoskin was accused by a series of local youths of being a paedophile. He was then tortured, drugged and led up to the Trenance viaduct in St Austell, where he fell to his death.

A similar thing happened to more than a dozen unrelated women who moved into new homes in various small, close-knit communities at around the time of the release of Maxine Carr, who was implicated in the Soham murders of two children in 2002. Each woman was mistaken for Carr. Although they looked almost nothing like her, each was subjected variously to months of abuse and violence. Bricks were thrown through their windows, they were taunted by mobs that kept them up all night. One of these women tried to kill herself. None of them had done anything to suggest that they were connected to these murders. What they shared was the fact that they were newcomers, and that in some cases they kept to themselves. As we know, this kind of behaviour can turn you into an object of suspicion in a small, closed community.

For those who were not victimized, the experience of living within a tightly knit local community was often one of feeling trapped. In *Estates*, a personal history of growing up on a council estate, Lynsey Hanley referred repeatedly to the 'wall in the head' that for many years kept her rooted to the area in which she grew up.

In *One Blood*, an account of contemporary British gangs, young men 'brutalized into territorialism' described a life in which they could not leave a particular postcode for fear of reprisals. A typical gang member 'sees only danger when he looks outside of his territory' and is excluded from a society predicated on mobility, experiencing instead 'a siege mentality'.

When the authors of another recent book, *The Spirit Level*, explained that 'among 21 developed market democracies, we found that Britain does worst on child wellbeing and badly on teenage births, imprisonment, drug abuse, trust, obesity, social mobility and mental illness', the areas in which these factors were most pronounced were those characterized by an extreme attachment to place and lack of spatial mobility.

Wherever you look, it seems that this singular vision of community, in which you must belong to the community of your neighbourhood or your estate, will often bring out the medieval villager within each of us. We become more suspicious of non-conformity and outsiders, we frown upon private space, we gravitate towards a more authoritarian and patriarchal take on the world, we become territorial and we look for witches in our midst.

Surely this is not a vision of community that any government should pour billions of pounds into promoting? I think there is another way of thinking about community in twenty-first-century Britain, one that embodies a confident rejection of life in a medieval village. At its heart is an understanding of how small groups actually work.

16

A New Ideal

The Future of Community

> In small groups, we are a clever species. In large groups,
> we are on a level roughly equivalent to that of pigeons.
> Or perhaps yeast.
>
> Elliott Bignell, online comment, *Guardian*

In 2002 I had my first white Christmas. I was in Sulaymaniyah, the capital of Kurdish Iraq. The invasion that would oust Saddam Hussein was about to begin, and the atmosphere in Sulaymaniyah was watchful and taut. Eyes met eyes a little faster than usual, and for most of Christmas Day it snowed. There were very few shadows. Pick-up trucks with machine-guns fixed to their beds rolled down the streets at a steady speed, looking like souped-up tumbrels, and there were snowmen on street corners. In shop windows you could make out pyramids of beer and cardboard Father Christmases propped up like scarecrows. The ice-cream had a peppery finish. The soldiers wore billowing, baggy trousers, and every day I spent in Sulaymaniyah a policeman, bodyguard or member of a local militia would accuse me of belonging to a group called Ansar Al-Islam.

This was the name given to a band of suicidal militants active to the north of Sulaymaniyah. As I soon found out, the combination of my slightly Mongoloid features and the beard I had grown in an attempt to fade into the background made me look as though I came from a central Asian state.

This was where the foot-soldiers of Ansar Al-Islam had grown up.

I remember finding out more about this group. It turned out that Ansar Al-Islam's chief objective was quite simple. They were killing themselves and others in order to recreate a particular community, that of seventh-century Medina around the time of the Prophet Muhammad. In other words, they wanted to construct a terrestrial paradise. A utopia.

What is so interesting about this utopia is that, like every other, it was to be a *place*. Where does this come from? Why is it that, when we dream of ideal communities, they are always rooted to one spot?

'Like a Gas'

Some 11,500 years ago the last Ice Age drew to a close. The humans that survived were genetically very similar to us, they were sociable primates who lived in groups that contained as many as 150 fellow humans, and they were nomadic. At some point during the millennia that followed, a strange and remarkable thing happened. Some of those bands of humans moving about over the earth began to settle.

The existence of a new wheat hybrid, improved domestication of various non-human animals and the development of specialized tools allowed a handful of human groups to farm and settle. They ceased to migrate with the seasons and instead built in close proximity to each other permanent structures from stone, thatch, mud and wood.

The size of these settlements expanded until these groups became larger than anything their ancestors had belonged to. They invented rules. They formalized their religious beliefs. Having once been mobile, some humans – by no means all – but some of these nomadic creatures chose to become sedentary.

This remains the defining shift of the last thirteen millennia of human history. It is the root of civilization. That the squiggles you are processing in your brain right now combine to form words that signify a succession of meanings is due, in part, to that momentous break with the past – the decision to be sedentary.

Many humans weren't interested. Perhaps they saw settlement as a waste of time, too much of a break with tradition, unnatural. We do not know. By their nature the sceptics left no trace other than their descendants: the Bedu, the Bakhtiari, the Bushmen of southern Africa, various Amazonian tribes, the Roma and the Sami reindeer herders, to name a few – people for whom sedentary life is a kind of death.

This tells us a little about where we come from, but it is also a reminder that many prehistoric communities chose not to settle down. This shift away from a nomadic existence was not universal and to begin with it was fraught with difficulties. Throughout the Old Testament you can see the strain of swapping one lifestyle for the other. Nomadism and motion become forms of divine punishment. They are portrayed as great hardships, the kinds of things you would not wish on your worst enemy. Wanderers are to be treated with suspicion. Cain's punishment for killing his brother is to 'be a fugitive and a wanderer on the earth', just as Grendel, the monstrous '*feond on belle*' in *Beowulf*, is the 'kin of Cain'. The 'wandering Jew' wanders in retribution for his supposed crime. Motion is a 'curse', a 'mark' and in every sense a burden.

This conflict between nomad and settled farmer has echoed down through the foothills of history, from the Old Testament to the guerrilla warfare of the last hundred years with Vietnamese, Iraqi and Afghan insurgents 'drifting about like a gas', as T. E. Lawrence put it, while their prey, the army of occupation, remains saddled to the land – lumbering and sclerotic.

It has meant that from the dawn of civilization we have created stories and mythologies that elevate our sedentary existence at the expense of a more peripatetic one. We have invented tales that justified the idea of settlement. It was our way of reassuring ourselves that being still was not so bad after all, that at least we weren't nomadic. To do this we traduced the idea of moving about, of wandering and not being fixed to one spot. We had to.

In short, as settled human beings we have developed and preserved a powerful and systematic bias against mobility. When we dream of utopias, the communities we imagine are settled, not because we are hard-wired to think like this but because the first settled humans set this up as an ideal. Our utopias are singular places – villages, gardens, cities, towns – not some*thing* but some*where*. Think of Plato's *Republic*, Milton's *Paradise Lost*, Bacon's *New Atlantis*, Harrington's *Oceana*, Babylon, the Garden of Eden, St Augustine's *City of God* or, as I found out in Sulaymaniyah, Medina in the seventh century.

Each was an expression of the same longing for a powerful attachment to place. They were born of the idea that mobility is a form of punishment and that a sedentary, static life in which you belong to a single community is the kind of paradise that we must aspire to. It is not. In twenty-first-century British society this bias against mobility has become out of date and is in need of revision. The medieval village is not an ideal that the government should be trying to roll out nationwide.

I think we need a new understanding of community, one that incorporates the reality of our mobility today as well as our social and intellectual desires. We need a vision of community that does not see geographic fluidity as a threat.

I want to propose a different kind of utopia – one that is both fluid and plural. Instead of a singular village like the one that Krentoma lived in, what about a society in which each of us can belong to an array of different groupings or communities? By 'community' I mean Aristotle's understanding of the word. One of these communities could be the community of your close family, your extended family, the community of people you work with, those who live around you or who go to the same church, mosque or synagogue as you – communities that now play a smaller part in many people's lives, but communities nonetheless – but they also include communities such as clubs, societies, teams, associations and other informal groups. Each of these is a community in its own right.

This embodies two major shifts. One is to do with the *number* of communities we belong to. The other is that very few of these groups are rooted to one spot. Yet this is more than a vision of how things could be. It is already happening in parts of Britain today. During the early twenty-first century, as we have seen, a growing number of Britons joined associations. For these people the experience of community became fractionally more plural, and it lost some of its emphasis on place. Belonging to a clutch of different communities is both an ideal and a reality; 89 per cent of the groups in my survey had members who belonged to at least one other association. One interviewee in a recent study of enthusiast groups said he belonged to ninety-eight different associations. This is a reminder – an extreme reminder, yes – that it is possible to belong to a great range of communities simultaneously. It no longer makes sense to think of community simply in terms of the people who live in your neighbourhood or those who share your faith. There is much more to it than that.

Community in Britain has not died, it has simply changed shape. Having once been public, religious and stationary, it has broadened to include groups that are private, voluntary and mobile. This is why it is now so much harder to spot and why we continue to talk about the death of community.

If you want to see community in twenty-first-century Britain, head to the back rooms of pubs, to community centres, village halls, living-rooms, Working Men's Clubs, bingo halls, sporting centres or out to our playing fields, our countryside and our parks. There is community spirit in a five-a-side football team that plays once a week after work, just as you can find this in a walking group, a charitable organization dedicated to rescuing stray cats, a group of trans-sexuals who meet in a club twice a week, a knitting circle, the residents of a cul-de-sac who organize a street party once a year or a prayer group that meets after church on Sundays. This vision of community does not exclude groups rooted to one spot; it merely includes those that are not and recognizes that we can belong to an array of them at the same time.

There are only really two things that stand in the way of this new ideal being embraced. The first is an outdated suspicion of private associations on account of the bonded social capital they encourage. The other obstacle is our attachment to the idea of life in a small, closed community – a village perhaps. As I have argued, living in one of these is rarely idyllic. The medieval village, no matter how cohesive it may sound from afar, how picturesque, cosy and non-industrial, is a false idol.

As the Health Education Authority Report urged in response to Robert Putnam's *Bowling Alone*, this deep-rooted yearning for a medieval version of community often blinds us to the social reality of the world in which we live. As Deborah Chambers explained, 'the report found little evidence in England of the atomised self-absorbed individualism identified by Putnam.' Instead, his idea of what community should be 'bore a greater resemblance to people's romanticised reconstructions of an idealised past than to people's accounts of the complex, fragmented and rapidly changing face of contemporary community life – characterised by high levels of mobility, instability and plurality'.

'What is the good life?' asked Etzioni. The good life is to belong to a society that is rich in community, in which we can join an array of groups that reflect our desires and aspirations, our past, present and future. If these communities don't exist, we can start them, because we have a capacity for membership and an understanding of how these groups work. We recognize the power of association. The good life embodies a confident rejection of life in a medieval village, and of monoculturalism. It sees mobility not as a threat but as an opportunity. The good life enshrines voluntarism and choice. Just as you choose to join a group, so you can choose to leave. The good life is a society in which it is possible to be eccentric, rebellious, misanthropic, unusual and in any other way the odd one out and have no fear of being stigmatized. The good life is to belong to a society in which you feel no pressure to join a particular group, in recognition of the fact that the groups that work are those we choose to join.

This is an answer to Etzioni's question that incorporates not just our recent historical past. It appeals as well to something more primeval.

17

The Men Who Hunt Elephants
Why Belonging to a Variety of Groups Comes Naturally

Our genes, unfortunately, are even stupider than we are.
Louis Menand in *The New Yorker*

Imagine a plain. Framed on one side by a lip of mountain, it unfurls to the horizon opposite. The light here is cloudless and bright, the ground brushed with scrub, grass, crumbling rock. In the middle distance you can make out a small group of upright creatures, not too tall, their hair matted down hard over their heads. They are spaced out in a shallow U and, as you watch, they jog forward in unison as though part of a web drawn towards an invisible point. Each is hunched a little forward. You follow the line of their gaze until you spot an elephant less than a mile away. In its proportions and the way its trunk threads in and out of the nearest tree it looks young. In spite of this, it is on its own.

There is a shout. This multiplies into a lovely rolling thunderclap of barking sounds that the she-elephant – we'll call it a she – hears. She looks towards it. Having seen the line of fifteen two-legged animals advancing towards her, she pulls away from the tree and in a blur of indecision trots at right-angles to the danger. There is fire in that direction. Broad and golden, it is strung out across the horizon like a range of dwarf hills. She has never seen anything like this, and yet, using a combination of perception, the ability to anticipate and imagine and her innate elephantine instinct, she reacts to it. She tacks away from the men and the fire. There is only one path she can take. Now she is moving towards safety. Now she is in a grassy declivity. Now she is moving down a narrow path, and on either side of her the banks become thick. The sound travels differently in here. *Poom-poom-poom-poom* go her feet as she thuds on towards safety.

The air cools and, as the shouts of the men become distant, the memory of what has just happened begins to form in her mind. Relief shudders through her as she slows down. At this point the ground gives way. *Thud, crack-crack, thud, tear.* She is in a freshly dug pit. The bone beneath the joint in her front right leg has snapped in two. There are fractures in both hind legs, some of the lower muscles in her neck are badly bruised, but much, much more worrying is the stake of wood that has slashed into her side. She has fallen into a trap. Of the five other sharpened wooden spikes only one did not shatter on impact, but it is enough.

The elephant is losing blood. The earth drinks its fill before a puddle starts to form. With no movement around her, the air is still but for the sound of liquid decanting into liquid. She tries to call out but cannot summon the breath to her lungs.

The blood continues to seep out of her like sewage from a plant, and now the soupy pool of it scums over with specks of earth and insects. Flies start to hurry about her wounds, until the smell of soil and blood blends with a different scent, that of lacerated flesh as it enters the initial stages of decomposition.

The men arrive. Soon after, the elephant is dead.

Fission–Fusion

At this point I should come clean. We do not know that this actually happened. There were no eyewitness accounts or scraps of CCTV footage. None of these men set down their story for posterity. Yet by combining the available evidence regarding the tools, society and communicative ability of humans alive some 70,000 years ago in the heart of Africa, we know that it *could* have occurred around this time, and that there were other groups in this part of the world behaving in a similar manner.

The reason why the idea of this elephant hunt matters to us is simple. It tells us something crucial about what it is to belong to an array of groups at the same time. It suggests that this kind of behaviour may come naturally to us.

You see, there are two things about this pack of elephant hunters that really stand out. First, their weapons were not at all sophisticated. They had neither barbed spears nor bows and arrows. Instead their most powerful weapon was the ability to communicate and work collaboratively as a group. They could make decisions and stick to them, they looked out for one another and shared information in order to achieve a shared goal. This was prehistory's answer to the laser-guided missile.

The other thing that stands out about this group is the fact that they were all men. Clearly this was not an independent group in its own right. Instead of being a complete tribe, the small group of men we imagined hunting a young elephant was in fact a sub-group that had broken away from a larger parent group containing as many as 150 people. They broke away with the intention of returning once their hunt had finished. While they were away from the main group, another sub-group might hive off on its own hunting trip. This too could last anything between a few hours and a few days. Then another group sets out, and so on. Over the years the group would migrate, for they are not rooted to one spot. They meander over and through the landscape, with sub-groups forever breaking away and returning, breaking away, returning.

We have a name for this. It is what's known as a 'fission–fusion' society. Humans are some of the only animals known to behave like this. The 'fission' part of the term relates to the act of breaking away from the parent group, while 'fusion' describes the return. A fission–fusion society is essentially an associational society. Those smaller units that break away from the main group are club-like. Belonging to one does not enforce a permanent break from the rest of the group, and at the same time each sub-group has a momentum and character of its own, with norms or rules that make it unique.

Fission–fusion societies are fluid and plural, and as a result their members have a much less rigid and defensive attachment to place. They are less territorial than those that stick together as a single unit and do not allow club-like sub-groups to hive off.

Most advanced hunter–gatherer societies functioned as fission–fusion societies. Even today, the !Kung San tribe in the Kalahari operate like this, with sub-groups containing as many as forty individuals breaking away from a parent group of about 150 tribesmen and women before returning later on.

Heredity

This matters in terms of our genetic heredity. Just as physical or anatomical traits that improve the fitness of successive human groups are often passed on by means of natural selection, so are behavioural inclinations. If fission–fusion was a consistently successful strategy, then there is a good chance that this is one of many behavioural traits that we have inherited.

One advantage of living like this is that the cost of group living is greatly reduced. Going after an elephant as an élite team of hunters rather than a massed tribe allows you to move faster. The feedback loop within your group becomes smaller, so you can adapt more easily to changing circumstances. Fission–fusion improves the group's overall ability to find food, as you could have several hunting parties on the go at the same time and these are more efficient, owing to their size. Meanwhile, those who are left behind with the main group can get on with their own tasks. Even if they cannot think what to do, then at least they expend less energy and require fewer calories to keep them going. Again, the overall cost of group living is reduced.

Fission–fusion societies can therefore adapt to a much wider range of environments. This makes them lighter on their feet. They can move away from the threat of conflict, drought, disease or flooding. Fission–fusion also allows the size of these groups to increase. A very similar thing happens among chimpanzees in Africa, who 'would be unable to live in any habitats where they currently occur' without functioning as fission–fusion societies. A community of chimpanzees that allows small groups to break away from time to time may contain as many as 130 members. Chimpanzees that stick together in single defensive units will rarely sustain more than twenty or thirty animals per group.

You would think that there is a catch to this. If a fission–fusion society is so beneficial, then why do more animals not behave like this? The only animals known to go in for fission–fusion are spotted hyenas, elephants, lions, bottlenose dolphins, humans and fellow primates such as spider monkeys, chimpanzees and gelada and hamadryas baboons.

The reason you are unlikely to see a 'club' of wildebeest wandering off from the main herd for a day's grazing, and why smaller-bodied primates generally stick together as one, is a fear of predation. Animals adopt a fission–fusion approach to life when they are at or near the top of their food chain. They behave like this because they *can*.

Since fission–fusion is a highly successful strategy, there is a good chance that this is a behavioural inclination that has been passed on within our species. That's not to say that anyone joins an association because their genes tell them to.

'It would be nice if we could justify our choices by pointing silently to our genes,' as the American cultural historian Louis Menand memorably explained. 'But we can't. Our genes, unfortunately, are even stupider than we are.' But that is not to say that we are 'blank slates'. Our behaviour and anatomy are a result of both our environment and our heredity. The key to understanding this heredity lies in our existence as sub-Saharan hunter–gatherers. Most of our anatomical traits and behavioural inclinations 'evolved in response to conditions that no longer exist', as the physical anthropologists Sherwood Washburn and Robert Harding put it. 'The human body and human nature are products of a succession of different ways of life, resulting in a peculiar, specialized kind of creature with great abilities and surprising limitations.'

One of those great abilities is the possibility of belonging to a variety of groups at the same time. For our prehistoric ancestors, human sociality was 'a peculiar balance of stability and fluidity, sociability and solitude'. One moment you could be within a tightly knit group of elephant hunters, the next you could be with your family, your children, another group, perhaps the band came together as one, or you could be alone. Your experience of society was fluid, and it was plural, as it became once again for a growing number of Britons in the early twenty-first century.

18

Case Study
Deerhurst

If men are to remain civilised or to become civilised, the
art of association must develop and improve among them
at the same speed as equality of conditions spreads.
Alexis de Tocqueville, *Democracy in America*

Andrew Leeke lives in the village of Deerhurst, less than
a mile from a powerful river. He is a middle-aged man of
average height and build, and has worked as a solicitor for
most of his life. Leeke is warm and outdoorsy, with a
lawyerly mind. He can't help it, he says, it's his job. For
more than two decades Leeke and his family have lived in
a Georgian building near the edge of Deerhurst. The other
twenty dwellings in this settlement form one or two neighbouring clusters set out over narrow lanes. Some of the
buildings are made from treacly Cotswold stone, others are
brick or timber-framed; there are two farms, an ancient
church and a Saxon chapel near the spot where King Cnut
and Edmond Ironside once divided England between them.
Beyond, dairy herds fill the fields, and just visible on the
horizon are the etiolated silhouettes of ageing oaks. Just out
of sight is the River Severn, silent and busy as it bullies on
towards the sea.

So what takes us to Deerhurst? I want to use this village
as a case study to illustrate what I mean by a new understanding of community, one that is more fluid and plural

than what we have become accustomed to. Part of the reason I've chosen Deerhurst is that, from a distance, it looks and sounds like a classic English village, the kind of settlement in which you'd expect to find a strong attachment to place and a very traditional understanding of community spirit. The reality is quite different.

By early 2007, while most residents knew the *name* of the other families in the village and could probably put a face to most of those names, there were some faces that would escape them. Any two residents of Deerhurst could go for weeks, perhaps months, without necessarily seeing one another.

This was not because they were at all mean-spirited or didn't get on. Their lifestyles simply did not require them to cross each other's paths on a daily basis. Only about a third of Deerhurst's population had lived there all their lives, and almost everyone in the village had access to a car. A small proportion divided their time between Deerhurst and another home in a nearby part of the country or further afield.

You could say a similar thing about countless streets, neighbourhoods and villages throughout twenty-first-century Britain. This is not unusual. As we have seen already, the combination of technological advance, changing patterns of employment, the fact that we move house more often and our dramatically increased spatial mobility has changed the way we connect with our neighbours.

In Deerhurst by the start of 2007 there were few occasions when the village met as one. Every two years the Deerhurst Flower Festival brought the village together, and there was always church on Christmas Day and Easter Sunday – although neither was guaranteed to get a full turnout. Otherwise there were no festivals or celebrations etched into the collective Deerhurst calendar.

The Deerhurst residents' experience of community had

become much more plural and less concerned with an attachment to place. A typical Deerhurster belonged to an array of communities. As well as being part of the village itself, they belonged to communities based on their families and the people they worked with. They might experience community in the local WI, the Parents', Teachers' and Friends' Association for the nearby school, Apperley Cricket Club, the parish council or the voluntary community drivers' scheme. There was a church flower rota for those who took it in turns to do the flowers in church on Sundays. Some might ride with the local hunt, attend a book group or a knitting circle, or do yoga and Pilates in nearby Apperley Village Hall or take part in local charities, walking groups, sailing clubs and any number of other associations, each one a community in its own right.

The same thing was happening all over the country. Take this email from a participant in my survey:

> Sir,
> I have filled in your questionnaire for the club I am involved with, but if our village is anything to go by you will only get a glimpse of how many clubs are about.
> In our village we have the following clubs: swimming, pigeon fliers, scooter, dramatics, operatics, allotment, brass band, football, cricket, rugby league, crown green bowls, British Legion club, sports club (footy, rugby, cricket) our own W.M.C. [Working Men's Club] with its interest sections.

For each resident of Deerhurst, the village itself was just one of many communities they might belong to. Yet by June 2007 this particular community – the community of Deerhurst itself – was unlikely to have been at the forefront of many villagers' minds. There was no real cause to bind them together. Yes, they lived in Deerhurst, but when one of them saw a fellow Deerhurster there was not necessarily an immediate surge of bonhomie or solidarity based on the fact that they lived in the same village.

That was about to change.

The Flood

In mid-July 2007 a meteorological depression settled over the Severn Vale. There followed a downpour of tropical intensity. A gigantic sponge of cloud that hung over Worcestershire, Gloucestershire and Warwickshire was wrung dry, and as the ground near the headwaters of the Severn and the Avon became saturated, the river broke its banks downstream near Deerhurst.

'Of course this kind of thing had happened before,' Leeke began. 'We had flood defences that had held out since 1947, so you couldn't say it was unexpected. You don't move to Deerhurst without knowing about the floods.'

Since then a new pumping station had been installed in the village, so nobody in Deerhurst was unduly worried when water began to creep up against the wall of earthen mounds that had kept them dry for the last sixty years. But on Sunday 22 July a fresh surge of water sloshed down the valley. Water began to slip over or around some of Deerhurst's defences, and the villagers embarked on a series of running battles in what some would later call 'Operation Cnut'.

'Some of us shovelled earth. A local builder added a stankboard to increase the height of a floodgate. One of the farmers got his hands on a JCB digger and started to move earth that way. Everyone threw themselves at it as best they could. But the water kept rising.'

More drastic measures were taken. Small trees were uprooted and holes dug into the earth like open wounds to feed more material on to the defences and make them taller.

'Towards the middle of the afternoon we thought we'd

managed it,' he went on. 'And it's amazing what you can get done in a short space of time with a few diggers.'

It was not to last. At around five o'clock that afternoon one of the farmers could be heard telling families to move their possessions to the upper floors. This was ominous. Farmers tend to be right about these sorts of thing.

'Not long after there was a further surge, and the water simply overtopped and came around the side of the existing defence. The village was inundated.' Of Deerhurst's twenty-one homes, eighteen now contained up to five feet of water. It would cost more than £2 million to repair what happened on that one afternoon.

The Response

'Never again', they muttered – to themselves, to their husbands, their wives, children, friends or anyone who cared to ask, including their neighbours. The sense of community among the villagers of Deerhurst was inflamed. There was an immediate and binding sense of solidarity between these people. They were fellow survivors, and in the days that followed there was a sense of togetherness in Deerhurst that had not been felt in years.

As the German social psychologist Kurt Lewin wrote in 1947, the year that Deerhurst was last flooded, recognizing a common fate pulls us together. We also know that this is one of the foundations on which associations can be built. Deerhurst was no exception.

Several weeks after the flood the villagers came together for a meeting – as we know, a rare event in Deerhurst. It was here that Leeke distributed a precise two-page document giving his analysis of the situation.

'Deerhurst is a collection of houses with a common enemy and a communal problem', he explained. As a small village,

Deerhurst was unlikely to be near the top of any government list of villages and neighbourhoods to assist, so they should not sit idly by and wait for the relevant arm of the state to come to their aid. Leeke argued that the best solution was to form an association that would 'reflect the views and aspirations of everyone concerned' and through this work to secure the village's flood defences.

Being a lawyer, he knew very well that as an unincorporated association this body would have no legal personality. This could leave the villagers liable at a later date. As the membership of the group was to be restricted to Deerhursters and the group's possessions would be owned in community, Leeke proposed a company limited by guarantee. There was a vote. The village agreed, and Leeke was nominated Chairman of Deerhurst Community Preservation (DCP).*

Ten days after that first meeting the DCP walked the defences to work out where the barrier should be raised and by how much. But it was a much smaller group that turned up that day. This is more important than it may sound. It gives us a valuable insight into what really happens when a neighbourhood or village comes together to get something done.

Although you may read about a local community uniting to oppose a nearby wind farm or the construction of a new supermarket, invariably you'll find that most of the work is done by a tightly knit cluster of residents bound together as an association. Usually the people who get involved like this are the ones who feel most passionately about the matter, those with more time to spare or, crucially, those with the necessary skills. It is very similar to an elite band of prehistoric hunters going after that elephant.

'Although the DCP had the mandate of the entire village, there was very much a central core of us that did most of

* For more on the different ways an association can reduce its liability, and why, see Appendix A.

the work,' Leeke told me. 'It became clear during that walk and over the next few weeks who those people were. I suppose the three people who felt most strongly were myself, Brian Leeke [no relation] and a young civil engineer named Brad Checkley. Between us we seemed to know how to do this sort of thing. I'm a lawyer so am used to the legal side of it. Brian Leeke has done all sorts of things with his life and has huge energy, even though he's seventy. He and the civil engineer really understood flood-banks. Then we had Will Morris, who was the go-between with the farmers, whose land the defences were on and who were most affected by it. I don't think we could have done it without him. John Rutter as the Treasurer completed the committee.'

Over the months that followed this nucleus of Deerhursters threw themselves into the task of securing the village against future floods. The first step was to contact the relevant government agencies and officials. The initial response was positive, but over the next few months nothing much happened. The task was lengthier and more complicated than had originally been thought.

Over the next three years the group continued to plug away at their objective. They negotiated a Herculean set of bureaucratic obstacles, enduring countless meetings, telephone conversations and emails to, from and with, variously, the Environment Agency, who answered to the Regional Flood Defence Committee, the developers who might pay to tip their earth on to the flood defences, the two farmers on whose land most of the defences were, the archaeologists from English Heritage as well as those from the Gloucestershire County Council (each with different remits), the Church, HM Revenue and Customs, and the Gloucestershire Wildlife Trust, whose main concern was the nearby colony of greater crested newts. Deerhurst happens to be a stronghold for these little amphibians, and the Wildlife Trust did not want to see any of them harmed during the shoring up of the village's defences.

By 2010, three years after the flood, the banks had been raised to a consistent height; taller and stronger floodgates now stood sentinel at the different entrances to the village, and new pumps had been installed. This virtually ruled out the possibility of Deerhurst being flooded again. Better still, none of the villagers had to pay a penny. All the money came from outside. Oh, and in case you were wondering, at a cost of £30,000 no newts were harmed.

Communities, Plural

In the story of Deerhurst before, during and after the great flood of 2007 there is a taste of almost everything we need to know about community in twenty-first-century Britain as well as the power of association. It is a reminder that the strength of feeling within any community will undulate with time. There will be moments when a group of people do not feel terribly close to each other, but a single event can change this and suddenly the sense of community is overwhelming. Moreover that transformation is unlikely to be triggered by a government initiative or corporate scheme. It must come from within.

What this also demonstrates is the peculiar power of association. If the feeling of togetherness within a neighbourhood or village can fade with time, it will do the opposite in an association. It grows steadily. By working together in the DCP, that nucleus of Deerhursters built on the sense of solidarity they felt in the weeks following the flood.

Yet among those villagers who were not part of the DCP inner core, the feeling of community gradually thinned in the years after the flood. Although they were certainly closer in 2010 than they had been before the village was inundated – three years on they were clubbing together to buy fuel at a discounted price and exchanging group emails about recommended chimney sweeps or suppliers of logs – the feeling was nothing like what it was at the heart of the DCP, among the Deerhursters who had battled to get the defences built.

We know exactly why this is. By coming together as an association and applying to this loose feeling of solidarity some kind of structure, you place it in aspic. In time, you become bound by the Power of Giving. With this comes a feeling of fellowship.

The story of the DCP is also a reminder that coming together as an association allows us to plug away at something indefinitely. What this group achieved during those three years, at no cost to themselves or the village, is a great illustration of what can be done when people come together as a room-sized association of volunteers with a shared objective. The Hothouse Effect explains how they were able to take their cause further than they might have done individually. They battled harder and they formed much stronger ties to each other along the way.

Another reason why Deerhurst gives us such a good snapshot of community in early twenty-first-century Britain is that these villagers belonged to a range of communities, from the village itself through to the many different associations and informal groups dotted around the area. Their experience of community was plural, and it was about much more than place.

What is the good life? One in which you can live in a small village like Deerhurst and belong to an array of communities. On the other hand, you might opt out and become a recluse. But you do so without the fear of discrimination. The good life is one in which we recognize the power of association, and that when a room-sized group of people come together of their own volition and agree to work towards a specific end, they can achieve remarkable things.

Conclusion

Man is said to be a Sociable Animal.

Joseph Addison, *Spectator*

During the early twenty-first century there appears to have been a nationwide surge of associational activity in Britain. This been the basic message of *Together*. It has meant that a growing number of Britons experienced a sense of community in small voluntary groups as well as or instead of their neighbourhoods or parish churches. The government has been slow to recognize this and instead has poured vast sums into promoting an archaic vision of community that places undue emphasis on where you live.

Society is changing shape. Community is becoming more plural and is less concerned with place. But is this a Good Thing? Should we be celebrating the fact that many more of us are joining associations and that the typical experience of community seems to be gravitating towards these small, mobile groups? I think so. Here are eight reasons why.

Physical and Mental Health

Belonging to one of these associations can improve your health. According to John Cacioppo, the healthy connection we experience within an association can slow the pace of our physical and mental decline. For the political scientist Paul Haezewindt, those of us 'who are more socially connected and have more social support, live longer, recover quicker from illness, suffer less from mental health problems, and engage less in behaviours damaging to health such as smoking'. Robert Putnam has argued that 'as a rough rule of thumb, if you belong to no groups but decide to join one, you cut your risk of dying over the next year *in half*. If you smoke and belong to no groups, it's a toss-up statistically whether you should stop smoking or start joining.'

Cacioppo also argues that belonging to an association improves your psychological equilibrium. He bases this on the idea that we connect with others on three different levels – the connection is either intimate or relational or collective. The intimate connections we have are usually with our children or our partners: yet many of us will form what D. H. Lawrence called an *égoisme à deux* and leave it at that. Our collective connections may be with co-religionists, fellow nationals or perhaps those who support the same internationally renowned football team. The 'relational' connections are with people who belong to the same association or community.

For Cacioppo, these three types of psychological connection are like the legs of a stool. Knock out one, and the whole thing will collapse. Belonging to an association feeds our need for a relational connection and can improve the psychological balance in our lives.

Fellowship and Social Satisfaction

The last question I asked in my survey was about the ways in which participants felt they benefited from belonging to their association. One of the themes that emerged clearly from the responses was the idea that these groups provided social satisfaction.

A member of the 32nd Regiment of Foot Cornwall Re-enacting Group praised the 'comradeship' and 'team spirit' in his group. A member of the Waltham Forest Hockey Club thought that 'keeping fit with humans is much more fun than with machines', adding that 'there is a wonderful camaraderie about being part of a team.'

Here we can see the Power of Giving working its magic. Within any group whose members help each other out over an extended period – whether it involves putting someone up for the night, exchanging passes as a hockey team, working together to put on a display or singing together – a feeling of camaraderie will eventually appear.

The benefits of that fellowship are impossible to measure. Perhaps it is best to leave it in the simplest terms – camaraderie feels good. Let's not over-complicate this. As one member of the Sussex Chorus explained, 'most people, at the end of a rehearsal, go away feeling happier than they did earlier in the evening.' A historian in North Cheshire Family History Society, in answer to my question about the benefit of belonging to their group, wrote simply: 'social satisfaction'.

Social satisfaction is a tonic to what Oliver James has called the 'affluenza virus', a mentality that can, at its worst, impel you to connect with the world around you only when convention or your career demands it. So 'you miss out on the large satisfaction to be gained from supporting others and feeling supported.' This is where associations come into their own. They give you the chance to support others. They offer a different way of being that is inherently less selfish.

A More Stable Relationship

Associations allow you to experience a different kind of relationship, one that can be more stable and secure than many of the friendships in your life. As Laura Wilkie said, 'even someone like my best friend I don't really see more than once every few months. She's always travelling, busy managing a company. I'm busy as well. But with the book group it's different. You know that you will see these people once a month, no matter what.'

Another member of the group, Jon, said something very similar: 'As you get older, you tend to move out of town, out of the city, and it's no longer possible to meet up in town and have a drink after work in the way that you might have done in your twenties. All our friends have slowly gravitated away from the centre, they have kids. The book group changes all that. It's a great way of keeping up without having to arrange anything. It takes away the pressure.'

Your relationship with someone who belongs to the same association will often have a degree of built-in permanence. This makes it less pressured than many friendships. With time these bonds can become some of the most important in your life. As one member of the Baldock and District Canoe Club put it, 'now my closest friends all come from the club.'

Making Your Money Go Further

Joining an association allows you to save money as well, and what little money you spend may go further. Take the Mendip Caving Group, whose members 'banded together to share resources such as ladders, ropes, a caving library and accommodation on Mendip. Members have use of the Group's cottage at reduced rates, free use of Group equipment and free access to the library. They also receive *MCG News* – the newsletter of the MCG and Occasional Publications.'

The point here is simple: associations provide an economy of scale. They are geared towards people doing favours for each other and as such they are money-saving vehicles. As Jeff Bishop and Paul Hoggett explained, 'if we were to attempt to calculate the economic value of the immense amount of time, materials, resources and simple cash which goes into communal leisure, the figures would be astonishing.'

We also know that whatever money you spend is bound to go further, in the sense that you will glean more pleasure from your purchases if they can be shared within an interpretive community.

Individualism, Consumerism and Infinite Choice

Belonging to an association also relaxes some of the emphasis we might otherwise feel on ourselves. It provides a moment apart from the pounding individualism and consumerism of mainstream British society. We can step back from the altar of infinite choice. Joining an association is a definite choice in a society that can place more emphasis on having an array of options rather than taking one and following through on it. As Tobias Jones wrote in *Utopian Dreams*, the lustre of infinite choice 'means we have less and less in common. It means we mourn what we haven't chosen rather than enjoy what we have. It means we can never feel at home because we have no notion of what the right choice might look like.'

Facing a choice is quite different from making one. The latter involves some kind of commitment, and that doesn't always sit so well within a consumerist society. As Andrew Welch of British Naturism explained: 'Back in the 1960s our members would come back from work, see that nothing's on television and then pop out to the local Naturist Club. But nowadays there are so many more things to do that a lot of people don't get round to it. Many people are happy to use one of our beaches, but they don't like the idea of signing up. They don't like the commitment to one thing. The words "Treasury Officer", "Annual General Meeting", or "Minutes of the Meeting" tend to scare off younger people because of that fear of commitment.'

Joining a group is indeed a small commitment. It is a choice that involves fractionally more courage than buying a new shirt or choosing a sofa, and in this sense becoming involved in an association is a small step away from consumerism. It is a taste of a more sociable, collective and definite way of living.

A Sense of Belonging

Belonging to an association can also add another layer to your identity. This has particular resonance today. Many of the more traditional identities that once defined our society were gently eroded over the course of the twentieth century. A typical Victorian man might have felt a strong sense of identity based on his race, where he lived, his religion, where he worked and his nationality.

For many Britons in the twenty-first century this quintet did not provide anything like the same sense of belonging. Our age has been described as materialist, but it is also one in which we long to belong. Joining an association satisfies some of that need. As we saw with the New Zealand Tendency, associations are very good at providing a sense of identity.

As one member of the Berkshire Family History Society explained, simply: 'I am a long-standing member [. . .] and [have] been Branch Chairman, Society Chairman and held many other positions. I feel involved.' For a member of the Hood Bikers, the benefit of belonging to this biking fraternity was 'knowing the support of the brothers is there' and the 'single identity' that goes with that.

Escape and Play

Not only do associations provide an extra layer of identity; they are also an excuse to escape. These groups are play-communities. Going to the meeting of an association that has its own rules and offices is not too different from playing at doctors and nurses. It is an adult form of play, which is why it can feel like going on a mini-mini-mini-break. These associations take us away from the monotony of daily life, leaving us refreshed and recreated. Without play we forget what it is to see through the eyes of a child, and we shrivel up like raisins in the sun.

Stephen Lord, of the American Civil War Society, said that what he liked about his society was that it allowed him 'to get away from work, the telephone, the modern lifestyle and go back to a simpler, stress free and slower lifestyle (I am a driving instructor).' For another member of the same society, belonging to this group 'enriched my life, [I] met my wife through the group and raised a family all of whom have participated, [and] escaped from stresses of modern life.'

Utility

'It makes me get things done,' explained one member of the Dulwich Quilters when asked what she liked about her group. Here we have the most obvious benefit of belonging to any association. It barely needs any explanation. Combine the Power of Giving and the Hothouse Effect, and you will probably get more done as a group over an extended period than you might as an individual. In an association you can take your interests further, learn more, campaign harder and for longer, and as a charity you can help more people.

The Good Life

These are the reasons why we should celebrate the fact that
so many more of us are joining associations. I want to return
now to Etzioni's question about the good life. For much of
the twentieth century the answer involved religion or ideology,
or it was about money in one way or another. Often it was to
do with the accumulation of wealth or it was some kind of
rejection of this, a desire to live more simply.

In *The Good Life*, the classic 1970s BBC TV sit-com, Tom
and Barbara live out their vision of sustainability. Tom leaves
a job that he hates, and the pair of them go back to the land.
Of course, what makes it funny is that they are doing this in
the London suburb of Surbiton. All around them is the life
they are trying to escape – a reminder, perhaps, of the difficulty of trying to live like this. You must cut yourself off
entirely if you are to do it properly, which is what makes it
so hard.

There is another approach to this question. I think the good
life is one that is rich in association. Whether you lust after
extreme wealth, a way of being that is monkish in its simplicity
or anything in between, it seems that if you can do this whilst
maintaining a balance in your life between the personal and
the collective, you are bound to enjoy what you are doing more.
You can take your interests further, you join a wider range of
social networks, you may become healthier and happier and
end up with a stronger sense of identity. You will experience
the regular burr of fellowship, the silliness of being around
people who know you well enough to tease you, you learn,
you achieve, you play, you escape. What's more, you contribute
to a society that can become much richer culturally.

Throughout history those societies with a thriving associational landscape have flourished in a cultural sense. Think
of Britain during the eighteenth century, or Athens in the
fifth century BC. Here for the first time was a city awash with

associations. Neighbouring city-states experienced nothing like the same freedom of association. In nearby Sparta, for example, men belonged to single groups such as a *phitidion* and did so on a permanent basis, living, fighting, sleeping and training with the same band of brothers.

Meanwhile, free Athenians could belong to an array of associations, such as the boisterous aristocratic political clubs called *hetaireiai*, with names like 'the Erections' or 'the Wankers'. 'True philosophers', Plato once sniffed, 'know nothing of [. . .] the enthusiasms of *hetaireiai* for offices, their meetings, dinner parties.' Yet they contributed to the rich fabric of Athenian social life. There were the bawdy *thiasoi*, or the hero cults to which slaves, migrants and women belonged. We know of guild-like unions of merchants and workers from particular professions, as well as formal dining clubs like the *syssition* and neighbourhood associations, burial-clubs and *epheboi*, made up of rowdy young Athenians. This efflorescence of associations coincided precisely with the golden age of Athens, in which the arts, learning and philosophy flourished as never before.

Yet I want to finish on a slightly different note. What I have been circling over the last few hundred pages has had less to do with the benefits to society of joining associations than a single decision, one that takes no more than a few seconds. It is not so much the decision to join a specific association as the moment when you think to yourself that this could be an interesting thing to do. That you might enjoy it. What kind of association you become a part of is a different matter. More important is becoming open to the idea. It is a small decision, and it takes only a few seconds, but it is one that I think can change your life.

Every day, all over Britain, a growing mass of people come together in different associations dotted all over the country. There will be cups of tea and biscuits, announcements and reunions as thousands of meetings come to order or games begin. Some of these people may settle down in low-lit living-rooms to indulge their love of books. Others will assemble in the back rooms of draughty village halls to learn more about the local bird population. Some will gather around fish-tanks to find out about the reproductive cycle of koi, or polish their boots before re-enacting a particular historical period. Others will arrange flowers, have sex with each other, make music, debate, knit, cycle, quilt, stitch, shoot, pray, bowl, paint, cave, sing or do Pilates. It could be anything. Perhaps the only thing we can say about what these people have in common is that when they leave these meetings most of them will be happier than when they went in.

Etzioni asked, what is the good life? I believe it is one in which we understand that remarkable things happen when we come together in small groups.

Appendix A
How 'Club' Came to Mean 'Club' – A Cunning Theory

In Shakespeare's day the word 'club' meant two things: it was the weakest of four suits in a pack of cards, often denoted by a dark-coloured trefoil; or it was an obdurate stick that you might use to bash someone over the head. The latter meaning came from the Old Norse *klubba*, and the Danish *klubbe*, meaning 'cudgel'. So to describe an association as a 'club' during the 1590s would have made as much sense as calling it a spade.

The etymological journey from 'heavy stick' to 'small group' is an unusual one. Nobody really knows how it came about. The *Oxford English Dictionary* describes the shift as 'obscure'. Some have suggested it was a derivation from the Anglo-Saxon words *clifian* or *cleofian*, meaning 'to cleave', but neither the meaning nor the sound of these earlier words is persuasive. Perhaps the idea of a club came about because when a group gathers together, they are so tightly packed that they resemble a heavy stick, a club. Again, it's not exactly convincing.

So how did this shift come about? With a nod to Baldrick, I have a cunning theory. It involves a riot, a line from Shakespeare, various gangs and a fragment of doggerel penned by Sir William D'Avenant, godson of Shakespeare. Hopefully, that link will be obscure no more.

The story begins on the night of 30 April 1517, when a series of riots broke out across London. They had an ugly, xenophobic feel and continued long into the next day. Most of the trouble was stirred up by gangs of young apprentices, or 'prentices', as they were known. These were young, boisterous men, eager to prove themselves and famous for bundling about London singing ballads about their manliness. A tavern called the London Apprentice had as its sign a young prentice tearing out with each hand the heart of a lion. They'd roam about town in packs and were forever getting into fights with retinues of servants or with more entitled young men working at the Inns of Court. As the historian John Stubbs wrote:

> Apprentices were famous for whoring, gaming and ale-drinking like virtually no other demographic banding; though also, paradoxically, for sweeping through the streets in hordes on certain public holidays to attack the very brothels and taverns they patronized so fervently under normal circumstances.

It was exactly this kind of reactionary conservatism that inspired the riots of 1517. Prentices had a 'historic dislike for foreigners and foreign fashions – since both, to the apprentices, constituted a threat to native goods and commerce'. On the eve of what would later be known as 'Evil May Day' in 1517 this boiled over once again.

There is one element of these riots that is of particular interest to us. According to most accounts the prentices marched about town bellowing out the slightly unusual battle-cry 'Prentices and clubs!' or 'Prentices! Prentices! Clubs! Clubs!' In the prelude to these riots an alderman had made the mistake of trying to accost a young prentice following some misdemeanour. In need of help, this prentice had cried out 'Prentices! Clubs!' Every prentice within earshot had grabbed a club and rushed to his defence. The alderman was seen off, and the prentices marched on, chanting, 'Prentices! Clubs!'

This battle-cry stuck, and during the decades that followed 'Prentices! Clubs!' slipped into the popular vernacular. It meant, very simply, 'come together', 'gather round' or 'unite'. It was about strength in numbers, defence and association in the face of a shared threat.

In Shakespeare's *Henry VI, Part I*, probably performed for the first time in 1592, the Mayor of London warns the Bishop of Winchester and the Duke of Gloucester:

'I'll call for clubs, if you will not away.'

This suggests that by the late sixteenth century 'calling for clubs' had become a well-known idiom. It was shorthand for summoning your gang, charging your fellows. But it was not until the 1620s that the meaning of the word entered a new phase and began to be used to describe specific groups.

In 1623, the same year that Ben Jonson's Sons of Ben began to meet in the Apollo Room, off Fleet Street, there was a sudden epidemic of gang-like activity in London. Groups with names such as the Order of the Fancy, the Tityre-tues, the Roaring Boys, the Bravadoes or the Order of the Bugle 'caused something of a storm' as one man wrote in his diary.

These gangs were similar to the London prentices in many ways. Their members were roughly the same age and gender; both had a love of drinking and brawling. So they rolled about in packs of twenty or so, like the ancient Greek *hetaireia*, and it follows that they might adopt the same battle-cry. It is easy to imagine one of these gangs in the 1620s tumbling out of their favourite tavern late at night, looking for trouble. Picture the street, poorly lit, with this gang meandering along as the sound of their laughter echoes on before them, when one of them sees a nervous watchman at the end of the street. The cry goes up, 'Clubs!' or just 'Club!'

By then the meaning of this cry had changed fractionally. It was no longer a practical injunction to go and fetch your club. Young men were unlikely to carry these about at the time. Instead they might have a sword, rapier, dagger or even a pistol. To call for clubs in the 1620s and 1630s had become metaphoric rather than literal. Technological advance had untethered the word from its original mooring, and it was at this point that the word 'club' seems to have become associated more directly with the group of people who responded to that call as much as the instruction itself.

It is during this period that we find the first uses of the word 'club' as we now know it. In his 'A Vision on the Muses of his Friend Michael Drayton', published in 1627, Ben Jonson assures the reader that he will not 'raise a rhyming club about the town'. Later, in *A Tale of a Tub*, Jonson refers to a 'politic club'. In *The New Inn*, performed in 1629, Barnaby asks Jordan:

How does old Staggers the smith, and Tree the saddler?
Keep they their penny club still?

More revealing is 'The Long Vacation in London', a good example of mock-verse in octosyllabic doggerel, if that's your thing, by Shakespeare's godson Sir William D'Avenant. It includes the line:

Our Mules are come! dissolve the Club!

This was published for the first time in 1673 as part of an anthology of D'Avenant's work, yet we can be sure that he wrote it long before then. The poem contains references to both the Globe and the Bull. By 1673 one of these was derelict, while the other had been pulled down during the 1640s. The historian Timothy Raylor has argued that this poem bears a strong resemblance in style and metre to the work of D'Avenant's close friends during the mid-1630s, and that it was almost certainly written during this period. There is also 'a considerable body of circumstantial evidence' to suggest that at the time D'Avenant was part of a group called the Order of the Fancy, another gang made up of gentlemen-poets. So there is a very good chance that this was the 'club' he wanted to dissolve in the poem.

Yet why didn't earlier groups of prentices refer to themselves as 'clubs'? It seems that these later gangs took the form and shape of their groups much further than the prentices. They swore oaths of secrecy to one another. There were passwords, strict rules of conduct. They used offices such as 'Prince', 'president' or 'treasurer'. The members of some groups referred to their fellow members as 'brother' and wore bugles or certain-coloured ribbons to denote membership. Crucially, they gave their groups names. It is at this point that the identity of any collective becomes more real, and this is what appears to have happened to groups like the one that D'Avenant belonged to. It was only when these young men gave their gangs a more formal structure that it made sense to talk about them as actual entities in their own right, as *clubs*.

Later, in 1660, we find Pepys referring to a 'Coffee club', or a 'club' he believed to be in existence at Cambridge. By then a growing number of educated literary men and women inferred from the word 'club' a group of people who came together regularly to share a meal or pursue a shared interest. From here the word went viral, in the best possible sense.

Appendix B
Running an Association

There seem to be three golden rules for running an association, although when I say 'golden' and 'rule', please don't think that there's anything solid about these. Think of them as pointers rather than commandments, from someone who has not run an association but has spoken to many people who have.

On the football team I used to play for, whenever a player went off on a run that ended in disaster (this happened a lot), there was one man who'd shout out, 'there's no "I" in team.' It's an annoying expression, but the sentiment is useful here. There's no 'I' in club either: if you want to join or start an association, you must be prepared to blend your will to that of the group. The most successful groups tend to be those whose members recognize this.

Another golden pointer has to do with identity. The happiest groups are often those with a clear sense of their own identity, of what sets them apart and makes them unique. This may sound like something you can't control, and either your group has it or it doesn't. But there are ways of stacking the odds in your favour. You can ensure that your group has a name (if it does not already), an insignia, a logo, a website, a motto, or you could work out its history or in any other way see that there is a shared understanding of what makes this body different. For more on this have another look at the chapter on the New Zealand Tendency.

Finally, it's important to remember the Power of Giving. This binds us together. It inspires us to give more and will often allow a group to keep going for many years. Groups that last are groups whose members give to each other as often as possible.

But there's more to running an association than this, and it can help to know the nuts and bolts of how these groups are seen in law, what steps you can take to reduce your liability, what a constitution involves and whether your group will ever need to pay tax. Here is a brief introduction to this, the more technical side of life in an association. But it is just that, an introduction, and if you need to know more then seek legal advice, not least because the law in this area continues to change.

In the Eyes of the Law

By judicial definition, when a group of people come together around an agreement to achieve a certain end, without seeking profit or attempting to break the law, they constitute an 'unincorporated association'.* Most of the groups in this book have been one of these, and so long as there is an agreement between these people that establishes why they have come together and what their obligations towards each other are – this agreement may be written or oral – then the association is said to exist in a legal sense. There is absolutely

---

*There is no statutory definition of these groups, but here is the next best thing, a judicial definition: in *Conservative and Unionist Central Office* v. *Burrell*, Lord Justice Lawton described these groups as 'two or more persons bound together for one or more common purposes, not being business purposes, by mutual undertakings each having mutual duties and obligations, in an organisation which has rules which identify in whom control of it and its funds rests and on what terms and which can be joined or left at will'. *Weekly Law Reports* (1982), vol. 1, p. 522.

no requirement for an unincorporated association to register with an authority or fill out forms. Nor does any government official have the power to see the accounts of a group like this or the details of its membership.

Of course, the corollary is that when a member of an unincorporated association feels that they've been hard done by, it is not always easy for them to appeal to the courts for help. There are several exceptions to this, including a proviso under the Literary and Scientific Institutions Act of 1854 that allows for any association 'established to promote science, literature or the fine arts, or to provide adult instructions, libraries, museums or art galleries' to appeal to the Department of Trade against an alteration to their society, association or club, if two-fifths of their membership agree. The Department can then reverse this alteration if it agrees that it is injurious to the group as a whole.

None of this changes the fact that an unincorporated association has no legal personality. This has several implications. First, the association cannot own property; however, it's not too hard to get round this. You could set up a trust and control the property through that. 'No legal personality' also means that in tort law and contract law the association itself is non-liable, so it cannot be sued. If a judge rules for or against an unincorporated association, the ruling will be struck out. Instead it is the members of the group who are liable.

For an association like, say, Laura's Book Group this is unlikely to be a problem. The group keeps to itself, and it is hard to imagine what kind of liability it could incur. Even if one day they got hold of a clubhouse – a pipe dream for Wilkie – and one of the members fell over and decided to sue her for damages, perverse as that may sound, any attempt to do this would be ruled inadmissible in court. There is no tortious liability between members of the same unincorporated association. As a member of that association, you are the occupier of a clubhouse as much as any other member.

But there are plenty of groups whose activities involve regular contact with the world outside, and as this increases, so does the potential liability of its members. Admittedly, the risk of being taken to court is still very, very small. But it can be enough to consider taking steps to reduce your collective liability. One of the ways to do this is to give the group you belong to, a legal form.

Acquiring a Legal Personality – Incorporation

The group could become incorporated. There are various ways of doing this. It might become a company in which the liability is limited by shares, or one limited by guarantee. This makes sense for most clubs and associations, especially if the group has a limited membership and it owns anything in community. The beauty of a company limited by guarantee is that each member's liability is limited to the nominal sum they pay on joining the group.

For many years these were the two principal forms a company would take. In 2005 this changed. Now, as an unincorporated association, you could also apply to become a Community Interest Company (CIC).

This legal entity is aimed predominantly at social enterprises – unincorporated groups constituted in such a way that when they generate a surplus it goes not exclusively to the group's owners or its shareholders but to specified social or environmental causes. Yet like unincorporated associations, social enterprises do not have legal personalities. CICs are more or less incorporated versions of these social enterprises; however, any profits they generate must go towards a 'community' cause rather than one that is merely social or environmental.

Within a CIC there will also be a cap on the dividends paid to shareholders, and each CIC is subject to an 'asset lock' – assets cannot be sold off on the cheap or given away, unless they go to another asset-locked group. In a similar sense, when or if the CIC is wound up, its assets cannot be transferred to the owners but must go to another asset-locked body.

The problem here, as ever, is the dreaded C-word. A CIC must benefit 'the community'. But how do you define this? According to CIC guidance, 'any group of individuals may constitute a community if they share a common characteristic which distinguishes them from other members of the community and a reasonable person might consider that they constitute a section of the community.'

As well as being vague and poorly worded, this places undue emphasis on what a 'reasonable person' imagines a community to be. Few people, whether reasonable or not, have a detailed understanding of what constitutes a community. Nor, by the sound of it, did the CIC Regulator. In late 2009 he, she or they drew up a list of sample 'communities'. These included:

The residents of Oldtown
People with learning difficulties
The elderly
The young unemployed
Small-scale produce growers in Africa
The XYZ charity
Sufferers from ABC disease
People wishing to learn to . . .
Youth of Oldtown needing sports facilities
Redundant car workers.

When I read this, I howled. To think that a specific charity is as much a community as 'the elderly' or 'the young unemployed' or the sufferers of a particular disease dilutes the meaning of 'community' until it becomes a vapid mess. You might as well refer to the stomach-sleepers of the world as a community, or how about the community of individuals with red hair who like to watch cricket on television? Nevertheless, if, somehow, you can persuade the CIC regulator that those who benefit from your group constitute a community in the eyes of a 'reasonable person', and you pass the 'community interest test', then your group can become a CIC.

The most obvious advantage of incorporation is that it becomes much harder for anyone to take the group to which you belong to the cleaners. But your group loses a degree of privacy and independence. You must file annual returns that are publicly available and comply with company law, and there will be added costs.

Acquiring a Legal Personality – as a Charity

Another way to reduce one's collective liability is to apply for charitable status. If your association has 'appropriate objects for the relief of poverty, the advancement of religion, the advancement of education or other purposes beneficial to the community', you can approach the Charity Commission to seek charitable status.

The main advantage of becoming a registered charity is that you don't have to pay income tax or capital gains tax; also, your group will enjoy a mandatory 80 per cent relief on property rates. The local authority could increase this to full exemption if they like your group. It should also become easier to attract funding, if that's what you're after. The disadvantages are that you cannot have any political agenda and that under charity law your group must comply with a raft of onerous regulations.

Acquiring a Legal Personality – as an IPS

If the prospect of incorporation does not grab you, nor the thought of charitable status, then you could turn your association into a Friendly Society or an Industrial and Provident

Society (IPS). Again this involves various restrictions, a small expense, publication of your accounts and a degree of external influence. There are different forms an IPS can take, such as 'community benefit society' or 'co-operative'. Essentially an IPS is a mutual aid society in which members club together to insure against future illness, injury, unemployment and retirement. For more on this, see the Co-operative and Community Benefit Societies and Credit Unions Act 2010.

Tax

Some groups need to pay tax. Even if your association is unincorporated, it could be required to pay corporation tax if it generates a profit above a certain threshold. There are exceptions to this: profit from the sale of donations or gifts in, say, a jumble sale cannot be taxed. If the club is considered to be a members' club rather than a proprietary club, then profits from trade within the club (involving refreshment) will be equally non-taxable. Trade with non-members is different.*

If your unincorporated association generates a taxable profit, then you need to track down a form with the alluring title 'CT41G (Clubs)'. Once this has been fed into the system, another form called a 'CT600' will make its way to you and on completion all will be well between you and the Inland Revenue.

I Demand To Be Let Into Your Club, I Have My Rights!

Interestingly, when it comes to joining an association, generally you do not. As the great sage of associations, Jean

*There is a good section on this at http://www.hmrc.gov.uk/manuals/bim manual/BIM24210.htm. Or get your hands on *The Taxation of Clubs, Societies and Voluntary Associations (IR46)*.

Warburton, has put it, 'no person has a [legal] right to become a member of an association.' Any group can 'refuse to admit any person to membership, however eligible they may appear to be. Nor need they give any reason for their decision. It is also perfectly legal to exclude someone on the grounds of gender (so long as your group is not geared towards profit). However, if the group has more than twenty-five members, you cannot exclude someone purely on the grounds of race, unless the group has been set up to benefit those who belong to a particular ethnicity (not race). It is also the case that if membership of a particular association is required in order to practise a certain trade, then when considering whether to let you in, the association is bound to 'reach their decision honestly, without bias and not in pursuance of any capricious policy'. They still don't need to give a reason for keeping you out.

There is a glimmer of hope for anyone who has been spurned by the club of their dreams: if the wording of that association's rules regarding admission is sufficiently loose and implies that 'anyone who agrees with their objects is eligible for membership', then by law the association cannot refuse someone who attempts to gain membership and is able to pay their subscription.

Rules

This brings us to rules and constitutions. A set of rules can be a good idea once the club grows beyond a certain size. This is not just to cover your collective back or to keep out those who threaten the character of the group, but, as Lord Romilly put it in 1867, rules are there to ensure 'a good understanding between all the members, and that nothing should occur that is likely to disturb the good feeling that ought to subsist between them!'

Of course, rules don't always work. However as Sir Robert

Megarry explained in a judgement made in 1970, 'nobody would suggest that rules are not rules unless they work perfectly'. Megarry also pointed out that

> usually there is a considerable degree of informality in the conduct of the affairs of such clubs, and I think that the courts have to be ready to allow general concepts of reasonableness, fairness and common sense to be given more than their usual weight. . . . In other words, allowance must be made for some play in the joints.

Let's say you wanted to draw up a constitution for your group. Roughly what should it look like? This memorandum, declaration or constitution should state in clear terms what the group is (its name, its aims, what it is that has pulled you together and who can join), as well as what kind of behaviour you don't want (criteria for expulsion), but it's also worth spelling out how you'd like the group to be constituted, if you feel it should be constituted in a certain way (whether you should have a president, chairman, secretary, how often they should change and, if so, how, whether there'll be an AGM and when, if and how an EGM can be called, how the club should be wound up, if it ever comes to that, and what the procedure should be if the rules are to be altered or added to). Finally, it's worth setting out what should happen to any money collected or raised by the group. Serious disputes within associations usually involve capital. A well-worded constitution can avoid any such conflict.*

Yet when doing this, always allow for a degree of flexibility and latitude, just as Megarry called for 'some play in the joints'. If the stated aims of any association are too narrow, they can stifle it. The rules should never dictate to the group against its collective will but rather they are there to maintain what Romilly called 'the good feeling' between members.

*For more on constitutions and roles within small associations see Ray Rogers, *How to Set Up and Run a Voluntary Club or Society* (Guildford: Ray Rogers, 2008).

Acknowledgements

'I haven't really had a life,' the late Sebastian Horsley once said. 'I've just sat in a room and died.' There have been times, in particular the sprint-to-the-finish that was the completion of this book, when writing has felt like a very solitary and room-bound affair. But almost as soon as I have had this thought, I have tried to remember the years that have led up to this frantic finale, and what has made this book such fun to write.

Although I like rootling around in libraries and hammering away at a laptop as much as the next person – in fact, a good deal more – what I have enjoyed most about writing this book has been the mass of conversations it has inspired. My thanks to everyone who took the time to talk to me about all things *group*, to let me into their world and to put up with my incessant questioning. This can't have been fun. I shudder at the thought of being on the receiving end of this traffic jam of needling, pernickety queries about the formal structure of one's group, its bye-laws, how many times it meets each year, its catchment area, or whether it has a 'character' of its own. Over the last three years I have become an associational trainspotter, and if any of these interrogations were boring to sit through or just confusing, I hope this book will shed light on what I was getting at.

On the subject of conversation, I should add that most of the speech reported in this book is a verbatim account of what was said to me (recorded using a minidisc and microphone). Some parts are based on my recollection of conversations and occasionally I have changed the order in which points were made to clarify the general meaning in a condensed passage. While I have tried to ensure that the details regarding specific associations are accurate, any errors that remain are my fault rather than that of the individuals I spoke to.

Throughout the text I refer to my online nationwide survey of associations that began in 2009. I am indebted to the groups that took part, and following this section you'll find a list of most of those involved (as well as associations I interviewed in person). This book would not have been possible without their input, and I want to thank each of them for taking part. They are the stars of *Together*.

Though the survey ended for the purposes of this edition of the book in 2010, it remains an ongoing project. There is so little survey-related material about voluntary associations that I plan to keep gathering data about these groups for as long as possible. If you belong to a small voluntary group that has been going for some time or, better still, you form one after reading this book, I would love to hear about it. Go to my website and there you will find the online survey as well as a section where you can write more fully about your group and what it does. There are several addresses for this website – www.henryhemming.com and www.henryhemming.co.uk – where you will find not only pages allowing you to enter information but a much fuller description of how the survey was conducted, as well as other titbits relating to clubs and small groups in Britain today.

For their help in promoting the survey, my great thanks to Sophie Rochester, as well as Justin Pollard, Lindsay Merriman, Jonathan Rowson at the RSA, Fiona Dodd at

TBR, the National Operatic and Dramatic Association and the National Society of Allotment and Leisure Gardeners. Larry Smith designed and maintained the website with immense skill and patience. At different points, I was also assisted by the talented Frank Brinkley. Not only was he able to liaise with a stream of different groups but he provided invaluable translation and commentary on various classical texts and helped with my research into Roman *collegia*. For a moment he was replaced by Rebecca Lee; my thanks to both of them.

The mass of statistics that make up most of Chapter 8 were gleaned from conversations with representatives of different national governing bodies or federations. With one exception, these organizations were extremely helpful and swift in their response. I would like to thank the Federation of British Historic Vehicle Clubs, Radio Society of Great Britain, British Astronomical Association, National Association of Flower Arranging Societies, English Golf Union, Badminton Scotland, Canoe Scotland, UK Athletics, Scottish Athletics, the National Association of Choirs, the National Women's Register, the Working Men's Clubs and Institutes Union, as well as John Tweddle at The Natural History Museum, David Bryant at Rotary International in Great Britain & Ireland, Susan Henderson of the United Grand Lodge of England, Gráinne Devery at Making Music, Suzie Thomas of Community Archaeology in the UK, Barry Goodman of the Morris Ring, Andrew St Ledger at Sport England, Bee at Motorbase, John Eady at KKP, Alex Teasdale at England Hockey, Sharon Smart at the Amateur Swimming Association, Alistair Hollis at Bowls England, William Ponissi at Welsh Athletics, Anna Avino at the National Federation of Young Farmers' Clubs, Ian Harvey at Civic Voice, Clare Bodel at The Scottish Football Association, Pippa Randolph at British Rowing, Sophie Curthoys at the Lawn Tennis Association, Tina Heeney at Badminton England, Nick Boothroyd at the

Rugby Football League, Robert Deacon at Canoe England, Arran Coggan at Grand National Archery Society and Andrew Welch at British Naturism.

If not getting in touch with these people or spending time with specific associations, the research for this book took place in the British Library. My thanks to the people who make coffee there, and in particular the men downstairs who put those wonderful patterns in the froth. I still do not quite understand how this happens, but I like it when it does. Also, many thanks must go to the kind people who dish out books.

For the time they spent looking through various parts of this book and their insights, I want to thank my sister Bea, and my father. For specific ideas, translations, suggestions and other shards of assistance, my thanks to Philip Winterbottom at the Royal Bank of Scotland, Chris Church, Sir Andrew Huxley, Philip Womack, Robin Lane Fox, Ben Wilson, Hubert Picarda, John Beauclerk, Jeff Bishop, Peter James, Victoria de Menil, Henry Trew, Peter Brown, Gill Seyfang, Hilary Geoghegan and Owen O'Rourke.

My unstinting thanks go to those at John Murray, to Nikki Barrow and Polly Ho-Yen for their superb publicity, to James Spackman for his marketing prowess, and of course to Roland Philipps and Victoria Murray-Browne for their great skill as editors. At a guess, this was not an easy book to edit. Certainly, it took on several different forms before reaching its final state. For a book about small groups and the marvellous power of discussion, it is apposite that its shape should owe so much to conversation and collaboration. So my thanks to both of them for their support and expert judgement, as well as their patience with regard to the *slight* lag between when I was due to hand in the manuscript and the joyous event itself.

Meanwhile, Jonathan Conway remains the platonic ideal of the literary agent. He really is very good. I can think of no better example of this than when I sent him an email asking about the meaning of the word 'macher', before spending the next half hour on the phone with him as he explained the nuances of what it implies in different settings. In my eyes, he is a literary macher. He gets things done, and is fearless to boot. I am enormously grateful for his support and advice over the years.

Finally, a word on Helena. During the past five years she has combined the unlikely roles of lover, critic, confidante, companion and playmate, and has done this in her own inimitable way. By the time this book is published we will be married – touch wood – so she may be bored of hearing these things, but I have yet to meet anyone who brings to the world the same mixture of intelligence, love, curiosity and silliness as well as surgical intellectual precision when and where it is required. She is a remarkable, stunning creature, and my life without her would be a monochrome version of what it has become. I am grateful for the way she coped as the book came to an end, for saying 'yes', and for being endlessly and effortlessly full of love; and it is for these reasons that this book is dedicated to her.

H. H., 13 August 2010

With thanks to:

The National Fancy Rat Society / Apperley Cricket Club / The Lower Wharfedale Group of the Ramblers / Hadleigh Bobbin Lace-Making Class / Pimlico Puffins / Knitting Hill / Christian Naturist Fellowship / Inverness Field Archery Club / Outdoor Swimming Society / Wimbledon Book Club / The Gay and Lesbian Humanist Association (GALHA) / The London Beer Meetup / London Pooches and Pals Meetup Group / The South-East London Meetup Group / The London Rock Meetup Group / Norwich Coin and Medal Society / London BookCrossing Group / Leeds Morris Men / Headingley Badminton Club / The West Yorkshire Fuchsia Society, Leeds / Littlehampton DollsHouse Club / Rutland Road Allotment Association / Subterranea Britannica / Sunday Hoop Club (aka London Hula Hoopers Meetup) / Croydon Natural History and Scientific Society Ltd / Stunners / London Photographic Meetup Group / Wye Valley Transport Interest Group / Queensway Allotment Association, Crosby, Merseyside / Thameside Sewing Bees / Coquet Yacht Club / The Real Book Club (TRBC) / University of Edinburgh Humanist Society (HS) / FireBeaters / The Young Georgians / Rotary Club of Stirling / Model Steam Road Vehicle Society / M5-M50-NGM / Briston Players / International Necronautical Society / Farnley Estate W. I. / Edinburgh University Philosophy Society / D.A.M.E. (Dolls' House and Miniature Enthusiasts) / Mini-Ness Dolls House Club / Bozeat Players / Mendip Caving Group / Alt Tuesdays Caving Collective / Cornwall

Bird Watching and Preservation Society / Wells Diving Group / Sevenoaks Allotment Holders Association / Calderdale Leisure Gardens Federation / The Association of Sustainability Practitioners / The Blackburn and East Lancashire Beekeepers Association / Ridgewood Sun Club / Altrincham and District Natural History Society / Berkshire Family History Society / 32nd (Cornwall) Regiment Foot 1808–1815 / American Civil War Society / Chesham & District Natural History Society / Dorset Geologists' Association Group / East Herts Geology Club / Shropshire Geological Society / Thorne & Hatfield Moors Conservation Forum / The British Gladiolus Society / Cleveland Naturalists' Field Club / Friends of Bunting's Wood / Wenvoe Wildlife Group / Colchester Natural History Society / Craven & Pendle Geological Society / Yorkshire Philosophical Society / Welford Women's Winter Reading Group / Wharfedale Gardeners / The Dell Angling Society / Matienzo Caving Expeditions / Strathclyde University Canoe Club / NUI Galway Kayak Club / Baldock and District Canoe Club / Meridian Canoe Club / Bristol Exploration Club / Hood Bikers / South Wales Caving Club / Mildenhall Naturist Swimming Club / The Desert Divas / Two Rivers Naturist Club / South Western Outdoor Club / The Preston Stroke Club / Stroke Care for Newbury and West Berkshire Support Groups / Macclesfield and District Young Stroke Society / Derby Younger Stroke Social Group / Plane Stupid / Stew / Little Moor Allotment Association / Historical Society of Frampton / Greater London Dutch Rabbit Club / Camborne-Redruth Natural History Society / South Downs Society / Broomhouse Lane Allotment Association / Norfolk Federation of Allotments / Furness Family History Society / North Cheshire Family History Society / The Northern Koi Club / Central Scotland Bat Group / Calthorpe Project Wednesday Evening 7:30 Athletic / Middlesex County Cricket League / Shropshire Ornithological Society / The Association of British Fungus Groups / Otley Aquarists Society / Essex Badger Protection Society / South Essex Natural History Society / Barnsley Naturalist and Scientific Society / Brandon & Wolston Young Farmers Club / Welford

Women's Institute / Leamington Hastings Young Farmers Club /
F. C. United of Manchester / Climate Rush / Laura's Book Group /
Barston & District Young Farmers Club / Welford School
Association / Berkshire and South Buckinghamshire Bat Group /
Network 2012 / Exeter Canoe Club / Dabbers Session / Hoover
Amateur Radio Club / The Calton Ramblers / The Remainders /
Bovey Book Group / Pub History Society / New Embroidery
Group / Dulwich Quilters / South London Women Artists / Dulwich
Dilettantes / Painswick Players / Denmead Operatic Society /
Gravesend & District Theatre Guild / Middle and East Greens
Allotment Association Morpeth / Herefordshire Goat Club /
Malvern Hills District Brass Band / Kippax Central W. M. C. /
Dawlish Black Swan Handbell Ringers / The Kentish VW Klub /
Bingley Amateur Swimming Club / Stockport Amateur Operatic
Society / Artful Dodgers / Waltham Forest Hockey Club / AFC
Snappers / South London Ladies Book Club / Stoke-on-Trent
Reading Group / Connect Group / Buddies / Leytonstone
Allotment Holders Association / Seven Kings and Goodmayes
Allotment Society / Gosport Musical Theatre Productions / North
Leigh Short Mat Bowls / The Bostock Singers / Liverpool Old
Swan Cage Birds Society / Yoga Group / Kent Iyengar Yoga
Institute (KIYI) / Wanderers / Essex Section / Southeast Koi club /
Scottish Outdoor Club / Areley Kings Players / Swansea & District
Leisure Club / Sussex Chorus / Birkbeck Early Modern Society /
Mabo Miniature Maniacs Dolls House Club / Tern Valley Vintage
Machinery Trust Ltd / 2nd Battalion, 95th Rifles Re-enactment
Group / The Thursday Club / Utrophia / Bristol Exploration Club /
Campaign for an English Parliament / Chantage / Deerhurst
Community Preservation / Genesis Order of Druids and Eclectic
Pagans / The New Zealand Golf Club / East London Advanced
Motorcyclists (ELAM) / Midland Vehicle Preservation Society

Notes

Introduction

1   'Man is a city-dwelling': 'City-dwelling' is one translation of *politikon*, which can also mean 'political'. Both make sense, as a free Athenian man would have been expected to engage in politics as a member of a *polis*.

2   F. C. United: For more on the story of F.C. United see Robert Brady, *An Undividable Glow* (Manchester: Rubberybubberyboy Parchment, 2006), or Steven Wood, *Trips on Glue* (Manchester: Trips on Glue, 2008).

4   'an area of social life': Jeff Bishop and Paul Hoggett, *Organizing around Enthusiasms: Patterns of Mutual Aid in Leisure* (London: Comedia, 1985), pp. 2, 121. This sentiment has been echoed by others including Konrad Elsdon who felt that 'both the public and the government remain in the dark' about small voluntary groups: 'National and local policies, in so far as they exist, rely on vague assumptions, often on prejudice.' See Konrad Elsdon, J. Reynolds and S. Stewart, *Voluntary Organisations: Citizenship, Learning and Change* (Leicester: National Institute of Adult Continuing Education 1995), pp. 1, 4.

4   'the "lost continent"': Lester M. Salamon, S. W. Sokolowski and H. K. Anheier, *Social Origins of Civil Society: An Overview* (Baltimore, MD: Working Papers of the Johns Hopkins Center for Civil Society Studies, 2000), p. 1.

4   'a loose and baggy': J. Kendall and M. Knapp, 'A Loose and Baggy Monster: Boundaries, Definitions and Typologies', in J. D. Smith, C. Rochester and R. Hedley (eds), *An Introduction to the Voluntary Sector* (London: Routledge, 1995), pp. 66–95.

4   report in 1995: Elsdon, Reynolds and Stewart, *Voluntary Organisations*, pp. 2–3, 39.

5   'one of the most pervasive': R. J. Morris, 'Clubs, Societies and Associations', *The Cambridge Social History of Britain, 1750–1950* (Cambridge: Cambridge University Press, 1990), vol. 3, p. 395.

5   'almost every parish hath': John Macky, *A Journey through England* (London: J. Hooke, 1722), p. 288.

5   'the whole British empire': William Hutton, *An History of Birmingham to the End of the Year 1780* (Birmingham, 1780), p. 294.

5   Friendly Societies: Simon Cordery, *British Friendly Societies, 1750–1914* (London: Palgrave Macmillan, 2003), p. 1. The figure of 6 million is from a calculation by Joseph Maria Baernreither, an Austrian who travelled through Britain in the 1870s looking at self-help associations, quoted in Jack C. Ross, *An Assembly of Good Fellows* (Westport, CT, and London: Greenwood Press, 1976), p. 246; the other figure is from the Registrar of Friendly Societies in a report to the Royal

Commission quoted in Ferdinand Mount, *Clubbing Together: The Revival of the Voluntary Principle* (London: W. H. Smith, 1993), p. 3.

7   Shopping habits: 'High Street Britain: 2015', All-Party Parliamentary Small Shops Group, 2006, pp. 10, 14–15, BBC News website, retrieved from http://news.bbc.co.uk/1/shared/bsp/hi/pdfs/15_02_06_highstreet.pdf on 23 August 2010; Jaap Favier and Michèle Bouquet, 'UK eCommerce Forecast 2006–2011', Forrester Research, March 2007, Forrester website, retrieved from http://www.forrester.com on 23 August 2010.

7   'if Christianity goes': T. S. Eliot, *Christianity and Culture* (New York: Harcourt, Brace, 1949), p. 200.

7   Church attendance in decline: Peter Brierley, 'Religion', in A. H. Halsey (ed.), *Twentieth-Century British Social Trends* (Basingstoke: Macmillan, 2000), p. 656.

8   going to church on Sunday: 'The Christian Research English Church Consensus 2005', quoted in Vexen Crabtree, 'Religion in the United Kingdom', 5 July 2007, retrieved from http://www.vexen.co.uk/UK/religion.html#BI-006 on 8 September 2009.

8   anxiety-ridden: Richard Wilkinson and Kate Pickett, *The Spirit Level: Why Equality is Better for Everyone* (London: Penguin, 2010), p. 3.

8   'the social glue': Danny Dorling, D. Vickers, B. Thomas, J. Pritchard and D. Ballas, *Changing UK: The Way We Live Now* (Sheffield: Social and Spatial Inequalities Group, Department of Geography, University of Sheffield, 2008), p. 29.

8   British Civil Society: Phillip Blond, *Red Tory* (London: Faber and Faber, 2010), p. 7.

1: Coming Together

15   'like that of a Grecian': Iain Grahame, *Amin and Uganda: A Personal Memoir* (London: Granada, 1980), p. 34.

19   'dozens of passengers': Rachel North, 'Kings Cross United 6 Months On', 6 January 2006, Rachel from North London blog, retrieved from http://rachelnorthlondon.blogspot.com/2006/01/kings-cross-united-6-months-on.html on 1 November 2009.

19   'interdependence of fate': Kurt Lewin, *Resolving Social Conflicts* (New York: Harper & Row, 1948), p. 184.

19   There are a handful of articles and books in support of this: Jacob M. Rabbie and M. Horwitz, 'Arousal of Ingroup-Outgroup Bias by a Chance Win or Loss', *Journal of Personality and Social Psychology*, vol. 13 (1969), pp. 269–77; Jacob M. Rabbie and M. Horwitz, 'Categories versus Groups as Explanatory Concepts in Intergroup Relations', *European Journal of Social Psychology*, vol. 18 (1988), pp. 117–23; D. Cartwright and A. Zander (eds), *Group Dynamics: Research and Theory* (New York: Harper & Row, 1969); and Leon Festinger, S. Schacter and K. Back, *Social Pressures in Informal Groups* (New York: Harper & Row, 1950).

21   'one-half of all': Cordery, *British Friendly Societies, 1750–1914*, p. 1.

22   'it seemed that': Henry Mayhew and John Binny, *The Criminal Prisons of London and Scenes of Prison Life* (London, 1862), pp. 41–2.

23   Charitable organizations: Quoted on Charity Commission website; retrieved from http://www.charity-commission.gov.uk/showcharity/registerofcharities/registerhomepage.aspx?&=& on 16 June 2010.

23   'cadence deep': Jonathan Swift, 'A Description of the Morning', *The Poetical Works of Dr Jonathan Swift* (London: Manson, Dilton, etc., 1736), vol. 1, p. 38.

23   'as if he had been': Edward Ward, *The Secret History of Clubs: Particularly the*

Kit-Cat, Beef-Stake, Vertuosos, Quacks, Knights of the Golden-Fleece, Florists, Beaus, etc. (London: J. Phillips, 1709), p. 352.

20 'old snarling Diogenes': Ward, *The Secret History of Clubs*, p. 353.

24 'Men of the best Wit': Ward, *The Secret History of Clubs*, p. 352.

24 'of the highest quality': From the title-page of the catalogue for the sale of Britton's musical collection shortly after his death in 1714, quoted in John Hawkins, *A General History of the Science and Practice of Music* (London: Novello, Ewer & Co., 1875), vol. 2, p. 792.

25 Pre-war associations: Peter Clark, *British Clubs and Societies, 1580–1800* (Oxford: Oxford University Press, 2000), p. 26.

25 'an Infinity': Macky, *A Journey through England*, p. 287. By the mid-eighteenth century as many as 20,000 men were thought to attend clubs each night; see Clark, *British Clubs and Societies, 1580–1800*, p. 89.

25 'clubs are established in England': Alexandre de La Rochefoucauld, *A Frenchman's Year in Suffolk*, trans. Norman Scarfe (Woodbridge: Boydell Press, 1988), pp. 188–9.

25 'which we find nowhere': Julius Rodenberg, *England, Literary and Social, from a German Point of View* (London: Richard Bentley & Son, 1875), p. 198.

26 'Keeping up good Humour': Macky, *A Journey through England*, p. 287.

26 'points wherein most men': Joseph Addison, *Spectator*, no. 9 (10 March 1711).

26 Prerogative courts: Clark, *British Clubs and Societies, 1580–1800*, p. 175.

26 Parliamentary blunder: This was the second relaxation of the English Licensing Act, yet there remained controls against blasphemy and a deep-rooted suspicion of anything that sounded Jacobite. See Ben Wilson, *What Price Liberty?* (London: Faber and Faber, 2009), pp. 70–1.

26 Pre-publication vetting: Ophelia Field, *The Kit-Cat Club* (London: Harper Press, 2008), p. 41.

27 'None shall be admitted': Addison, *Spectator*, no. 9 (10 March 1711).

27 'there is no religion': Quoted in Hippolyte Taine, *History of English Literature* (Edinburgh: Edmonston and Douglas, 1871), p. 389.

27 'The divine art': John Aubrey, Nicholas L'Estrange and John Collet, *Anecdotes and Traditions*, compiled by William John Thoms (London: Nichols & Son, 1839), p. 102.

27 Praise for Thomas Britton: See Thomas Hearne, *Hemingi Chartularium Ecclesiae Wigorniensis* (Oxford: E Theatro Sheldoniano, 1723); Horace Walpole, *Anecdotes of Painting in England* (London: Thomas Kirgate, 1765); and Hawkins, *A General History of the Science and Practice of Music*.

27 'happy was the man': Ward, *The Secret History of Clubs*, p. 19.

28 'a Companion': Ward, *The Secret History of Clubs*, p. 352.

28 'Every man has his': 'Sua cuique quum sit animi cogitatio, / Colorque privus'. 'Privus' should really be 'proprius', which is where 'particular' comes from; see Plato, *Phaedrus*, Prologue to Book IV. Richard Steele, *Guardian*, no. 144 (26 August 1713).

31 'capacity for membership': George C. Homans, *The Human Group* (London and New Brunswick, NJ: Transaction Publishers, 1992), p. 315.

2: The Power of Giving

36 Brain nuclei: William T. Harbaugh, U. Mayr and D. Burghart, 'Neural Responses to Taxation and Voluntary Giving Reveal Motives for Charitable Donations', *Science*, vol. 316, no. 5831 (15 June 2007), pp. 1622–5.

36 A stronger bond following gift-exchange: Robert Axelrod, *The Evolution of Cooperation* (New York: Basic Books, 2006), p. 17.

37 'bears fruit': Lewis Hyde, *The Gift: How the Creative Spirit Transforms the World* (Edinburgh: Canongate Books, 2006), p. 38.

38 'an agent of social': Hyde, *The Gift*, p. 36.

39 'sharing a good activity': Bernard Yack, *The Problems of a Political Animal: Community, Justice and Conflict in Aristotelian Political Thought* (London and Berkeley, CA: University of California Press, 1993), p. 29; see Aristotle, *Politics*, 1252a1, and Aristotle, *Nicomachean Ethics*, 1156a–1157b.

39 'little platoon': Edmund Burke, *Reflections on the Revolution in France* (London: Rivingtons, 1868), p. 57.

39 'understanding developed': Alexis de Tocqueville, *Democracy in America*, ed. J. P. Mayer, trans. George Lawrence (New York: Anchor Books, 1969), p. 515.

39 'The foundation of cooperation': Axelrod, *The Evolution of Cooperation*, p. 182.

40 The need for balanced input: Bishop and Hoggett, *Organizing around Enthusiasms*, p. 118.

40 'none but traitors': Burke, *Reflections on the Revolution in France*, p. 57.

40 'old ends': Ben Jonson, Prologue to *Volpone*, quoted in Michelle O'Callaghan and Adam Smith, *Authors at Work: The Creative Environment*, ed. Ceri Sullivan and Graeme Harper (Cambridge: D. S. Brewer, 2009), p. 159.

41 'strengthens the spirits': Hyde, *The Gift*, p. 39.

41 'by them, for us': Bishop and Hoggett, *Organizing around Enthusiasms*, p. 41.

43 'disproportionately effective': Alex MacGillivray, Chris Wadhams and Pat Conaty, *Low Flying Heroes* (London: New Economics Foundation, 2001), p. 1.

45 The Preston Stroke Club: Correspondence with Mrs Ann Waqaruddin, 1 June 2010.

46 Putnam on social capital: Robert D. Putnam, *Bowling Alone: The Collapse and Revival of American Community* (New York: Simon & Schuster, 2000), p. 19.

47 'get ahead': See Xavier de Souza Briggs, 'Doing Democracy Up Close: Culture, Power, and Communication in Community Building', *Journal of Planning Education and Research*, vol. 18 (1998), pp. 1–13.

47 'sociological WD40': Putnam, *Bowling Alone*, p. 23.

47 'may also create': Putnam, *Bowling Alone*, p. 23.

48 Social capital references: 'References to social capital in academic publications 1994–2008', Academic Search Premiere database.

48 'negative effects occur': Paul Haezewindt, 'Investing in Each Other and the Community: The Role of Social Capital', *Social Trends*, no. 33 (2003), pp. 25–6.

49 'In one section': J. H. Morgan, *Leaves from a Field Note-Book* (London: Macmillan, 1916), p. 271.

49 'Mr Boche': Stair Gillon, *The Story of the 29th Division: A Record of Gallant Deeds* (London: Thomas Nelson and Sons, 1925), p. 77.

49 'Let 'em': Ian Hay, *The First Hundred Thousand* (Edinburgh: Blackwood, 1916), p. 236.

50 'these people evidently': Geoffrey Dugdale, *'Langemarck' and 'Cambrai'* (Shrewsbury: Wilding & Son, 1932), p. 95.

50 Citations of Axelrod's book: See Axelrod's personal page at University of Michigan website, retrieved from http://www-personal.umich.edu/~axe/ on 1 December 2009.

50   'replace the Gideon': Axelrod, *The Evolution of Cooperation*, p. xvi.

50   'the wars of this': Wendy Barnaby, 'Do Nations Go to War over Water?', *Nature*, vol. 458 (19 March 2009), pp. 282–3.

51   Serageldin later wrote in to *Nature* to explain that he had in fact said, 'The wars of this century have been on oil, and the wars of the next century will be on water . . . unless we change the way we manage water.'

51   'between 1948 and 1999': Barnaby, 'Do Nations Go to War over Water?', p. 282.

51   'killed my book': Barnaby, 'Do Nations Go to War over Water?', p. 283.

53   'their prowess': Axelrod, *The Evolution of Cooperation*, p. 79.

53   'the same small units': Axelrod, *The Evolution of Cooperation*, p. 77.

53   'enmity has not been': Amartya Sen, interviewed in 'Mummy of Hornedjitef', *A History of the World*, BBC Radio 4, 18 January 2010.

54   'most beautiful proof': Henry Walter Bates, 'Contributions to an Insect Fauna of the Amazon Valley: Lepidoptera: Heliconidae', *Transactions of the Linnaean Society*, vol. 23 (1862), p. 513; quoted in Hugh Raffles, *In Amazonia: A Natural History* (Princeton, NJ: Princeton University Press, 2002), p. 119.

54   'true Darwinism': Peter Kropotkin, *Memoirs of a Revolutionist*, ed. James Allen Rogers (London: Century Hutchinson, 1988), p. 300.

3: The Hothouse Effect

57   'I suppose you could say': Margaret Atwood, *The Book Group Book: A Thoughtful Guide to Forming and Enjoying a Stimulating Book Discussion Group*, ed. E. Slezak (Chicago, IL: Chicago Review Press, 2000), foreword.

58   'interpretive community': H. Jenkins, *Textual Poachers: Television Fans and Participatory Culture* (London: Routledge, 1992).

59   'my heart sank': Alyson Rudd, 'How a Book Club Changed My Life', *The Times* (5 March 2010).

59   'We call this': Jay Hall, 'Decisions, Decisions, Decisions', *Psychology Today*, vol. 5, no. 6 (November 1971), p. 53.

59   'Conflict, effectively managed': Hall, 'Decisions, Decisions, Decisions', p. 88.

61   'a number of microphones': Cardigan Big Art website retrieved from http://www.cardiganbigart.com/ on 11 May 2010.

62   'a minor civil war': Tom Whipple, 'Tall, Slim and the Public Love Her', *The Times* (9 May 2009).

64   Matthew Syed and table tennis: Matthew Syed, *Bounce: How Champions are made* (London: Fourth Estate, 2010).

65   'such an odd': Ward, *The Secret History of Clubs*, p. 18.

65   'a nice Beau': Ward, *The Secret History of Clubs*, p. 18.

65   'Bird-Fanciers': Ward, *The Secret History of Clubs*, p. 176.

65   'One of the things': Interview with the author, 1 April 2010.

66   'those who resemble': Aristotle, *Nicomachean Ethics*, 1155a32, quoted in Émile Durkheim, *The Division of Labour in Society*, transl. W. D. Halls (London: Macmillan, 1984), p. 16; Aristotle, *Politics*, 1261b5.

66   'When people have the chance': 'Immigration: The Inconvenient Truth', *Dispatches*, Channel 4, 21 April 2008.

67   'a knowledge-intensive': Jonathan Gershuny, *A New Measure of Social Position: Social Mobility and Human Capital in Britain*, Institute for Social and Economic Research Working Papers, no. 2, Colchester: Institute for Social and Economic Research (2002), p. 9.

67   'for the first time': Ed Smith, 'Are We Too Professional?', *INTELLIGENT LIFE* (Winter 2009).

68   'priority was': Luiz Felipe Scolari, quoted in Smith, 'Are We Too Professional?'.

69   'success, like happiness': Victor Frankl, *Man's Search for Meaning* (New York: Pocket Books, 2004), p. 12.

4: Going to Extremes

71   Death threats to former pupil: The pupil was Michael Jacobs; Miranda Carter, *Anthony Blunt* (London: Macmillan, 2001), p. 478.

71   'supercilious lack of patriotism': *The Times* (21 November 1979).

71   'the pursuit of truth': Henry Sidgwick, quoted in Robert Skidelsky, *John Maynard Keynes, 1883–1946: Economist, Philosopher, Statesman* (London: Pan Books, 2004), p. 72.

72   'Did I tell you': quoted in W. C. Lubenow, *The Cambridge Apostles, 1820–1914* (Cambridge: Cambridge University Press, 1998), p. xi.

72   Apostolic meetings: Skidelsky, *John Maynard Keynes, 1883–1946*, p. 72; Paul Levy, *Moore: G. E. Moore and the Cambridge Apostles* (Oxford: Oxford University Press, 1981), p. 65.

73   Communist sympathies: Skidelsky, *John Maynard Keynes, 1883–1946*, pp. 514–15.

73   'seething with Communist': Anthony Blunt, 'Memoir', British Library, Add. MS 88902/1, p. 23; *The Times* (21 November 1979).

73   Persuasive Guy Burgess: Blunt, 'Memoir', p. 14.

73   'so naive': Blunt, 'Memoir', p. 26. This particular sentence has a quite different feel from any other line in the handwritten version of the manuscript. The direction of the line wobbles for once; the letters are larger and a little wild; the line becomes thicker and angrier; you can see that the pen has been pushed right into the paper.

73   'aware of the presence': Blunt, 'Memoir', p. 17.

74   Group polarization:- Donald C. Pennington (ed.), *The Social Psychology of Behaviour in Small Groups* (Hove: Psychology Press, 2002), p. 177; D. Cartwright (attrib.), 'Risk Taking by Individuals and Groups: An Assessment of Research Employing Choice Dilemmas', *Journal of Personality and Social Psychology*, vol. 20 (1971), pp. 361–78; K. L. Dion, R. Baron and N. Miller, 'Why Do Groups Make Riskier Decisions than Individuals?' in L. Berkowitz (ed.), *Advances in Experimental Social Psychology*, vol. 5 (New York: Academic Press, 1970).

75   'the usual paraphernalia': Skidelsky, *John Maynard Keynes, 1883–1946*, p. 72.

76   'the more pleasant associations': Levy, *Moore: G. E. Moore and the Cambridge Apostles*, p. 27.

76   'the higher sodomy': Carter, *Anthony Blunt*, p. 62.

77   'Is it monomania': Quoted in Skidelsky, *John Maynard Keynes, 1883–1946*, p. 74.

77   'urban terrorism': *Guardian* (21 January 2009).

5: The New Zealand Tendency

81   'the character of a group': Thomas Hobbes, *Leviathan* (London, 1651).

82   'an entity *sui generis*': Louis Wirth, 'Social Interaction: The Problem of the Individual and the Group', *American Journal of Sociology*, vol. 44 (1939), p. 965.

82   'different from': This has become known as the 'social mould' perspective. See Homans, *The Human Group*, p. 317, and Bishop and Hoggett, *Organizing around Enthusiasms*, p. 3.

82   'I hate and detest': Jonathan Swift in a letter to Alexander Pope, 29 September 1725; quoted in Irvin Ehrenpreis, *Swift: The Man, His Works, and the Age*, vol. 3 (London: Methuen, 1983), p. 150.

82   Social Identity Theory: Henri Tajfel and John C. Turner, 'An Integrative Theory of Intergroup Conflict' in William G. Austin and Stephen Worchel (eds), *The Social Psychology of Intergroup Relations* (Monterey: Brooks/Cole, 1979), pp. 37–47.

84   The origins of the New Zealand: T. D. P. Emblem, *Around and about New Zealand Golf Club* (Whitstable: Whitstable Litho Printers, 1989), p. 87.

85   'tyrant Chairman': W. Lionel Fraser, *All to the Good* (London: Heinemann, 1963), p. 219.

85   'Both': Emblem, *Around and about New Zealand Golf Club*, p. 53.

87   'Hang up': Panel over the door to the Apollo Room, collection of Child & Co.

87   The Sons of Ben: Joshua Scodel, *Excess and the Mean in Early Modern Literature* (Princeton, NJ: Princeton University Press, 2002), p. 206.

87   'Luther's beer': Ben Jonson, 'Epigram 51: Inviting a Friend to Supper', *The New Oxford Book of Seventeenth-Century Verse*, ed. Alastair Fowler (Oxford: Oxford University Press, 1991), pp. 129–30.

87   'Sober Bigots': Ben Jonson, 'Rule 11', *The Works of Ben Johnson*, vol. 6. (London, 1716), pp. 422–3.

87   Drinking moderation: See Erasmus, *Convivium religiosum* (1522), in which a group of Christians at a dinner party talk about the woes of excessive drunkenness and the virtue of moderation, or *The Profane Feast*, where again the emphasis is not so much on ritual or expensive food as on conversation and camaraderie.

87   'the milk of *Venus*': Panel over the door to the Apollo Room, collection of Child & Co.

87   'Let the Contests': Ben Jonson, 'Rule 12', *Works*, vol. 6, pp. 422–3.

87   'moderate Bottle': Ben Jonson, 'Rule 11', *Works*, vol. 6, pp. 422–3.

87   'guilty': Ben Jonson, 'Rule 24', *Works*, vol. 6, pp. 422–3. See Martial, *Epigrams*, trans. Walter Ker (London: Heinemann, 1968, Book 10, no. 48). This one bears a strong resemblance to the last line of a poem by Martial.

90   'we shape our buildings': Winston Churchill, speech to the House of Commons, 28 October 1943, in *Never Give In!* (London: Pimlico, 2003), p. 358.

91   'worthy of Michelangelo': George Woodbridge, *The Reform Club, 1836–1978* (London: Reform Club, 1978), p. 67.

91   'the political centre': William Molesworth, letter to his mother, March 1836, quoted in Woodbridge, *The Reform Club*, p. 8.

91   'massive Reformatorium': Quoted in Russell Burlingham and Roger Billis, *Reformed Characters: The Reform Club in History and Literature* (London: Reform Club, 2005), p. 52.

92   Character of the group as God: Ara Norenzayan and Azim Shariff, 'The Origin and Evolution of Religious Prosociality', *Science*, vol. 322, no. 5898 (3 October 2008), pp. 58–62; Elizabeth Culotta, 'On the Origin of Religion', *Science*, vol. 326, no. 5954 (6 November 2009), pp. 784–7.

92   'I see many things': Alexis de Tocqueville, *Journeys to England and Ireland*, ed. J. P. Mayer, trans. George Lawrence and K. P. Mayer (New York: Anchor Books, 1968), pp. 74–5.

94   Keeping out exceptionally good or bad players: See the story of Southfields Dynamos in Leicester, in Bishop and Hoggett, *Organizing around Enthusiasms*, pp. 106–8.

95   'Dunces, Fools': This is a theme on which Jonson expands in his 'An Epistle

answering to One that Asked to be Sealed of the Tribe of Ben': Ben Jonson, *The Complete Poems*, ed. George Parfitt (New Haven, CT, and London: Yale University Press, 1982), pp. 191–3. The use of the word 'sealed' is interesting in terms of the connection it makes to guilds and companies, which would literally seal their documents with stamped blobs of molten wax; Jonson, 'Rule 11', *Works*, vol. 6, pp. 422–3.

95   '*Learned* and *Witty*': 'Rule 3', Johnson, *Works*, vol. 6, pp. 422–3.

95   'all the snobs': Fraser, *All to the Good*, p. 219.

95   'manifestly indecorous': Roger Fulford, *Votes for Women* (London: Faber, 1957), p. 64.

96   Aronson and Mills experiment: Elliot Aronson and Judson Mills, 'The Effect of Severity of Initiation on Liking for a Group', *Journal of Abnormal and Social Psychology*, vol. 59, no. 2 (1959), pp. 177–81.

96   'fuck, cock': Aronson and Mills, 'The Effect of Severity of Initiation on Liking for a Group', p. 178.

96   'Participants spoke dryly': Aronson and Mills, 'The Effect of Severity of Initiation on Liking for a Group', p. 179.

6: Rules and Roles

99   Two-penny Club: The 'Two-penny Club' was 'a knot of artisans and mechanics' that met in an alehouse in London around this time. Joseph Addison, *Spectator*, no. 9 (10 March 1711).

103   6,500 WIs: Women's Institute website retrieved from http://www.thewi.org.uk/section.aspx?id=12 on 10 March 2010.

103   '*President, Secretary*': Macky, *A Journey through England*, p. 288.

103   'the most morose': Ward, *The Secret History of Clubs*, pp. 9–10.

103   'exemplify'd at large': Ward, *The Secret History of Clubs*, p. 2.

104   'Upon reaching': Georg Simmel, 'Quantitative Aspects of the Group', *The Sociology of Georg Simmel*, ed. and trans. Kurt H. Wolff (London: Collier-Macmillan, 1964), pp. 87, 96.

105   Details of *collegia*: Julius Caesar, *The Commentaries of C. Julius Caesar, The Civil War* (Oxford: Clarendon, 1880), Book 1, 23.2, p. 13; Livy, *Titi Livi ab urbe condita libri iterum* (Lipsiae: B. G. Teubner, 1889), Book IV, 38.2; Tacitus, *Histories, Book I*, ed. Cynthia Damon (Cambridge: Cambridge University Press, 2003), no. 70, p. 65.

105   Guild nomenclature: Virginia Rosalyn Bainbridge, *Guilds in the Medieval Countryside: Social and Religious Change in Cambridgeshire c.1350–1558* (Woodbridge: Boydell Press), 1996, p. 138.

105   Modern-day dub nomenclature: Jean Warburton, *Unincorporated Associations: Law and Practice* (London: Sweet and Maxwell, 1992), p. 19.

106   'Neither noisie': Ben Jonson, 'Rule 13' and 'Rule 14', 'Leges Convivales', *Works*, vol. 6, pp. 422–3.

106   'bear no unmusical': Ben Jonson, 'Rule 20', *Works*, vol. 6, pp. 422–3.

106   'with wisdom and': Surah 16, Aya 125, *The Holy Qur'an*, trans. Yusuf Ali.

107   'free state': Ben Jonson, 'Rule 3', 'Leges Convivales', *Works*, vol. 6, pp. 422–3.

107   'escaping the home': Bishop and Hoggett, *Organizing around Enthusiasms*, p. 60.

107   'the only place': Denys Forrest, *The Oriental Club* (London: Batsford, 1979), p. 119.

107   'It seems to me': Johan Huizinga, *Homo Ludens: A Study of the Play-Element in Culture* (London: Routledge & Kegan Paul, 1949), foreword.

109 Aristotle on philia: Aristotle, *Nicomachean Ethics*, 1155a1–1172a15.

110 'of sharing something': Huizinga, *Homo Ludens*, p. 12.

110 'Places where': T. Gent, *History of Hull* (York, 1735), p. 80.

110 'the lethargy of custom': Samuel Taylor Coleridge, *Biographia Literaria* (New York: George P. Putnam, 1848), p. 442.

7: Machers and Maintainers

113 'a bit of a starlet': Jessica Brinton, 'Tamsin Omond: Eco Starlet', *The Times* (14 December 2008).

115 'exceed that of any': Field, *The Kit-Cat Club*, p. 242.

116 'a flower grown': Field, *The Kit-Cat Club*, p. 246.

116 'our club is dissolved': Charles Seymour, 6th Duke of Somerset, quoted in William Roberts, *The Earlier History of English Bookselling* (London: Sampson Low, 1889), p. 173.

118 'the kudos': Tamsin Omond, *Rush!* (London: Marion Boyars, 2009), p. 13.

118 'She became Project Manager': Omond, *Rush!*, p. 114.

118 'Both of us': Omond, *Rush!*, p. 115.

119 'For most newspapers': Omond, *Rush!*, p. 170.

121 'above all, his duty': Sir Robert Megarry, *John* v. *Rees*, Law Reports, Chancery Division (3rd series), 1970, pp. 345, 377.

122 Research into group leaders: Bishop and Hoggett, *Organizing around Enthusiasms*, p. 65.

122 'Every child': Quoted in Lilless McPherson Shilling and Linda K. Fuller, *Dictionary of Quotations in Communications* (Westport, CT: Greenwood, 1997), p. 46.

122 'Every human being': Joseph Beuys quoting the German Romantic author Novalis in 1973, translated into English by Caroline Tisdall, *Art into Society, Society into Art* (London: ICA, 1974), quoted in Charles Harrison and Paul Wood, *Art in Theory: 1900–2000* (Oxford: Blackwell, 2003), p. 929.

123 'that a group's level': Suzie Thomas, 'Community Archaeology in the UK', Council for British Archaeology, 29 April 2010, p. 60, Council for British Archaeology website, retrieved from http://www.britarch.ac.uk on 15 May 2010.

123 Transition Towns Survey: Gill Seyfang, *Green Shoots of Sustainability* (Norwich: University of East Anglia, 2009), p. 4.

123 'socio–emotional': Robert F. Bales, 'How People Interact in Conferences', *Scientific American*, vol. 192 (1955), pp. 31–5.

124 'silly little girls': Fiona Pryor, 'Clarkson Plays Down Dung Dumping', BBC News website, 3 October 2009.

125 Georgian associational life expectancy: Clark, *British Clubs and Societies, 1580–1800*, p. 60.

125 'I am not sure': Fraser, *All to the Good*, p. 217.

126 'cooperation based on': Axelrod, *The Evolution of Cooperation*, p. 174.

127 'that un-English thing': George Orwell, 'As I Please 13', 25 February 1944, in Paul Anderson (ed.), *Orwell in Tribune* (London: Politico's, 2006), p. 102.

8: The Evidence

133 Declining neighbourliness: There are plenty of reports like this; see the research commissioned by AXA Home Insurance into the state of community spirit conducted by OnePoll in March 2010.

133 Households with single-occupancy: 'Household Projections to 2031, England', Communities and Local Government, 11 March 2009, Department for

Communities and Local Government website, retrieved from http://www.communities.gov.uk/documents/statistics/pdf/1172133.pdf on 16 October 2009; this report also states that by 2006 some 13 per cent of the total population lived alone.

134 'pulled apart from': Putnam, *Bowling Alone*, p. 27.

134 Trades Unions membership in 2000: Haezewindt, 'Investing in Each Other and the Community', pp. 19–20.

134 Trades Unions membership in 2010; TUC website, retrieved from http://www.tuc.org.uk/ on 6 May 2010.

134 WI membership: Women's Institute website, retrieved from http://www.thewi.org.uk/section.aspx?id=12 on 10 March 2010.

134 Rotary Clubs membership: According to Rotary International in Great Britain and Ireland website, retrieved from http://www.ribi.org on 27 April 2010; correspondence with Rotary International in Great Britain and Ireland.

134 Freemasonry membership: 'Masons Appeal for New Recruits', *The Independent* (23 January 1999).

134 Working Men's Clubs figures: According to conversation with the WMCIU, 24 May 2010.

134 Interdisciplinary research group: Social and Spatial Inequalities (SASI) group, Department of Geography, University of Sheffield.

134 'Life in UK': BBC News website, 1 December 2008.

134 'Britain has become': Nicole Martin, *The Daily Telegraph* (1 December 2008).

134 'Britain has become a': Steve Doughty, 'Britain has become a "lonelier" place over the past 30 years, where even your neighbour's a stranger', *Daily Mail* (2 December 2008).

135 'New research': *The Camden Private Tenant*, issue 2 (Winter 2008–9).

135 'Life in the UK': Pat Ashworth, 'Stoke-on-Trent Bucks Loneliness Trend', *Church Times* (5 December 2008).

135 'sense of trust': Peter A. Hall, 'Social Capital in Britain', *British Journal of Political Science*, vol. 29 (1999), p. 444; Haezewindt, 'Investing in Each Other and the Community', p. 20; 'National Accounts of Well-Being', NEF, p. 32.

135 'Brits increasingly': Thomas Sander, Social Capital Blog, 2 December 2008, retrieved from http://socialcapital.wordpress.com/2008/12/page/2/ on 2 March 2009.

135 levels of loneliness: Dorling et al., *Changing UK: The Way We Live Now*, p. 23.

135 Congdon's study: Peter Congdon, 'Suicide and Parasuicide in London: A Small-Area Study', *Urban Studies*, vol. 33, no. 1 (1996), pp. 137–58.

136 'both positively correlated': Congdon, 'Suicide and Parasuicide in London: A Small-Area Study', p. 140.

136 Variable impact of factors: Congdon, 'Suicide and Parasuicide in London: A Small-Area Study', p. 157.

136 2003 suicide rates: 'UK Suicides Reach 30 Year Low in 2003', Office for National Statistics, 10 March 2005; Ray Fitzpatrick and Tarani Chandola, 'Health', in A. H. Halsey (ed.), *Twentieth-Century British Social Trends* (Basingstoke: Macmillan, 2000), p. 105.

136 'the sociological term': Dorling et al., *Changing UK: The Way We Live Now*, p. 23.

136 First use of 'anomie': Émile Durkheim, *The Division of Labour in Society*, trans. W. D. Halls (London: Macmillian, 1984), p. 304.

137 'comparable to the effect': John T. Cacioppo and William Patrick, *Loneliness* (New York: W. W. Norton & Co., 2008), p. 5.

138 'level of incomprehension': Alastair Donald, 'A Death Greatly Exaggerated', in D. Clements, A. Donald, M. Earnshaw and A. Williams (eds), *The Future of Community* (London: Pluto, 2008), p. 183.

138 'at least 1.3 million': Elsdon, Reynolds and Stewart, *Voluntary Organisations*, p. 4.

139 'draws its membership': Elsdon, Reynolds and Stewart, *Voluntary Organisations*, pp. 2–3, 39.

139 Community buildings: Paul Marriott, *Forgotten Resources? The Role of Community Buildings in Strengthening Local Communities* (York: York Publishing Services, 1997), p. 3.

139 'no equivalent erosion': Hall, 'Social Capital in Britain', p. 417.

139 'even a conservative': Hall, 'Social Capital in Britain', p. 427.

139 'micro social enterprises': MacGillivray, Wadhams and Conaty, *Low Flying Heroes*, p. ii.

140 Civil society organisations: National Council for Voluntary Organisations website, retrieved from http://www.ncvo-vol.org.uk/uploadedFiles/NCVO/What_we_do/Research/Almanac/Almanac2008ExecutiveSummary.pdf on 18 December 2009; Jenny Clark, D. Kane, K. Wilding and J. Wilton, *The UK Civil Society Almanac* (London: National Council for Voluntary Organisations, 2010).

140 Britons who belong to clubs: Kate Fox and Leicha Richards, *Sport and Leisure: Results from the Sport and Leisure Module of the 2002 General Household Survey* (London: Office for National Statistics, 2004).

140 1988 British Social Attitude Survey: Quoted in Charles Leadbeater and Paul Miller, *The Pro-Am Revolution: How Enthusiasts Are Changing our Economy and Society*, DEMOS, November 2004, p. 26, DEMOS website, retrieved from http://www.demos.co.uk/files/proamrevolutionfinal.pdf on 7 March 2009.

140 'associations or groups': Rossy Bailey and Alison Park, 'Britain at Play: Should We "Do" More and View Less?', in Alison Park et al., (eds), *British Social Attitudes* (London: National Centre for Social Research, 2009), p. 188.

141 Nationwide survey of the voluntary arts: *Our Creative Talent: The Voluntary and Amateur Arts in England* (London: Department of Media, Culture and Sport and Arts Council England, 2008).

141 Music societies: The total membership grew by 18 per cent between 2005 and 2008: 'Making Music Membership Survey 2005', Making Music Website, retrieved from http://www.makingmusic.org.uk/html/159.shtml on 6 May 2010; *Mapping Our Music Makers* (London: Making Music, 2008), p. 1.

141 Choirs: Conversation with the Membership Secretary of the National Association of Choirs.

141 Bands: This is the weakest figure in this book (apart from *Changing UK*'s 'loneliness indices') and is based on a recollection by a music industry figure of a survey carried out by myspace.com in 2008. If this survey did take place and that was the figure, the number of actual bands will be much higher, as many do not go near this website.

141 'reading groups are': Jenny Hartley, *Reading Groups* (Oxford: Oxford University Press, 2001), p. vii.

141 'fantastically diverse': Alison Flood, '"Book Group of Lifestyle" wins Orange/Penguin prize', *Guardian* (28 August 2008).

142 'there is a': 'Natural History Societies and Recording Schemes in the UK', unpublished report by Natural History Museum and OPAL, 2009.

314 *Notes to pages 142–143*

142 Allotment associations: There were almost five times as many people on these waiting lists in 2009 as in 1996. Margaret Campbell and Ian Campbell, 'A Survey of Allotment Waiting Lists', Transition Town West Kirby and National Society of Allotment and Leisure Gardeners, June 2009, retrieved from National Society of Allotment and Leisure Gardeners website www.nsalg.org on 10 May 2010.

142 Archaeological groups: Thomas, *Community Archaeology in the UK*; the one caveat to add to this is that the two contrasting figures are based on slightly different survey criteria, with the 2009 survey addressing a wider range of groups.

142 Beekeeping groups: Conversation with British Beekeepers' Association, 25 May 2010.

142 Family history societies: Conversation with Federation of Family History Societies, 24 May 2010.

142 Astronomical associations: Conversation with British Astronomical Association, 24 May 2010.

142 Flower-arranging societies: Conversation with National Association of Flower Arranging Societies, 24 May 2010.

142 Historical vehicle clubs: Conversation with Federation of British Historic Vehicle Clubs, 24 May 2010.

143 Amateur radio clubs: Conversation with Radio Society of Great Britain, 24 May 2010.

143 Morris dancing: Although there were no accurate figures as to what their numbers were, the President of the Morris Ring, Barry Goodman, insisted that the scene was 'as strong as it's ever been, and if anything, stronger' and described an upsurge in rapper sword dancing, molly dancing and border dancing, part of a broader revival within the folk tradition.

143 Sporting participation: 'Participation Rates in Various Sporting Activities in the Past Month, General Household Survey sample members aged 20–40, 1977–97', quoted in Jonathan Gershuny and Kimberly Fisher, 'Leisure', in A. H. Halsey (ed.), *Twentieth-Century British Social Trends* (Basingstoke: Macmillan, 2000), p. 641.

143 '25.1 per cent': Active People Survey, Sport England, 2005–6. It's worth adding that the 2002 figure came from a different survey (the General Household Survey), so any comparison should be taken lightly, Sport England website, retrieved from http://www.sportengland.org/research/active-people-survey/active-people-survey-1.aspx on 16 June 2010, also from conversation with Andrew St Ledger at Sport England on 17 June 2010. The figure for 2010 is based on the second quarterly report from Active People Survey 4, April 2009–April 2010. During 2007–8 the figure dipped slightly, to 10,078,700.

143 Rugby Union clubs: Conversation with John Eady at Knight, Kavanagh & Page, 25 June 2010.

143 Hockey clubs: By 2010 there were 960 hockey clubs affiliated to England Hockey, with about 100,000 participants. Correspondence with Alex Teasdale, National Manager, Clubs and Facilities, England Hockey, 18 June 2010.

143 Swimming clubs: Correspondence with Sharon Smart at the Amateur Swimming Association, June 2010.

143 Bowling clubs: Correspondence with Alistair Hollis at Bowls England, 22 June 2010.

143 Golf clubs: Conversation with representative of English Golf Union, 17 June 2010.

144 English Football clubs: Haezewindt, 'Investing in Each Other and the Community', pp. 19–20.

144 Scottish Football clubs: Correspondence with Clare Bodel at the Scottish Football Association, 1 July 2010.

144 Rowing clubs: Correspondence with Pippa Randolph at British Rowing, 22 June 2010.

144 Tennis clubs: Correspondence with Sophie Curthoys at the Lawn Tennis Association, 21 June 2010.

144 English badminton clubs: Conversation with Tina Heeney at Badminton England, 22 June 2010.

144 Scottish badminton clubs: Conversation with Badminton Scotland, 29 June 2010.

144 Rugby League clubs: Correspondence with Nick Boothroyd at Rugby Football League, 14 July 2010.

144 English canoe clubs: Correspondence with Robert Deacon at Canoe England, 25 June 2010.

144 Scottish canoe clubs: Conversation with Canoe Scotland, 29 June 2010.

144 Northern Irish canoe clubs: '1995–2008 Trends in Outdoor Recreation', Countryside and Access Network, Belfast, Countryside Recreation website, retrieved from http://www.countrysiderecreation.com/ on 29 June 2010.

144 Archery clubs: Conversation with Arran Coggan at Grand National Archery Society, 28 May 2010.

144 English athletics clubs: Conversation with UK Athletics, 22 June 2010.

144 Scottish athletics clubs: Conversation with William Ponissi at Scottish Athletics, 29 June 2010.

145 Welsh Athletics clubs: Conversation with Welsh Athletics, 29 June 2010.

145 National Women's Register: Details supplied by NWR Membership Co-ordinator, 11 May 2010.

145 Neighbourhood Watch: Based on British Crime Survey 2000, Home Office website, retrieved from http://www.crimereduction.homeoffice.gov.uk/partnerships31.htm on 6 May 2010. Neighbourhoodwatch.net, retrieved from http://www.neighbourhoodwatch.net/index.php?func=PageUKNWT on 30 April 2010.

145 Young Farmers' Clubs: According to correspondence with National Federation of Young Farmers' Clubs in 2010.

145 User groups: Jan Wallcraft and Michael Bryant, 'The Mental Health Service User Movement in England', Sainsbury Centre for Mental Health, May 2003, Centre for Mental Health website, retrieved from http://www.centreformental health.org.uk on 1 May 2010.

145 Civic Society groups: Civic Society Initiative, 'Own the Future', October 2009, Civic Society Initiative website, retrieved from http://www.civicsociety initiative.org.uk on 1 May 2010.

145 Transition towns: Gill Seyfang, 'Green Shoots of Sustainability,' University of East Anglia, July 2009, p. 3, Transition Culture website, retrieved from http://transitionculture.org on 1 May 2010.

145 Nationwide survey: For more on this survey see www.henryhemming.com.

146 Population growth: On census day 2001 the population of the UK was 58,789,194. An estimate from mid-2009 put it at 61,792,000, a growth of 3,002,806 or 5.1 per cent (Office for National Statistics).

147 'people assemble for': Pliny the Younger, Correspondence with Trajan from Bithymia (Warminister: Aris and Phillips, 1990), p. 32.

147   closure of *collegia*: Jonathan Scott Perry, *The Roman 'collegia': The Modern Evolution of an Ancient Concept* (Leiden: Brill, 2006), p. 6.

147   guilds and fraternities: Clark, *British Clubs and Societies, 1580–1800*, p. 20; Ross, *An Assembly of Good Fellows*, p. 165; Joseph Lambert, *Two Thousand Years of Guild Life* (Hull: Brown, 1891), p. 31; George Unwin, *The Guilds and Companies of London* (London: Frank Cass & Co., 1963), p. 352; Charles Coote, *The Romans of Britain* (London, 1878); Charles H. Pearson, *History of England during the Early and Middle Ages* (Bell and Dalduy, 1867).

148   'They who conquered': Andrew Marvell, '*A Dialogue between Two Noted Horses*', *The Poems and Satires of Andrew Marvell* (London: Vincent, Brooks, Day and Son, 1870), p. 174.

148   'we have numberless': *The Times* (8 January 1785).

148   Combination Acts: The term 'combination' made its début in statute and common law in 1721 with The Tailors' Combination Act: 7 Geo. 1, st. 1, c. 13 (1721); *Rex* v. *Journeymen-Taylors of Cambridge*, 8 Mod. 10, 88 Eng. Rep. 9 (KB 1721).

148   Unlawful Oaths Act: 37 Geo. III, c. 123 (1797).

148   Unlawful Societies Act: 39 Geo. III, c. 79 (1799).

148   Seditious Meetings Act: 57 Geo. III, c. 19 (1817).

148   'a wise and strong': 1902 Encyclopedia website, retrieved from http://www.1902encyclopedia.com/C/CLU/club.html on 16 April 2009.

149   'membership, expulsion': Warburton, *Unincorporated Associations:* p. 12.

149   'the greatest single': Robert Nisbet, *The Quest for Community* (New York: Oxford University Press, 1953), p. 265.

9: The Internet

151   'Common love': Joseph Priestley, quoted in Jenny Uglow, *The Lunar Men* (London: Faber and Faber, 2002), p. xiv.

151   'at the leading': Uglow, *The Lunar Men*, pp. 500–1.

151   'their passionate': Uglow, *The Lunar Men*, p. xv.

151   Inter-meeting pause: There may actually be a reason for this pause between sessions. One study has shown that, if a group meets more than once every three weeks, its members may begin to enjoy their sessions less. See Putnam, *Bowling Alone*, 333–4. In my survey the average number of meetings per year was twenty-seven – a little over twice a month – although that figure was distorted by the number of groups organizing weekly or bi-weekly meetings that did not require full attendance. The most popular response to the question 'how often do you meet' was 'monthly'.

152   'Newspapers make associations': De Tocqueville, *Democracy in America*, p. 518.

152   'converse every day': De Tocqueville, *Democracy in America*, p. 517.

153   'One does not': Martin Mayer, 'The Telephone and the Uses of Time', in Ithiel de Sola Pool (ed.), *Social Impact of the Telephone* (Cambridge, MA: MIT Press, 1977), p. 228.

153   Internet access: 'Internet Access', Office for National Statistics, 28 August 2009, Office for National Statistics website, retrieved from http://www.statistics.gov.uk/CCI/nugget.asp?ID=8 on 18 December 2009.

157   Eighteenth-century publicity: Clark, *British Clubs and Societies, 1580–1800*, p. 173.

158   'before a thousand': De Tocqueville, *Democracy in America*, p. 517.

161 Internet users in 1990s: 'Adults Who Have Used the Internet by Their Characteristics: Individual Internet Access', Office for National Statistics, July 2000–February 2003, Office for National Statistics website, retrieved from http://www.statistics.gov.uk/StatBase/Product.asp?vlnk=5672 on 7 January 2009.

161 'time-space': Deborah Chambers, *New Social Ties* (London: Palgrave Macmillan, 2006), p. 152.

164 The waggle dance: Aristotle, *Historia animalium*, IX, 624b; Karl von Frisch, *The Dancing Bees*, trans. Dora Ilse (London: Methuen, 1954), pp. 101–3.

165 'so important that': Albert Mehrabian, *Silent Messages* (Belmont, CA: Wadsworth, 1971), p. iii.

165 'had the naïve': William S. Condon, 'Cultural Microrhythms', in Martha Davis (ed.), *Interaction Rhythms* (New York: Human Sciences, 1982), p. 54; for a more detailed analysis of this (in less playful language) see William S. Condon, 'Sound – Film Microanalysis: A Means for Correlating Brain and Behavior', in Frank Duffy and Norman Geschwind (eds), *Dyslexia: A Neuroscientific Approach to Clinical Evaluation* (Boston, MA: Little, Brown, 1985), pp. 123–56.

166 'You can't break': Condon, 'Cultural Microrhythms', p. 54.

167 Prehistoric communion: Nicholas R. E. Fisher, 'Greek Associations, Symposia, and Clubs', in Michael Grant and Rachel Kitzinger (eds), *Civilization of the Ancient Mediterranean* (New York: Scribners, 1988), vol. 2, p. 1170.

168 Ultra sociability: We even cultivate this extreme sociability in the animals we keep. The social cognition of puppies born to domesticated dogs is far superior to that of those born to wild dogs. See Esther Herrmann, J. Call, M. Hernández-Lloreda, B. Hare and M. Tomasello, 'Humans Have Evolved Specialized Skills of Social Cognition: The Cultural Intelligence Hypothesis', *Science*, vol. 317 (2007), pp. 1360–66; and Brian Hare, M. Brown, C. Williamson and M. Tomasello, 'The Domestication of Social Cognition in Dogs', *Science*, vol. 298, (2002) pp. 1634–6.

10: The Decline of Traditional Community, 1

170 'Church of England': Morris, 'Clubs, Societies and Associations', p. 420.

170 'And who or what': Thomas Hardy, 'God's Funeral', *The Complete Poems*, ed. James Gibson (Basingstoke: Palgrave, 2001), p. 328.

171 'almost religious': Anthony Blunt, 'Memoir', pp. 18, 28.

171 'one cannot have': George Orwell, 'As I Please 14', 3 March 1944, *Orwell in Tribune*, pp. 106–7.

172 'originally [religion] extended': Durkheim, *The Division of Labour in a Society*, p. 119.

172 WIs: Thomas Kelly, *A History of Adult Education in Great Britain* (Liverpool: Liverpool University Press, 1992), p. 301.

173 Post-war Christian revival: Callum G. Brown, *The Death of Christian Britain* (London: Routledge, 2001), p. 6.

173 'experienced more secularisation': Callum G. Brown, 'The Secularisation Decade: What the 1960s Have Done to the Study of Religious History', in Hugh Mcleod and Werner Ustorf (eds), *The Decline of Christendom in Western Europe, 1750–2000* (Cambridge: Cambridge University Press, 2003), p. 29.

173   1963: Brown, *The Death of Christian Britain*, p. 1; Philip Larkin, 'Annus Mirabilis', *Collected Poems* (London: Faber and Faber, 1988), p. 167.

173   Baptisms and weddings: Brown, *The Death of Christian Britain*, p. 6.

173   Age and ethnicity of congregants: The Church of England website, retrieved from http://www.cofe.anglican.org/info/statistics/2005provisional attendance.pdf on 23 February 2009; 'Minorities Prop Up Church-Going', BBC News, 18 September 2006, BBC News website, retrieved from http://news.bbc.co.uk/1/hi/uk/5349132.stm on 8 September 2009.

173   Divine qualities of Jesus Christ: Brown, *The Death of Christian Britain*, p. 4.

173   Ipsos MORI Poll: 'Three in Five "Believe in God"', Ipsos MORI, 9 September 2003, Ipsos MORI website, retrieved from http://www.ipsos-mori.com/research publications/researcharchive/poll.aspx?oItemId=773 on 25 January 2010.

174   'is second only': Putnam, *Bowling Alone*, pp. 247–8.

174   Joining years: Putnam, *Bowling Alone*, p. 18.

11: The Decline of Traditional Community, 2

176   Working-age population changing address: A report in April 2003 by Sylvia Dixon of the Labour Market Division, Office for National Statistics.

176   Four moves in a typical lifetime: Dorling et al., *Changing UK*, pp. 12–13.

176   British households in 2005: General Household Survey 2005, Office for National Statistics, November 2006, Table 4.13, p. 341, Office for National Statistics website, retrieved from http://www.statistics.gov.uk on 1 March 2010.

176   'spend all [our] lives': Andrew Marr, *A History of Modern Britain* (London: Macmillan, 2007), p. 43.

176   'for the best': T. S. Eliot, *Notes towards the Definition of Culture* (London: Faber and Faber, 1948), p. 52.

177   Second home ownership: This is according to a report by Seema Shah for Capital Economics, but it is hard to know precisely how many second homes there are in this country. Council Tax Returns of 2005 suggest 166,000, while other reports indicate as many as 300,000.

177   Personal mobility: National Travel Survey, Department for Transport; Family Expenditure Survey, Office for National Statistics; General Household Survey (Longitudinal), Office for National Statistics, 2009.

177   Average distance travelled: Nicholas Christakis and James Fowler, *Connected* (London: HarperPress, 2009), p. 264.

177   'would rather drive': Research commissioned by AXA Home Insurance into the state of community spirit and conducted by OnePoll in March 2010 among 2,000 adults.

178   'the most drunken': Clark, *British Clubs and Societies, 1580–1800*, p. 30.

178   'neighbours came together': Clark, *British Clubs and Societies, 1580–1800*, p. 31.

178   Medieval urban centres: Jonathan Clark (ed.), *A World by Itself* (London: William Heinemann, 2010), p. 121.

179   Activities of guilds and fraternities: Clark, *British Clubs and Societies, 1580–1800*, p. 20.

179   An emphasis on burial: A well-attended funeral and careful observance of subsequent obits would speed one's passage through purgatory, and this was important within most guilds. Susan Reynolds, *Kingdoms and Communities in Western Europe, 900–1300* (Oxford: Clarendon, 1984), p. 78.

179   Economic need to join a guild: David J. F. Crouch, *Piety, Fraternity, and*

Power: Religious Guilds in Late Medieval Yorkshire, 1389–1547 (Wood-bridge: York Medieval Press, 2000), p. 15; Ross, *An Assembly of Good Fellows*, p. 142.

180 'Man's economy': Karl Polanyi, *The Great Transformation* (Boston, MA: Beacon, 1957), p. 46.

181 Friendly Societies: Cordery, *British Friendly Societies, 1750–1914*, p. 1.

181 Imperial clubs: Jessica Harland-Jacobs, *Builders of Empire* (Chapel Hill, NC: University of North Carolina Press, 2007), p. 13; Mrinalini Sinha, 'Britishness, Clubbability, and the Colonial Public Sphere', in Tony Ballantyne and Antoinette Burton (eds), *Bodies in Contact: Rethinking Colonial Encounters in World History* (Durham, NC: Duke University Press, 2005), p. 184.

182 Imperial Masonic lodges: Harland-Jacobs, *Builders of Empire*, p. 3.

182 'the centre and': Quoted in Sinha, 'Britishness, Clubbability, and the Colonial Public Sphere', p. 184.

182 'the *necessity* of being': Quoted in Harland-Jacobs, *Builders of Empire*, p. 1.

183 Hobbyists and neighbours: Leadbeater and Miller, *The Pro-Am Revolution*, p. 42; the survey was for the programme *Curiosity Culture*, Discovery Channel, 2000.

12: The Elevation of Interest

185 'a congestion of': John Evelyn, *Fumifugium, or the Inconvenience of the Aer and Smoak of London Dissipated*, quoted in Liza Picard, *Restoration London* (London: Weidenfeld & Nicolson, 1997), p. 6.

187 'gentry, tradesmen': Anon., *The Rules and Orders of the Coffee House* (London, 1674), line 3.

187 'each man seems': 'The Character of the Coffee-House' (1673), in Gwendolen Murphy, *A Cabinet of Characters* (London: Humphrey Milford, 1925), p. 322.

188 'probably the greatest': Michael White, *Isaac Newton: The Last Sorcerer* (London: Fourth Estate, 1997), pp. 163–4, 190; Ross, *An Assembly of Good Fellows*, pp. 218–19.

190 'machine for debate': Markman Ellis, *The Coffee-House* (London: Phoenix, 2005), p. 46.

190 The Rota: Clark, *British Clubs and Societies, 1580–1800*, p. 51.

191 'the most ingeniose': John Aubrey, *Brief Lives*, ed. Oliver Lawson Dick (London: Secker and Warburg, 1960), p. 125.

191 'very good': Samuel Pepys, *The Diary of Samuel Pepys*, ed. Robert Latham and William Matthews (London: G. Bell and Sons, 1971), vol. 1, p. 20.

191 Whig political clubs: Ross, *An Assembly of Good Fellows*, p. 216.

191 Associations of archers and florists: Ross, *An Assembly of Good Fellows*, pp. 230, 246.

191 Nonconformist groups: These groups formed in the face of vicious persecution by Archbishop Laud and his henchmen and, like many other groups, designed offices for each other, collected subscriptions, developed sartorial distinctions and addressed each other as 'thou' or 'thee'. They were fraternal, voluntary and run on the principles of self-defence and mutual aid.

192 1960s university: Hall, 'Social Capital in Britain', p. 435; see also R. D. Laing, *The Politics of Experience* (London: Penguin, 1965).

192 Full-time students: A. H. Halsey, 'Further and Higher Education', in Halsey (ed.), *Twentieth-Century British Social Trends*, pp. 222, 223.

193 'it is well-established': Hall, 'Social Capital in Britain', p. 435; Bailey and Park, 'Britain at Play: Should We "Do" More and View Less?', p. 188.

193 Educational qualifications among the elderly: Future Foundation, nVision Service, 2004 (www.futurefoundation.net), quoted in Leadbeater and Miller, *The Pro-Am Revolution*, p. 57.

193 Leisure time: Gershuny and Fisher, 'Leisure', p. 629; 2005 Time Use Survey, Office for National Statistics; Putnam, *Bowling Alone*, p. 222.

194 'I think we live': *The Today Programme*, BBC Radio 4 (Guest Editor: Zadie Smith), 29 December 2008.

195 'explosion of': Leadbeater and Miller, *The Pro-Am Revolution*, p. 45.

196 Life expectancy: 'Table 3.1 Life Expectancy at Birth, England, Wales and Scotland, 1901–96', in John Benson, *Affluence and Authority* (London: Hodder Arnold, 2005), p. 8, based on Fitzpatrick and Chandola, 'Health', p. 95.

196 Britons getting older: 'Aging population', National Council for Voluntary Organisations, Third Sector Foresight Website, retrieved from http://www.3s4.org.uk/drivers/ageing-population on 18 December 2009; Benson, *Affluence and Authority*, p. 13.

197 Part-time employment: Gershuny and Fisher, 'Leisure', p. 629.

197 Household size: General Lifestyle Survey 2008, Overview Report, Office for National Statistics.

198 Lone parents: General Lifestyle Survey 2008, Overview Report, Office for National Statistics.

198 'create a culture': Vinspired website, retrieved from http://www.vinspired.com/ on 3 March 2009.

198 Young volunteering: Brian Harrison and Josephine Webb, 'Volunteers and Voluntarism', in Halsey (ed.), *Twentieth-Century British Social Trends*, p. 613.

13: The Case Against

199 'each possessing': John Timbs, *Curiosities of London* (London: Longmans, Green, Reader and Dyer, 1868), p. 239.

200 Hanwell Community Centre: *Heavy Metal Britannia*, BBC 4, first broadcast on 7 March 2010.

200 The Thatched House: John Timbs, *Clubs and Club Life in London* (London: John Camden Hotten, 1872), p. 511.

201 Number of pubs: According to a survey reported by the British Beer and Pub Association, quoted in the *Daily Telegraph* (21 March 2009). BBPA website, retrieved from http://www.beerandpub.com/pub_facts.aspx, on 8 September 2009.

201 Pub-less villages: Luke Leitch, 'Beer Today, Gone Tomorrow', *The Times* (12 March 2009).

201 'traffic': Paul Kingsnorth, *Real England* (London: Portobello, 2008), p. 30.

201 Community centres: Paul Marriott, *Forgotten Resources?*, pp. 3, 44, 13, based on Chartered Institute of Finance and Public Accountability 1996/7 estimates.

202 British churches and their maintenance: In 2000 that figure was well over 48,000. See Peter Brierley, 'Religion', in Halsey (ed.), *Twentieth-Century British Social Trends*, pp. 668–9; National Church Trust website, retrieved from http://www.nationalchurchtrust.org/churches.html on 19 January 2010; figures from Christian Research quoted by Ruth Gledhill, 'Thousands of Churches Face Closure in Ten Years', *The Times* (10 February 2007).

202 Hub to adult ratio: This is on the basis that the adult population in Britain was

approximately 50 million in 2005 and 51 million in 2008, the years that these surveys relate to.

202   'there is widespread': *Our Creative Talent: The Voluntary and Amateur Arts in England* (London: Department of Media, Culture and Sport and Arts Council England, 2008).

203   'the place of Peace': John Ruskin, *Sesame and Lilies* (London: Dent, 1911), p. 59.

203   DIY: 63 per cent of adults did some kind of DIY in 1999. Leadbeater and Miller, *The ProAm Revolution*, p. 29.

203   IKEA: Retrieved from http://www.ikea.com/ms/en-GB/about-ikea-new/ press-room/pr-files/IKEA-21_Years-PP.pdf on 11 October 2009.

204   Non-domestic rates: *Liverpool Roman Catholic Archdiocesan Trustee Inc.* v. *Mackay (Valuation Officer), Rating Appeals*, 1988, p. 90, quoted in Warburton, *Unincorporated Associations*, p. 57.

204   A school in the grounds of a mosque: Warburton, *Unincorporated Associations*, p. 57.

204   'spiritual welfare': 'Exemptions' (Schedule 9, Part II, Group 7, Item 10), Value Added Tax Act 1994, 94 (3).

205   'whose main objects': Warburton, *Unincorporated Associations*, p. 58.

205   VAT exemptions: Value Added Tax Act 1994, 94 (3), Office of Public Sector Information website, retrieved from http://www.opsi.gov.uk/Acts/acts1994/ plain/ukpga_19940023_en#pt3_11g46 on 27 February 2009.

206   'should be seen': Marriott, *Forgotten Resources?*, p. 5.

207   'a concerted effort': Marriott, *Forgotten Resources?*, p. 5.

207   'The pub is the hub': Prince of Wales website, retrieved from http://www.princeofwales.gov.uk/personalprofiles/theprinceofwales/initiatives/ the_pub_is_the_hub_1916389644.html on 7 January 2010.

207   'Community Right to Buy': Third Sector website, retrieved from http://www.thirdsector.co.uk/news/Article/968781/Tories-propose-community-right-buy-scheme/ on 7 January 2010.

207   'Asset transfer': 'Room for Improvement, Strategic Asset Management in Local Government', Audit Commission, June 2009, p. 6, quoted in Blond, *Red Tory*, p. 214.

207   'central government': Blond, *Red Tory*, p. 217.

208   'The drive to play': Denise Hicks and Ray Stone, 'Unlucky for Some: The Social Impact of Bingo Club Closures', The Bingo Association, August 2007, pp. 4, 5, Department for Culture, Media and Sport website, retrieved from http://www.culture.gov.uk on 12 May 2010.

208   Cost of community centres: Marriott, *Forgotten Resources?*, pp. 3, 44, 13, based on Chartered Institute of Finance and Public Accountability 1996/7 estimates.

208   Hubs as generators of social capital: Jeffrey Hill, *Sport, Leisure and Culture in Twentieth-Century Britain* (Basingstoke: Palgrave, 2002), p. 132.

209   NHS: NHS website, retrieved from http://www.nhscareers.nhs.uk/ details/Default.aspx?Id=796 on 11 September 2009.

209   The Civil Service: Civil Service website, retrieved from http://www. civilservice.gov.uk/about/who/statistics/index.aspx on 16 October 2009.

209   Public sector employees: 'Public Sector Employment as % of Total Employment', Office for National Statistics, 8 September 2009, Office for National Statistics website, retrieved from http://www.statistics.gov.uk/statbase/TSDdownload2.asp on 16 October 2009.

209   Government expenditure: Angus Maddison, *The World Economy: A Millennial*

Perspective (Paris: Organisation for Economic Co-operation and Development, 2001), p. 135; *Economic Forecast* (Luxembourg: Office for Official Publications of the European Communities, spring 2009).

209   'the greatest argument': Winston Churchill, *Complete Speeches, 1897–1963*, ed. Robert Rhodes James, vol. 3, p. 2664, quoted in Ben Wilson, *What Price Liberty?* (London: Faber and Faber, 2009), p. 190.

209   'a kick in the': Wilson, *What Price Liberty?*, p. 202.

210   Emergency Powers Act: Wilson, *What Price Liberty?*, p. 210.

210   The Beveridge Report: Nicholas Timmins, *The Five Giants* (London: HarperCollins, 2001), pp. 23, 25.

211   'a British Revolution': William Beveridge, *Social Insurance and Allied Services: A Report by Sir William Beveridge* (London: HMSO, 1942), paragraph 31, p. 17.

211   Support for the proposals: Timmins, *The Five Giants*, p. 43.

211   National Insurance Acts: Mount, *Clubbing Together*, p. 6.

211   Friendly Societies in decline: Appendix to William Beveridge, *Voluntary Action: A Report on Methods of Social Advance* (London: Allen & Unwin, 1948); Harrison and Webb, 'Volunteers and Voluntarism', p. 605.

211   'the extinction of': Mount, *Clubbing Together*, p. 6.

211   Paid staff in community centres: M. K. Smith, 'Community Centres (Centers) and Associations'; the encyclopedia of informal education website, retrieved from www.infed.org/association/b-comcen.htm on 4 March 2009.

212   'voluntary effort': Ministry of Education, *Community Centres* (London: His Majesty's Stationery Office, 1944).

212   'a skilled and difficult': H. A. Mess and H. King, 'Community Centres and Community Associations', in H. A. Mess (ed.), *Voluntary Social Services since 1918* (London: Kegan Paul, Trench, Trubner and Co.), 1947, quoted in Smith, 'Community Centres (Centers) and Associations'.

214   'feels, and he is': Durkheim, *The Division of Labour in a Society*, pp. 119–20.

214   'polish one another': Anthony Ashley-Cooper, 3rd Earl of Shaftesbury, quoted in Clark, *British Clubs and Societies, 1580–1800*, p. 177.

215   'When men are': Joseph Addison, *Spectator*, no. 9 (10 March 1711).

218   'a global': Lester M. Salamon, 'The Nonprofit Sector at a Crossroads: The Case of America', *Voluntas*, vol. 10, no. 1 (1999), p. 5.

218   'from the developed': Lester M. Salamon, 'The Rise of the Nonprofit Sector', *Foreign Affairs*, vol. 73 (July/August 1994), pp. 111–24.

14: The Community Agenda

225   A communal animal: Aristotle, *Eudemian Ethics*, 1242a25.

225   The Athenian community: J. M. Cooper, 'Political Animals and Civic Friendship', in Günther Patzig (ed.), *Aristoteles' 'Politik'* (Göttingen: Vandenhoeck & Ruprecht, 1990), p. 220.

226   'know most of': Benedict Anderson, *Imagined Communities: Reflections on the Origin and Spread of Nationalism* (London: Verso, 2006), p. 6.

227   'aggregate': David Buchanan and Andrzej Huczynski, *Organizational Behaviour: An Introductory Text* (Harlow: Pearson Education, 2007), p. 281.

228   'Real communities': MAIDeN website, retrieved from http://www.maiden. gov.uk/aboutAboutus.asp on 30 January 2010.

231   Governmental definitions of community: 'Glossary', Department of Communities and Local Government website, retrieved from http://www.communities.gov.uk/ communities/communityempowerment/aboutcommunityempowerment/whatis

community/glossary/ on 24 October 2009; 'Useful definitions', Improvement & Development Agency website, retrieved from http://www.idea.gov.uk/idk/core/page.do?pageId=10773112 on 23 July 2009.

231 'the strongest defence': David Blunkett, 'What Does Citizenship Mean Today?', *The Observer* (15 September 2002).

231 Community Justice centres: Blunkett, 'What Does Citizenship Mean Today?'; Community Justice was first introduced to Liverpool and Salford, and by 2009 similar centres had appeared in eleven other areas in England and Wales.

231 Confident Communities: Hazel Blears, 'Confident Communities', speech at Oxford Town Hall, 17 September 2007, Department of Communities and Local Government website, retrieved from http://www.communities.gov.uk/speeches/corporate/confidentcommunities on 25 September 2009.

231 Communitybuilders: Communitybuilders website, retrieved from http://community buildersfund.org.uk on 7 January 2010.

231 'a ten-point action': 'Blears – £50 Million Investment in Community Cohesion', Department for Communities and Local Government, 6 October 2007, Department for Communities and Local Government website, retrieved from http://www.communities.gov.uk/news/corporate/500395 on 21 October 2009.

232 Community Empowerment: Improvement and Development Agency website, retrieved from http://www.idea.gov.uk.idk/core/page.do?pageId=7381994 on 20 October 2009.

232 Community practitioners: The Community Development Challenge, Department for Communities and Local Government, December 2006, p. 9. Department for Communities and Local Government website, retrieved from http://www.communities.gov.uk on 22 October 2009.

233 'our desire for': Richard Williams, 'Public Space: Designing-in Community', in Clements, Donald, Earnshaw and Williams (eds), *The Future of Community*, p. 49.

233 'to anyone in': *Private Eye*, no. 1248 (30 October 2009), p. 7, quoting *BBC News*.

234 The Parekh Report: The Runnymede Trust, *The Future of Multi-Ethnic Britain: The Parekh Report* (London: Profile Books, 2000).

234 20,000 local communities: Based on a figure quoted at length in MacGillivray, Wadhams and Conaty, *Low Flying Heroes*.

235 Fashionability of community: Deborah Chambers, *New Social Ties* (London: Palgrave Macmillan, 2006), p. 160.

235 'to begin the job': Byrne, 'Do People Need Communities Anymore?'

235 Community and Society: It is important to add that Tönnies was not suggesting that any community or society could necessarily be labelled as either *Gemeinschaft* or *Gesellschaft*. Instead, these were two normal types.

236 'All praise of': Ferdinand Tönnies, *Community and Society*, trans. Charles Loomis (Mineola, NY: Dover, 2002), p. 35.

237 'politics [. . .] is not': David Willetts, 'The Spirit of Co-operation', *Prospect Magazine* (March 2010).

15: Witches and the Problem with Localism

238 Panará contact: For more on this and other contacts in the Amazon during the twentieth century see John Hemming, *Die If You Must* (London: Macmillan, 2003).

239 'nobody cried': Elizabeth Ewart, 'Living with Each Other: Selves and Alters

amongst the Panará of Central Brazil', D.Phil. thesis, London School of Economics and Political Science, 2000, p. 106.

239 Witch accusations: R. H. Heelas, 'The Social Organisation of the Panará, a Gê Tribe of Central Brazil', D.Phil. thesis: St Catherine's College, Oxford, 1979, p. 121, quoted in Ewart, 'Living with Each Other'.

241 Terrorism and territory: Robert Pape, *Dying to Win: The Strategic Logic of Suicide Terrorism* (New York: Random House, 2005).

243 'male and from': Women Against Fundamentalism and Southall Black Sisters, 'Commission on Integration and Cohesion', January 2007, Women Against Fundamentalism website, retrieved from http://www.womenagainst fundamentalism.org.uk/ on 15 September 2009.

244 'Plural monoculturalism': Quoted in 'Amartya Sen and the Dilemmas of Multiculturalism and Plural Monoculturalism', February 2006, Larvatus Prodeo website, retrieved from http://larvatusprodeo.net/2006/02/22/amartya-sen-and-the-dilemmas-of-multiculturalism-and-plural-monoculturalism/ on 15 July 2009.

244 'can be a good way': Amartya Sen, *Identity and Violence* (New York: W. W. Norton, 2006), p. xii.

244 'massive rise': Justin Davenport, 'Police Tackle Massive Rise in "Honour" Violence Cases', *Evening Standard* (7 December 2009).

245 'I know from': Jasvinder Sanghera, 'It is not Part of Anyone's Culture to be Abused', *The Times* (18 December 2009).

245 'would not be allowed': Jason Burke, 'Love, Honour and Obey', *The Observer* (8 October 2000).

245 'it's rare for': Tracy McVeigh, 'Ending the Silence on "Honour Killing"', *The Observer* (25 October 2009).

245 Bradford police community officer report: Burke, 'Love, Honour and Obey'.

247 'brutalized into territorialism': John Heale, *One Blood* (London: Simon and Schuster, 2008), p. 37.

248 'a siege mentality': Heale, *One Blood*, p. 37.

248 'among 21 developed': Richard Wilkinson and Kate Pickett, 'A Broken Society, Yes, but Broken by Thatcher', *Guardian* (29 January 2010).

16: A New Ideal
251 'be a fugitive': Genesis 4:12.

253 Belonging to 98 associations: Most of these related to his interest in natural history and subterranean construction. Hilary Geoghegan, 'The Culture of Enthusiasm: Technology, Collecting and Museums', PhD thesis for Royal Holloway, University of London, 2008, p. 79.

254 'the report found': Quoted in Deborah Chambers, *New Social Ties* (London: Palgrave Macmillan, 2006), p. 97.

17: The Men Who Hunt Elephants
258 The size of prehistoric human groups: Estimates as to how large bands of human beings were around this time range from fifteen to 200, but average out at around 150. This is the figure on which Dunbar places great emphasis. See Paul Rubin, *Darwinian Politics: The Evolutionary Origin of Freedom* (New Brunswick: Rutgers University Press, 2002), p. 7; Robin Dunbar, 'Brains on Two Legs: Group Size and the Evolution of Intelligence', in Frans B. M. de Waal (ed.), *Tree of Origin: What Primate Behavior can Tell Us about Human Social Evolution* (Cambridge, MA: Harvard University Press, 2001); Robert. L. Kelly, *The Foraging Spectrum: Diversity in Hunter–Gatherer Lifeways* (Washington

DC: Smithsonian Institution Press, 1995); Lance Workman and Will Reader, *Evolutionary Psychology: An Introduction* (Cambridge: Cambridge University Press, 2004, p. 273); Robin Dunbar, *Grooming, Gossip and the Evolution of Language* (London: Faber and Faber, 1996), p. 192.

258 Fission–fusion: Jane Goodall, *The Chimpanzees of Gombe: Patterns of Behaviour* (Cambridge, MA: Harvard University Press, 1986), quoted in Julia Lehmann, A. Korstjens and R. Dunbar, 'Fission–Fusion Social Systems as a Strategy for Coping with Ecological Constraints: A Primate Case', *Evolutionary Ecology*, vol. 21(2007), pp. 613–34.

259 !Kung San: Dunbar, *Grooming, Gossip and the Evolution of Language*, pp. 119–20.

260 'would be unable': Lehmann, Korstjens and Dunbar, 'Fission–Fusion Social Systems as a Strategy for Coping with Ecological Constraints: A Primate Case', pp. 613, 630.

260 A fear of predation: Lehmann, Korstjens and Dunbar, 'Fission–Fusion Social Systems as a Strategy for Coping with Ecological Constraints: A Primate Case', p. 630.

261 'It would be nice': Louis Menand, 'What Comes Naturally', *The New Yorker* (25 November 2002).

261 Sub-Saharan hunter-gatherer: This is the widely accepted 'Out of Africa Theory'. There are others who argue a 'Separate Origins' take on prehistory, whereby different chunks of humanity have descended from separate clusters of *Homo erectus* who would have made an exodus out of Africa approximately 1.7 million years ago and/or at some point between 840,000 and 420,000 years ago.

261 'evolved in response': Sherwood L. Washburn and Robert S. O. Harding, 'Evolution and Human Nature', in David A. Hamburg and H. Keith H. Brodie (eds), *American Handbook of Psychiatry: New Psychiatric Frontiers*, vol. 6, 2nd edn (New York: Basic Books, 1975), p. 4.

261 'a peculiar balance': Lars Rodseth, R. W. Wrangham, A. M. Harrigan and B. B. Smuts, 'The Human Community as a Primate Society', *Current Anthropology*, vol. 32, no. 3 (June 1991), p. 240.

18: Case Study

266 'Deerhurst is a': Andrew Leeke, letter to residents of Deerhurst, 8 August 2007.

269 Newts kept safe: 'No Newts Is Bad Newts Project Is Going Strong', Gloucestershire Wildlife Trust website, retrieved from http://www.gloucestershire wildlifetrust.co.uk/Gwt/Gwt.Nsf/WEBARTICLE?OpenFrom&id= 368861D7A9 E60423802575E1005156B4 on 27 January 2010.

Conclusion

272 Mental and physical decline: Cacioppo and Patrick, *Loneliness*, p. 12.

272 'who are more': Haezewindt, 'Investing in Each Other and the Community: The Role of Social Capital', p. 25.

272 'as a rough rule': Putnam, *Bowling Alone*, p. 331.

273 'you miss out': Oliver James, *Affluenza* (London: Vermilion, 2007), p. 24.

275 'if we were': Bishop and Hoggett, *Organizing around Enthusiasms*, p. 2.

275 Infinite choice: Christopher Lasch, *The Culture of Narcissism* (London: Abacus, 1980).

275 'means we have': Tobias Jones, *Utopian Dreams* (London: Faber and Faber, 2007), p. 47.

278 Athenian associations: See also Aristotle's distinction between the Athenian political club and the Spartan 'common mess' in Aristotle, *Politics*, 1272b36.

279 'True philosophers': Plato, *Theatetus*, 173d.

279 *thiasoi*: Aristotle refers to *thiasôtês*, meaning members of a *thiasos*. Aristotle, *Nicomachean Ethics*, 1160a19.

279 Further Athenian Associations: Ross, *An Assembly of Good Fellows*, p. 97.

Appendix A

281 'obscure': *Oxford English Dictionary*, 2nd ed, vol. III (Oxford: Clarendon Press, 1989), p. 366.

282 'Apprentices were famous': John Stubbs, *Donne: The Reformed Soul* (London: Penguin, 2007), p. 39.

282 'historic dislike': Stubbs, *Donne: The Reformed Soul*, p. 39.

282 'Prentices and clubs!': *The Home Friend*, no. 79 (1854), p. 562.

283 *Henry VI, Part 1*: William Shakespeare, *The Complete Works*, ed. Stanley Wells and Gary Taylor (Oxford: Clarendon Press, 1988), p. 153.

283 'I'll call for': William Shakespeare, *Henry VI, Part 1*, Act 1, scene 4 (although sometimes scenes two and three are lumped together, in which case it is scene 3).

283 Tityre-tu: Most of the members of the Tityre-tu served in a regiment raised in 1622 by Lord Vaux to fight in the Low Countries. Their name is a reference to the opening line of Virgil's first *Eclogue*. See Timothy Raylor, *Cavaliers, Clubs, and Literary Culture: Sir John Mennes, James Smith, and the Order of the Fancy* (Newark, DE: University of Delaware Press; London: Associated University Presses, 1994), p. 76; Ross, *An Assembly of Good Fellows*, p. 238; Thornton Shirley Graves, 'Some Pre-Mohock Clansmen', *Studies in Philology*, vol. 20, no. 4 (1923), pp. 395–421. For more see Walton B. McDaniel, 'Some Greek, Roman and English Tityretus', *American Journal of Philology*, vol. 35 (1914), pp. 52–66.

283 'caused something': Walter Yonge, *Diary of Walter Yonge, Esq., 1604–28*, ed. George Roberts (London: J. B. Nichols and Son, 1848), p. 70.

284 Long Vacation in London: 'The Long Vacation in London, in Verse Burlesque, or Mock-Verse', *The Works of Sir William D'Avenant* (London: Henry Herringman, 1673), p. 289.

284 Poem probably written during 1630s: Raylor, *Cavaliers, Clubs, and Literary Culture*, p. 90; Julius Rodenberg, *England, Literary and Social, from a German Point of View* (London: Richard Bentley & Son, 1875), p. 199.

285 The Order of the Fancy: Raylor, *Cavaliers, Clubs, and Literary Culture*, p. 87.

285 D'Avenant's club: Raylor, *Cavaliers, Clubs, and Literary Culture*, pp. 84, 90.

285 Rules and passwords: For a lively account of the Tityre-tues apparently swearing allegiance to each other, see Yonge, *Diary of Walter Yonge, Esq., 1604–28*, p. 70.

285 Uniform: Later that century the Levellers would be known for the green ribbons they wore. Later still there was the Whig Green Ribbon Club (broken up in the 1680s after various members were accused of plotting against the King).

285 'Coffee club': Samuel Pepys, *The Diary of Samuel Pepys*, ed. Robert Latham and William Matthews (London: G. Bell and Sons, 1971), vol. 1, p. 20.

285 'club': Pepys, *The Diary of Samuel Pepys*, vol. 1, p. 67. A different sighting is in the 1911 *Encyclopaedia Britannica* (Cambridge: Cambridge University Press, 1910–11). Aubrey's line – 'we now use the word clubbe for a sodality at a taverne or drinking house' – was attributed to 1659, but in fact it was published in the late 1680s. The *Encyclopaedia* attributes it to Aubrey's *Letters by Eminent Persons*, written in 1659, but it appears to be from Aubrey's 'The Remaines of Gentilisme

and Judaisme' (1687–9), Lansdowne MS 231, which remained unpublished until it appeared in John Aubrey, Nicholas L'Estrange and John Collet, *Anecdotes and Traditions*, compiled by William John Thoms (London: John Nichols & Son for The Camden Society, 1839), p. 94.

Appendix B

288 No forms to fill out: Warburton, *Unincorporated Associations*, p. 1; Warburton's book remains the authority on the legality of most elements of associational 288.

288 The Literary and Scientific Institutions Act: Warburton, *Unincorporated Associations*, p. 4.

288 Tortious liability: Warburton, *Unincorporated Associations*, p. 74.

290 'any group of individuals': Regulation 5, as amended by the Community Interest Company (Amendment) Regulations 2009; CIC Guidance Notes, Updated October 2009, Community Interest Companies website, retrieved from http://www.cicregulator.gov.uk/guidance/Chapter%202%20-%20October% 202009%20(version%203%20Final).pdf on 14 June 2010.

291 'appropriate objects': Warburton, *Unincorporated Associations*, p. 7.

293 'refuse to admit': Warburton, *Unincorporated Associations*, p. 67.

293 'reach their decision': Warburton, *Unincorporated Associations*, p. 67.

293 'a good understanding': *Hopkinson* v. *Marquis of Exeter*, 1867, quoted in Warburton, *Unincorporated Associations*, p. 11.

294 'nobody would suggest': Sir Robert Megarry, 'Woodford v. Smith', *Weekly Law Report*, vol. 1 (1970), pp. 806, 814.

294 'usually there is': Sir Robert Megarry, 'Re G. K. N. Bolts and Nuts Ltd. (Automotive Division) Birmingham Works, Sports and Social Club', *Weekly Law Report*, vol. 1 (1982), pp. 774, 776.

Index

The heading 'associations, aspects of' is used generically to include all types of affiliations including clubs, groups, organizations and societies.